THE
HISTORY OF
FINLAND

THE
HISTORY OF
FINLAND

Jason Lavery

The Greenwood Histories of the Modern Nations
Frank W. Thackeray and John E. Findling, Series Editors

Greenwood Press
Westport, Connecticut • London

Library of Congress Cataloging-in-Publication Data

Lavery, Jason Edward.
  The history of Finland / Jason Lavery.
    p. cm.—(Greenwood histories of the modern nations, ISSN 1096–2905)
  Based on a lecture course given since the summer of 1992 for the
Helsinki Summer University in Finland.
  Includes bibliographical references and index.
  ISBN 0–313–32837–4
  1. Finland—History. I. Title.
  DL1032.L384 2006
  948.97—dc22   2006021333

British Library Cataloguing in Publication Data is available.

Library of Congress Catalog Card Number: 2006021333
ISBN: 0–313–32837–4
ISSN: 1096–2905

First published in 2006

Greenwood Press, 88 Post Road West, Westport, CT 06881
An imprint of Greenwood Publishing Group, Inc.
www.greenwood.com

Printed in the United States of America

The paper used in this book complies with the
Permanent Paper Standard issued by the National
Information Standards Organization (Z39.48–1984).

10 9 8 7 6 5 4 3 2 1

To S. K. W.

Contents

Series Foreword

The *Greenwood Histories of the Modern Nations* series is intended to provide students and interested laypeople with up-to-date, concise, and analytical histories of many of the nations of the contemporary world. Not since the 1960s has there been a systematic attempt to publish a series of national histories, and, as editors, we believe that this series will prove to be a valuable contribution to our understanding of other countries in our increasingly interdependent world.

Over thirty years ago, at the end of the 1960s, the Cold War was an accepted reality of global politics, the process of decolonization was still in progress, the idea of a unified Europe with a single currency was unheard of, the United States was mired in a war in Vietnam, and the economic boom of Asia was still years in the future. Richard Nixon was president of the United States, Mao Tse-tung (not yet Mao Zedong) ruled China, Leonid Brezhnev guided the Soviet Union, and Harold Wilson was prime minister of the United Kingdom. Authoritarian dictators still ruled most of Latin America, the Middle East was reeling in the wake of the Six-Day War, and Shah Reza Pahlavi was at the height of his power in Iran. Clearly, the past 30 years have been witness to a great deal of historical change, and it is to this change that this series is primarily addressed.

With the help of a distinguished advisory board, we have selected nations whose political, economic, and social affairs mark them as among the most important in the waning years of the twentieth century, and for each nation we have found an author who is recognized as a specialist in the history of that nation. These authors have worked most cooperatively with us and with Greenwood Press to produce volumes that reflect current research on their nations and that are interesting and informative to their prospective readers.

The importance of a series such as this cannot be underestimated. As a superpower whose influence is felt all over the world, the United States can claim a "special" relationship with almost every other nation. Yet many Americans know very little about the histories of the nations with which the United States relates. How did they get to be the way they are? What kind of political systems have evolved there? What kind of influence do they have in their own region? What are the dominant political, religious, and cultural forces that move their leaders? These and many other questions are answered in the volumes of this series.

The authors who have contributed to this series have written comprehensive histories of their nations, dating back to prehistoric times in some cases. Each of them, however, has devoted a significant portion of the book to events of the last thirty years, because the modern era has contributed the most to contemporary issues that have an impact on U.S. policy. Authors have made an effort to be as up-to-date as possible so that readers can benefit from the most recent scholarship and a narrative that includes very recent events.

In addition to the historical narrative, each volume in this series contains an introductory overview of the country's geography, political institutions, economic structure, and cultural attributes. This is designed to give readers a picture of the nation as it exists in the contemporary world. Each volume also contains additional chapters that add interesting and useful detail to the historical narrative. One chapter is a thorough chronology of important historical events, making it easy for readers to follow the flow of a particular nation's history. Another chapter features biographical sketches of the nation's most important figures in order to humanize some of the individuals who have contributed to the historical development of their nation. Each volume also contains a comprehensive bibliography, so that those readers whose interest has been sparked may find out more about the nation and its history. Finally, there is a carefully prepared topic and person index.

Readers of these volumes will find them fascinating to read and useful in understanding the contemporary world and the nations that comprise it. As series editors, it is our hope that this series will contribute to a heightened sense of global understanding as we embark on a new century.

Frank W. Thackeray and John E. Findling
Indiana University Southeast

Preface

Readers will quickly learn from this book that Finland is an officially bilingual country. In most cases, names of geographic places and important terms will be expressed first in Finnish, followed by the Swedish-language name given in the first case that the place is named, for example, Helsinki (Helsingfors). Readers will more easily recognize some terms and place names in their Swedish form, such the Åland Islands (in Finnish, Ahvenanmaa). In these cases, the Swedish term will be used first and the Finnish version will be explicitly identified. Many places in Finland do not have a Swedish-language name, or the Swedish name is not frequently used even in Swedish. In these instances, obviously only a Finnish name will appear. Finnish and Swedish have two letters that do not appear in the English alphabet: *ä* and *ö*. In Finnish (and Finland Swedish), *ä* is pronounced like the *a* in the English word hat, *ö* like the -er in soldier. Swedish also has an additional letter, *å*, which most frequently sounds like the *o* in so. In both Finnish and Swedish, the frequently occurring diphthong -ei is pronounced like the -ay in the English word hay. The Finnish diphthong -ai is pronounced like the English word eye.

Over the course of a project of this scope, one collects many debts. In some cases, the debts span decades. This book is based on a lecture course that I have given since the summer of 1992 for the Helsinki Summer University in Finland. I owe special thanks to the Summer University's director, Eeva Martinsen, as well as its curriculum planner, Katja Kuuramaa, for entrusting me with such a rewarding opportunity. Parts of this book were scrutinized by many expert colleagues: Seppo Hentilä, Kristiina Kalleinen, Pauli Kettunen, Mika Lavento, and Päiviö Tommila. Professor Andrew Nestingen of the University of Washington read through the entire manuscript and offered me an opportunity to present some of my work at his institution. Georg Haggrén read some book chapters and has been an unfailing source of advice. At various junctures I received useful suggestions and or support from Leena Ahtola-Moorhouse, Paul Bushkovitch, Terje Leiren, Pirjo Lyytikäinen, Jyrki Nummi, Mikko Salmela, George Schoolfield, and Petteri Takkula. The Oklahoma State University Cartographic Service drew the maps. Oklahoma State University and its Department of History together provided me a year of sabbatical leave for research and writing. Research costs were underwritten by grants from the Oklahoma Humanities Council, Oklahoma State University, the Alfred Kordelin Foundation, and the Finnish Cultural Foundation. I hope that this work will represent at least a small return on the generous investments made by these organizations. The author assumes responsibility for all errors.

My wife, Dr. Susanne Weinberger, provided encouragement at a time of great challenge for our family. This book is dedicated to her.

Finland and the Baltic Sea region. Adapted from Byron J. Nord-strom, *The History of Sweden* (Westport, CT: Greenwood Press, 2002), xii. Reprinted with permission.

Timeline of Historical Events

1548	Mikael Agricola publishes the New Testament in Finnish
1550	Founding of Helsinki
1593	Uppsala Decree formally establishes Lutheranism in the Swedish kingdom
1595	Peace of Teusina
1596–1597	The War of the Clubs peasant rebellion
1617	Peace of Stolbova
1640	Foundation of university in Turku
1642	Full Bible published in Finnish
1695–1697	Crop failures and epidemics decimate Finland's population by a third
1700–1721	The Great Northern War
1713–1721	Russian armies occupy Finland
1721	Peace of Nystad
1741–1743	The Hats' War
1788–1790	Gustav's War and the Anjala League
1808–1809	The War of Finland, annexation of Finland to Russian Empire
1809	Porvoo Diet, in which Emperor Alexander I of Russia confirms Finland's laws and religion (March 25–July 19)
1812	Helsinki named Finland's new capital
1828	University moved to Helsinki from Turku
1835	Elias Lönnrot publishes *The Kalevala*
1860	The introduction of the mark as Finland's currency
1863	Language Rescript makes Finnish co-official with Swedish
c. 1890–1914	Finland's artistic Golden Age
1899	February Manifesto reduces Finland's autonomy
1904	Assassination of Governor-General Nikolai Bobrikov
1906	Creation of unicameral Parliament
1914–1918	World War I

1917	Collapse of the Russian monarchy, March 16 (old style, 3 March 1917)
1917	Finland's Parliament passes Enabling Act (July)
1917	Bolshevik Revolution, November 7 (new style)
1917	Parliament approves declaration of independence from Russia (December 6)
1918	Civil War (January–May)
1919	Parliament ratifies republican constitution (July)
1920	Peace of Tartu (Dorpat) between Finland and Soviet Russia
1929–1932	Rise and fall of the Lapua Movement
1937	Social Democratic Party and Agrarian League form red earth coalition
1939	F. E. Sillanpää wins the Nobel Prize for literature
1939–1940	The Finnish–Soviet Winter War
1941–1944	The War of Continuation (World War II) against the USSR
1944–1945	The Lapland War against Germany
1945	A. I. Virtanen wins the Nobel Prize in chemistry
1945–1948	Big three Center-Left coalition Government
1946–1956	J. K. Paasikivi is Finland's president
1946	Finland signs Treaty of Friendship, Cooperation, and Mutual Assistance Treaty (YYA Treaty) with USSR
1952	Finland completes payment of war reparations to USSR
1952	Helsinki hosts Olympic summer games
1955	Finland becomes a member of the United Nations and the Nordic Council
1956–1981	Urho Kekkonen is Finland's president
1958	Finnish–Soviet Night Frost Crisis (August–December)
1961	Finnish–Soviet Note Crisis (October–November)
1966–1982	Big three or popular front Center-Left coalition

1975	Conference on Security and Cooperation (CSCE) conference produces Helsinki Accords
1982–1994	Mauno Koivisto is Finland's president
1987–1991	Social Democratic-Conservative (blue-red) coalition
1990–1994	Finland's economy in depression
1991–1995	Conservative-Center coalition
1992	Finland applies for European Union membership
1994–2000	Martti Ahtisaari is Finland's president
1995	Finland joins European Union
1995–2003	Rainbow coalition Government
2000–	Tarja Halonen is president of Finland
2000	New constitution
2003	Red earth coalition returns to power
2006	Rock group Lordi wins Eurovision song contest

1

An Introduction to Finland

Finland has a recorded past of several thousand years. This long time frame involves four major periods. The first of these, the prehistoric period, begins with the first definitive evidence of human habitation in Finland around 10,500 years ago. Small, tribal groups populated prehistoric Finland. Finland as understood today still lay thousands of years away. The second period consists of Finland's experiences as part of the kingdom of Sweden, traditionally dated from about the year 1155 until 1809. In the twelfth and the thirteenth centuries, much of the Finnish Peninsula came under the rule of the Swedish king. At the same time, the principality of Novgorod, which in turn later became a part of Russia, absorbed some eastern parts of Finland. As a part of the Swedish kingdom, Finland served as a battlefield between the Swedish king and the rulers of Russia. As a result of one of these wars in 1808–1809, Russia annexed Finland. With his new conquest, Russian Emperor Alexander I created the Grand Duchy of Finland, an autonomous part of the Russian empire where the legal and religious traditions from the Swedish era were allowed to continue. During this third major era, the so-called Age of Autonomy or Imperial Era (1809–1917), modern-day Finland began to take shape.

As a result of the turmoil in Russia unleashed by World War I, Finland's leaders in December 1917 declared the country's political independence. Finland then entered its fourth and current period, the Age of Independence.

GEOGRAPHY AND CLIMATE

Situated in Europe's northeastern corner, Finland shares a border with Sweden to the west and Norway to the north. To the east lies Russia. The Baltic Sea surrounds the rest of the country. In a global context, Finland lies between 60 and 70 degrees north latitude, roughly as far north as Alaska. Finland's capital, Helsinki, and Anchorage, Alaska are both located approximately at 60 degrees north latitude. About one-third of Finland lies north of the Arctic Circle.

Finland's regional place in Europe often creates confusion because of the use of the term Scandinavia. Some consider Scandinavia a geographic shorthand that includes the countries of the Scandinavian Peninsula, that is, Sweden and Norway. Others use Scandinavia as a cultural-linguistic label to include Norway, Sweden, Denmark, and Iceland—all of whose languages are related. Others see Scandinavia as a broader region with a common culture and history, as well as similar political and social institutions. This latter understanding of Scandinavia includes Finland. Sometimes the Scandinavian word *Norden,* often translated as "the Nordic region" is used in respect to all five countries. Since no consensus exists on the use of the word Scandinavia, and the use of *Norden* and Nordic region is complicated on several levels, this book will use the term Scandinavia in the broadest sense to encompass the countries of Finland, Sweden, Denmark, Norway, and Iceland.

Finland encompasses a surface area of 338,000 square kilometers (130,599 square miles). It is the seventh-largest country in Europe (including European Russia), ranking in size between Germany and Poland. It is slightly smaller than the American state of Montana. The country is divided into five distinct topographical regions. Its coasts are lined with thousands of islands; the Åland Islands (Ahvenanmaa) in the southwest form Europe's largest archipelago. The sandy or agrarian zone is a lowland (200 meters/656 feet above sea level at the highest) that covers southwestern Finland and an enclave on the west coast around the city of Vaasa (Vasa). This sandy soil is Finland's most fertile agricultural land. Most of west-central Finland forms a region consisting largely of swamps or drained swampland. In the central and southeastern parts of the country lies the Lake District, home of most of Finland's nearly 190,000 lakes. Finland's forested hill country covers the eastern border regions of Kainuu, Savolax, North Karelia, and all but extreme northern Lapland. In the far north lies the higher and less-forested mountain district. Finland's highest mountain, Halti (1,328 meters/4,357 feet), lies in this area.[1]

Finland's northern location has a significant impact on its climate. Winters are indeed long and cold. Winter usually begins in mid-October in Lapland, moving southward until it reaches the Åland Islands in December. During the winter, average temperatures throughout the country remain below freezing. In Helsinki, the average high in January is −4 degrees C (24 degrees F). The

Finland today.

average low reaches −12 degrees C (13 degrees F). In the town of Sodankylä, one of the coldest spots in Lapland, temperatures average between highs of −8 degrees C (18 degrees F) and lows of −19 degrees C (−2 degrees F). The snow cover reaches maximum depth around mid-March, with an average of 60 to 90 centimeters (25 to 53 inches) in the east and north and 20 to 30 centimeters (8 to 12 inches) in the southwest. Lakes freeze over in late November and early December. Icebreakers keep coastal ports open in the winter months.

Nonetheless, Finland's climate is milder than that of similarly northern locations, such as Siberia, Greenland, or Alaska. The major moderating force is water: Finland's inland lakes, the Baltic Sea, and the North Sea, warmed by the Gulf Stream, moderate winter temperatures. Summers in Finland are warmer as well. Summer usually begins in late May in the south, reaching Lapland a month later. Helsinki in July has an average high of 21 degrees C (70 degrees F). This average prevails throughout the entire country in July with the exception of Lapland, where average temperatures are only a few degrees cooler.

Another characteristic of Finland's climate is light—or the lack thereof. North of the Arctic Circle people experience the so-called polar night, during which the sun does not clear the horizon. In the most northern parts of Finland, this period lasts 51 days during December and January. Winter offers a bit more light to Finland's south, where the shortest day in Helsinki lasts about six hours. In short, Finns go to work and school in the dark and come home in the dark during December and January. The dayless days yield to nightless nights in the summer. Above the Arctic Circle, the sun remains above the horizon for as long as 73 days. In southern Finland, the longest day at the summer solstice is nearly 19 hours long. In agriculture, the length of the days helps compensate for the shorter growing season. It also allows golfers to tee off at 10:00 p.m. [2]

POPULATIONS AND LANGUAGES

Finland has a population of more than 5.2 million inhabitants. Most of the population lives in the country's southern third. One in five inhabitants lives in the four communities that comprise the capital city area: Helsinki (Helsingfors), the capital and largest city (559,046); Espoo (Esbo), Finland's second-largest city (227,472); Vantaa (Vanda), the country's fourth-largest city (185,429); and Kauniainen (Grankulla) (8,465). The other three cities with populations of more than 100,000 are Tampere (Tammerfors) in south-central Finland (202,932), Turku (Åbo) in the southwest (174,824), and Oulu (Uleåborg) on the northwestern coast (127,226). This high degree of urbanization has occurred very quickly. Before 1969, the majority of Finns lived in rural areas. Despite this urbanization, Finland remains one of the least densely populated countries in Europe. Finland's population density of 15 people per square kilometer (24 people per square mile) makes Finland the third least densely populated country in Europe, behind Iceland and Norway. By another point of comparison, the United States has 31 people per square kilometer and the United Kingdom has 244. [3]

More than 93 percent of the population speaks Finnish as its first language. Finnish stands out as anomalous among Europe's languages. It is one of a few that does not belong to the Indo-European family of languages. Finnish is in the Finno-Ugric (or Uralic) family; the significant languages most closely related to Finnish are Karelian and Estonian. More distant relatives are Hungarian and languages spoken in central Russia, such as Mari, Udmurt, and Komi. From the standpoint of a speaker of English most and other Indo-European languages, Finnish has many peculiarities. For example, there are no definite or indefinite articles. The word *talo* means "house," "a house," and "the house." Prepositions are added to the end of the noun in question. "In a (or the) house" is in Finnish *talossa* (*talo* + *ssa*). Finnish has no grammatical gender. The pronoun *hän* means both he and she. Finns frequently point with pride at how difficult Finnish is for foreigners to learn. There are, however, two important mitigating circumstances for the foreign learner. First, Finnish is fully phonetic. For every sound there is one letter. Finnish has no silent letters or multiple ways of spelling the same sound. Second, Finnish grammar has many rules but few exceptions.

Slightly less than six percent of the population speaks Swedish as its first language. Swedish, a Germanic language, is closely related to Norwegian and Danish. More distant relations include Icelandic, German, Dutch, and English. Swedish speakers are concentrated along the western and southern coasts of Finland, and they define themselves as a linguistic rather than an ethnic minority. They share a common sense of nationhood and ethnicity with the Finnish-speaking majority. Thus the terms *Swedish* or *Finland Swedish,* when applied to Finland's linguistic minority, denote language rather than ethnicity or nationality.

The Swedish language enjoys many legal protections. Both Swedish and Finnish are official languages. The Language Act of 1922 entitles a Finnish citizen to use Finnish or Swedish in courts of law and in dealings with national authorities. Swedish enjoys official status in local governance as well. In the Åland Islands, where well over 90 percent of the population speaks Swedish as its first language, Swedish is the sole official language. Elsewhere, a municipality is officially classified as bilingual if a minority of at least eight percent of the population, or a minimum of 3,000 people, speaks the other language. One can easily tell if a community is bilingual by looking at the street signs: two sets of street signs mean that a community is bilingual. In Helsinki, for example, the name of the city's main street is Mannerheimintie in Finnish and Mannerheimvägen in Swedish.

Educational institutions protect the use of Swedish as well. In addition to having separate schools for the two language groups, students of both language communities must study the other language beginning in seventh grade. While Swedish-speaking youngsters feel more pressure to master Finnish than vice versa, Finnish speakers who aspire to positions in the country's elites find a command of Swedish to be very helpful. In fact, evidence suggests a recent increase in the use of Swedish. Until the 1990s, children of mixed-language families were almost invariably placed in Finnish-language schools; now the trend is moving in the other direction. Parents are attracted to Swedish-language schools because they are often smaller. Going through a Swedish-language curriculum better ensures that a child becomes truly bilingual. If this trend continues, it will help stem the decline of a minority group whose percentage of the population has dwindled by more than half since Finland's independence in 1917.[4]

Finland has several small ethnic minorities—communities that claim a separate sense of culture and society in respect to the majority population. The best-known of these groups is the Sámi, formerly called the Lapps. For millennia the Sámi have inhabited the northern reaches of Scandinavia known as Lapland. Like Native Americans or the Maori of New Zealand, they are internationally recognized as a "first people," a people that inhabited an area before its conquest and colonization, or the drawing of modern boundaries. The Sámi number between 60,000 and 100,000, and most of them inhabit a crescent ranging from central Sweden and Norway to the Kola Peninsula in Russia. The prevalence of reindeer herding as a major economic occupation distinguishes their way of life.

Over 6,000 Sámi live in Finland, two-thirds of whom inhabit the Sámi region that consists of Finland's three most northern municipalities: Enontekiö, Inari, Utsjoki, as well as the northern part of Sodankylä. The Sámi have self-governance in cultural and educational affairs. They have the right to use their language in dealings with government officials. About half of Finland's Sámi speak the Sámi language, a Finno-Ugric language, which actually consists of 10 closely related but distinct languages. Most Sámi in Finland speak North Sámi, the most frequently used of the languages and the *lingua franca* of among the Sámi.[5]

Another well-established ethnic group is the Rom, previously known as Gypsies. They number as many as 10,000, concentrated mostly in the urban south. It is estimated that about a third of Rom adults speak Finland's dialect of Romany, but nobody speaks it as a first language. The Rom first arrived in Finland in significant numbers in the seventeenth century, from central Europe. They historically have been a target of discrimination in Finland, as in other parts of Europe. Since the 1980s, the Finnish state has worked to enhance legal and cultural protections for the Rom.[6]

In contrast to its Scandinavian neighbors, Finland does not have large immigrant communities. In the century before the 1980s, Finland was a net exporter of people, primarily to North America and neighboring Sweden. At the same time, Finland's immigration laws were very strict. Since the early 1990s, several factors have opened up a steady stream of immigrants. Finland's leaders have bowed to both domestic and foreign pressure to accept more refugees. The collapse of the Soviet Union in 1991 opened the eastern border, and many arrivals from the former USSR have skills desired by Finland's employers. The country's entrance into the European Union (EU) in 1995 eased the movement of EU citizens into Finland. These various factors have helped to create a diverse immigrant population. Most of the immigration has come from countries belonging to the former Soviet Union, primarily from Russia and Estonia. The number of immigrants nearly quadrupled in the years 1990–2002. Nonetheless, the immigrant population of over 100,000 in the year 2004 still pales in comparison to that of Finland's Scandinavian neighbors both in absolute and relative terms.[7]

RELIGIONS

Finland's religious communities fall into two groups: those that historically have received state support and those that have not. The distinction is a remnant of centuries of European history in which subjects had to accept the religion of the monarch. The ruler, in turn, supported the church. Finland's historical legacy as a place between Eastern and Western Europe has given it two state-supported churches: the Evangelical Lutheran Church and the Orthodox Church. About 84 percent of Finns belong to the Evangelical Lutheran Church, which is a legacy of Finland's time as a part of the Swedish kingdom. About one percent belongs to the second-largest religious community, the Orthodox Church. The status of the Orthodox Church stems from the varying degrees of Russian rule over Finland before its independence in 1917.

The non-state-supported religious communities, combined, command the allegiance of about two percent of the population. This small but diverse group includes various Protestant churches. Roman Catholics number more than 7,000. Finland's Jewish community has about 1,000 members. Islam has had a small presence since the nineteenth century when Tatar soldiers in the Russian army settled in the country. Those claiming Tatar ancestry today number about 900. The number of Muslims has increased with recent immigration. About 13 percent of the Finnish population claims no religious affiliation.

Although the level of religious affiliation is very high, regular church participation, as in the rest of Western Europe, is low. A recent study revealed that less than two percent of Lutherans in Finland attend church services on a weekly basis. Nonetheless, the Lutheran Church exercises considerable moral authority on ethical, moral, and social issues. Weekly church attendance tends to be higher within the smaller religious communities. In fact, although the Lutheran Church has experienced slow but steady erosion in membership in recent years, many of the smaller denominations have experienced increases. [8]

EDUCATION AND INNOVATION

If Finns as a society value anything, it is the importance of education. In international studies, Finland's schoolchildren rank near or at the top in mathematics, science, and reading. According to a recent study, 36 percent of women aged 25 to 64 have a degree from an institution of higher education—the highest in the European Union. Among men of the same age, 29 percent have degrees. Among all EU countries, men in the United Kingdom and Ireland surpass Finland's men by only one percent.[9]

Finland belongs to a handful of countries in Europe where compulsory education begins at age seven, rather than six. More than 90 percent of six-year-olds, however, attend preschool. After the ninth grade, youngsters can choose between two educational paths. About half choose a general upper secondary school that provides university preparation (comparable to an American high school, a German *Gymnasium,* or a French *lycée*). The other half chooses to study for a specific trade in a vocational upper secondary school. The course of study in the general upper secondary school lasts for three years; most vocational training programs last as long.[10]

The two tracks continue into the realm of higher education. For those who have completed either track of upper secondary education, there are 29 polytechnics. These schools seek to train and retrain workers with specific skills designed to meet the needs of business and industry. The completion of a degree at a polytechnic takes about four years. On the other path of higher education there are 20 universities: 10 comprehensive universities, 3 universities of technology, 3 universities of economics and business administration, and 4 art academies. Entry into one of these institutions is based on exit examination scores in upper secondary school and the university's entrance examination results. Universities engage in broad-based theoretical research and education. The universities' basic degree has been the master's degree, which takes an average of six to seven years to complete. Some universities now confer a bachelor's degree, which takes about four years to earn.[11]

This educated population has used its learning in the creation of new technologies and knowledge. Finland leads the industrialized world in the number of people employed as researchers as a percentage of the workforce, and ranks among the world leaders in public and private investment in research and development. Among EU member states in 2002, Finland led by a large margin in the number of patents per million inhabitants in the field of information technology. In total patents per million inhabitants, in 2001 Finland ranked fourth in the world, behind Japan, Germany, and the United States. Recent inventions created in Finland include the cancer drug interferon, cholesterol-reducing margarine, the cavity-fighting sweetener xylitol, and the Linux computer operating system.[12]

ECONOMICS

This investment in education has had a decisive influence in creating one of the world's wealthiest economies. Finland's economic success over the last two centuries has also stemmed from its ability to export products to larger markets. For centuries, forest products (primarily wood and paper) have led Finland's export economy. With more than three-quarters of its land covered with trees, Finland is Europe's most heavily forested country. Wood is the only natural resource in which Finland is self-sufficient. In the years since

World War II, Finland's exports of metal and engineering technologies, as well as machinery, have risen to an equal position—slightly more than one-fourth of its total exports. This sector produces for export such goods as tractors, elevators, and machinery and technology for processing wood and wood products.[13]

Over the last 20 years, electronics and information technology have grown to comprise a slightly larger share of Finland's exports. Finland was late in creating an industrial economy but it has been a pioneer in the creation of a postindustrial information society. Finland's most visible enterprise in this transformation is Nokia, a world leader in providing people with what many consider a twenty-first century necessity—the mobile telephone. According to the 2004–2005 report of the respected World Economic Forum, Finland ranks just behind Singapore and Iceland in the use of information and communications technologies. This use of new technologies has kept Finland's economy one of the most competitive in the world.[14]

Along with education and exports, a third "e" serves as a basis for economic development in Finland—equality. In the economy there is a relatively high level of gender and social equality. A significant amount of the wealth created over the last half-century has been channeled into the creation of a welfare state that provides a comprehensive array of benefits for citizens from cradle to grave, such as paid maternity leave, day care for all children, and universal health care. For these benefits, Finns pay some of the highest tax rates among industrialized countries. High taxes on the wealthy and income transfers have helped make the gap between rich and poor one of the narrowest in the world.[15]

Successful in creating and spreading wealth, Finland's economy does suffer from some longstanding systemic problems. Unemployment has been a challenge, even in times of high economic growth. During the years of growth in the 1960s and 1970s, the low unemployment rates of two to three percent were masked by the migration of hundreds of thousands of working-age Finns to Sweden, where jobs abounded. Finland achieved nearly a full-employment economy in the 1980s, only to see unemployment rise to nearly 20 percent during the depression of the early 1990s. Despite high rates of growth since the end of the depression in 1994, unemployment hovered around nine percent in 2002—high for a developed economy. In addition to the problem of joblessness, Finland's overall cost of living is among the highest in Europe. Economic development since World War II has been geographically uneven. Finland's southern third has experienced a disproportionate share of the economic growth. Even in economically good times, many communities in northern and eastern Finland suffer from high unemployment and declining populations of working-age people. The reasons for these problems stem from many sources. Proposed solutions fuel a constant national discussion.

GOVERNMENT

Finland's democratic form of government explicitly places the people as the ultimate source of public power. Article II of the constitution states, "The powers of the state in Finland are vested in the people, who are represented by the Parliament."[16] This article reveals the preeminence of the country's legislative body in relation to the executive and the judicial branches of government. Citizens 18 years of age and older elect the 200 members of Finland's Parliament. Members of Parliament (MPs) are chosen by proportional representation, that is, each party receives approximately the number of seats in Parliament that corresponds with its percentage of the overall vote. Unlike in many countries with proportional representation, the voters, not the parties, determine the candidates a party will send to Parliament. Members of Parliament are elected to four-year terms. Early elections can be called if the president agrees to the prime minister's request for early elections.

Several parties, ranging from the far Left to the populist far Right, are represented in Finland's legislature. An overwhelming majority of Finns vote for parties between the two extremes: the Social Democrats, the Center, the Conservatives, or the Greens. As in many other small countries in Europe, political decision-making in Finland relies more on consensus than conflict. In contrast to many countries in Western Europe, several parties, not just one or two, have molded modern Finland's political history.

Both the president of the republic and the Government, or the Cabinet, exercise executive power. A recent round of constitutional reforms, culminating in the new constitution in 2000, focused on reducing some of the president's powers to the benefit of the Government and Parliament. The president is elected every six years; he or she can serve a maximum of two consecutive terms. The president has many important powers as head of state. He or she is commander-in-chief of the armed forces, although the president, with Cabinet approval, has the right to give that task to another citizen. In concert with the Government, the president determines the county's foreign policy. The president names the head of the Government, the prime minister, upon the recommendation of Parliament. The prime minister recommends other Government ministers to the president for appointment. The president signs into law bills passed by Parliament. He or she cannot expressly veto a bill but can leave a bill unsigned; a simple majority in Parliament can put an unsigned bill into law. The president can dissolve Parliament and call elections for a new Parliament at the request of the prime minister.

The conduct of daily governance belongs to the Government or Cabinet. In Finland, as in most countries, a distinction is made between *government*, which consists of all of those who exercise public or state power, and the *Government*, which is the highest executive body. Finland's Government consists of the prime minister and other ministers who lead the major ministries, such as social affairs, defense, finance, and foreign affairs. Most recent Cabinets have had 16 to 18 ministers. The Cabinet's authority to govern rests on the confidence of a majority in Parliament. For this reason, the larger parties generally form Cabinets after an election. Ideally, the Government's ministers represent parties that, combined, control a parliamentary majority. In Finland's multiparty system, that means building coalitions among several parties.

In terms of more local levels of governance, Finland is divided into six provinces. These are purely administrative channels for the central authorities in Helsinki. The one exception among the provinces, the Åland Islands, enjoys both wide-ranging autonomy and a provincial assembly. Finland's municipalities do have elected councils and significant responsibilities in education, social services, the environment, and infrastructure.

Finland has an independent judiciary. The court system is divided into two major subsections. One adjudicates criminal and civil cases, which are first presented to district courts. Finland does not have a jury system, but district court judgments are often rendered by a panel consisting of a judge, another legally trained person (usually another judge), and three so-called lay judges—citizens elected by the municipal or city council for four-year terms. Like jurors, they perform their tasks as a civic duty, not a profession. A district court's decisions can be challenged before a court of appeal. In turn, the Supreme Court can review an appellate court's judgment. The other body of courts, the administrative courts, adjudicates disputes concerning decisions of governing authorities. Verdicts can be appealed to the Supreme Administrative Court. All courts seek to interpret specific laws with respect to specific cases; they do not question a law's constitutionality. Legal thinking in Finland is based on the assumption that Parliament would not pass an unconstitutional law. As a bill goes through Parliament, the committee process vets its constitutionality.[17]

A high level of gender equality characterizes Finland's political culture. In 1906, Finnish women were the first in Europe to receive the right to vote for their national legislature. In the Parliament elected in 2003, 75 of 200 members were women. Finland has long competed with its Scandinavian neighbors over which country's legislature has the highest percentage of women in the world. In recent years, women have made serious gains in the executive branch as well. In the current Government, women hold 8 of 18 ministerial portfolios. In 2000, Finns elected their first female president, Tarja Halonen. In that same election, three of the top four finishers were women. In 2003, Finland for two months had its first female prime minister, Anneli Jäätteenmäki. Women also hold visible positions in the judiciary. In 2006, a woman, Pauliine Koskelo, assumed the presidency of Finland's Supreme Court.

FOREIGN RELATIONS AND NATIONAL SECURITY

Since achieving independence in 1917, the shadow of the Russian bear has guided, and in some cases misguided, Finland's foreign policy. Until the end of the World War II, independent Finland sought allies to neutralize the perceived threat from the Soviet Union. The failure of this search left Finland alone against the USSR during the Winter War of 1939–1940. After the war, Finland aligned itself with Germany in its invasion of the USSR in June, 1941.

With Germany defeated at the end of World War II and no reliable alternative counterweight to Soviet power available, Finland had to change its conduct of foreign relations. Formally, Finland maintained a policy of neutrality in the ensuing Cold War between the Soviet Union and the United States. In practice, Finland pursued a foreign policy that first and foremost sought to appease the USSR This policy, known as the Paasikivi-Kekkonen Line, was named after Finland's two postwar presidents, J. K. Paasikivi (1946–1956) and Urho Kekkonen (1956–1981). This policy created for Finland a more secure place in Europe. The development of trade with the Soviet Union contributed to Finland's economic transformation into one of the world's wealthiest countries. The cost of this policy was a persistent growth of Soviet influence in Finland's domestic politics, especially during the Kekkonen era.

Finland's comfortable niche between East and West began to disappear at the beginning of the 1980s. In the East, the Soviet empire was disintegrating. At the same time, Western Europe's democracies were taking steps toward greater political and economic integration. Finland's decision to join the process of Western European integration was motivated in part by the fear of an unstable post-Soviet Russia, in part by a desire to secure continued access to Western European markets. In 1995, Finland joined the EU—the most significant institution in the process of European integration. In 1999, Finland joined 11 other EU members in introducing the single European currency, the euro.

The end of the Cold War has not yet shaken Finns' reluctance to integrate themselves in formal military alliances. Finland relies on its own resources for national defense. Finland's armed forces consist of about 32,000 soldiers. More than half serve in the army, the rest in the navy and air force. The strength of Finland's armed forces lies in the support that they command in society. All male Finnish citizens are required to complete a term of military service of 180, 270, or 362 days, depending on the level of training and rank the draftee desires. More than 80 percent of those drafted annually (mostly 19- and 20-year-olds) complete a term of military service. Many of the best educated spend the longest period of military service in order to receive officer training. Less than 10 percent of draftees choose alternative nonmilitary service, one of the lowest rates among the world's democracies that have conscription. In 1995, the armed forces were opened to women on a voluntary basis. After completing military training, citizens enter the reserves. Reservists are liable for recall to refresher training until the age of 60. This large reservoir of reservists—almost half a million—would be mobilized to defend the country against attack. This wealth in human capital contrasts with a small defense budget. Finland spends slightly more than one percent of its gross national product on defense, compared to two percent in neighboring Sweden and seven percent in the United States. In addition to defending the nation, Finland's soldiers have contributed to the maintenance of international peace. Since 1956, more than 40,000 Finns have served in 25 United Nations peace-keeping operations around the world.[18]

FINLAND, EUROPE, AND THE WORLD

This book will survey Finland's past, with an emphasis on the nineteenth and twentieth centuries. For those interested in European and world history, Finland's past offers three special perspectives. First, since prehistoric times Finland has occupied the political, cultural, religious, and economic border-lands between Eastern and Western Europe. Second, despite its geographi-cally peripheral position, the country has found itself in the mainstream of developments that have created modern Europe, such as nationalism, indus-trialization, liberal democracy, world wars, as well as current political and economic integration.

Third, although it is a small country, Finland has made a wide array of im-portant contributions to European and world civilization, as well as to popular culture. The structures of Finnish architect Alvar Aalto (1898–1976) are found in countries ranging from the United States to Iran. The compositions of Jean Sibelius (1865–1957) are played in concert halls around the world. The films of Aki Kaurismäki (1957–) have received international acclaim. In sports, Finland has established a large reputation for a small country. The runner Paavo Nurmi is recognized by many as the greatest athlete of the first half of the twentieth century. In more recent times, the country's winter athletes have been leaders in cross-country skiing and ski jumping. Fans of ice hockey in North America know Finnish players Jari Kurri, Saku Koivu, and Teemu Se-länne, among others. Aficionados of Formula One auto racing are acquainted with Finnish drivers Keke Rosberg, Mika Häkkinen, and Kimi Räikkönen.

Finland's best-known cultural export is the sauna. Most adaptations of the sauna outside of Finland flout traditional Finnish sauna culture. In Finland, one does not read a newspaper or wear shoes in a sauna. Men do not sit in saunas with women. In Finland, saunas are definitely not associated with prostitution.

In world politics, Finland has attracted world attention on a handful of occasions, two of which are of lasting importance. The first was the Finnish–Soviet Winter War of 1939–1940, in which Finland miraculously repulsed an invasion by its much larger eastern neighbor. This conflict resulted in Finland losing about 10 percent of its land but maintaining its independence. Finland's second major moment on the world's stage was the Conference on Security and Cooperation in Europe in 1975. At this meeting in Helsinki, leaders of Europe and North America signed the Helsinki Accords that lessened Cold War tensions and gave hope to dissidents in Communist Eastern Europe. The conference became a permanent organization, the Organization for Security and Cooperation in Europe (OSCE), which seeks to maintain peace and human rights in Europe.

In examining any history, a few general points are helpful to keep in mind. The first is that the past, to paraphrase historian David Lowenthal, is always a foreign country, regardless of whether that past is that of one's own country or a foreign land. Using the example of Finland's history, a Finn hurtled 100 years back into Finland's past would feel about as foreign as a non-Finn placed in the same place in time. Second, one should avoid the temptation of reading history from the present to the past. In the case of Finland, there is a tendency to want to understand Finland and the Finns of the past in today's terms. Such an attempt blinds one to the richness of Finland's past; it runs counter to the evidence. Third, history is not only the study of the past, but also of change over time. Seldom is this change immediate, linear, or inevitable. Fourth, history is a problem-solving discipline. Historians do not spend their days memorizing dates. They are primarily concerned with understanding the past based on available evidence. For historians, the past is an equation to be solved. Fifth, contrary to the well-worn saying, history does not repeat itself. However, the past is constantly being rewritten. New generations of scholars, new approaches to old questions, new historical sources, as well as current events have a constant impact on the study of history. New scholarship does not always mean better scholarship.

The above-mentioned points apply to studying any period of history. Two specific suggestions apply to reading national histories such as this one. First, despite the current process of globalization, nationalism still molds the allegiances and politics of the world's peoples. The independent nation-states of the world today are not historical inevitabilities. This is particularly true of small, independent nations such as Finland. Many turning points in the past could have taken Finland far from its present place as a member of the family of nations. Second, national identities are constantly being redefined. At the beginning of the twentieth century, most people in Finland believed that a nation had to have one language. By the beginning of World War II, the Finnish nation was redefined to include both of the country's major language groups. Until recently, Finns defined their country as separate from Europe. In the early 1980s, when this author came to Finland for the first time, he was frequently asked if he had ever been to Europe! Finland was, according to many, "the most American country in Europe." Now, as a member of the EU,

Finland's national identity is being defined within the context of Europe. One aspect of Finland that has endured through the centuries is its location at the borderlands of Eastern and Western Europe.

NOTES

1. Kalevi Rikkinen, "Luonnonmaantieteelliset alueet," in *Suomen maantiede*, ed. Kalevi Rikkinen (Helsinki: Otava, 1980), 52–53; *Statistical Yearbook for Finland 2005* (Helsinki: Statistics Finland, 2005), 589.

2. "Climate in Finland—The Seasons," web site of Finnish Meteorological Institute, http://www.fmi.fi/weather/climate_4.html (accessed 5 January 2006); Finnish Meteorological Institute temperature statistics, http://www.fmi.fi/saa/tilastot_61.html#6 (accessed 5 January 2006).

3. *Statistical Yearbook for Finland 2005*, 72, 77, 90, 589–592.

4. Finlands Svenska Folketing, *Svenskt i Finland* (Ekenäs: Ekenäs Tryckeri, 2001); Anna Junger, "Swedish in Finland," web site of Virtual Finland, http://virtual.finland.fi/finfo/english/finnswedes.html (accessed 5 January 2006).

5. Veli-Pekka Lethtola, *Saamelaiset: Historia, yhteiskunta, taide* (Inari: Kustannus-Puntsi, 1997), 7–17; Veli-Pekka Lethtola, "The Sámi in Finland," web site of Virtual Finland, http://virtual.finland.fi/finfo/english/saameng.html (accessed 5 January 2006).

6. Martti Grönfors et al., "Suomen romaniväestö: Unohdettu kulttuuriryhmä," in *Suomen kulttuurivähemmistöt*, eds. Juha Pentikäinen and Mirja Hiltunen, Suomen Unesco-toimikunnan julkaisuja 72 (Helsinki: Yliopistopaino, 1997), 149–179.

7. *Statistical Yearbook for Finland 2005*, 116–117.

8. Kimmo Kääriäinen, "Churches and Religion," web site of Virtual Finland, http://virtual.finland.fi/finfo/english/uskoeng.html (accessed 6 January 2006); "Kirkon sana alkanut taas painaa," *Helsingin sanomat*, 18 May 2003; "Kirkossa käynti väheni edelleen,"*Helsingin sanomat*, 6 May 2003.

9. "Suomalaiskoulu tehokas OECD-maiden vertailussa," *Helsingin sanomat*, 30 October 2002; "Suomen naiset EU:n koulutetuimpia," web site of Finnish Broadcasting Corporation, http://ww2.yle.fi/pls/show/page?id = 218774 (accessed 5 March 2003); "Suomi kunnostautuu Unicefin kouluvertailussa," *Helsingin sanomat*, 27 November 2002. Among other studies concerning elementary education, see PISA studies by the Organization for Economic Cooperation and Development, http://www.minedu.fi/minedu/education/pisa/PISA.html (accessed 6 January 2006).

10. "The Finnish Education Policy—General Education," web site of Finnish Ministry of Education, http://www.minedu.fi/minedu/education/general_education.html (accessed 6 January 2006).

11. "The Finnish Education Policy—Polytechnics," web site of Finnish Ministry of Education, http://www.minedu.fi/minedu/education/polytechnic.html (accessed 6 January 2006); "The Finnish Education Policy—University Education," web site of Finnish Ministry of Education; http://www.minedu.fi/minedu/education/university_edu.html (accessed 6 January 2006).

12. "Suomen tiede pärjää tilastoissa," *Helsingin sanomat*, 5 November 2003; various statistics e-mailed from Finnish Patent Board, 2 September 2003.

13. "Finland at a Glance," web site of Virtual Finland, http://virtual. finland.fi/finfo/english/glance.html (accessed 6 January 2006); Foreign trade statistics, Finnfacts web site, http://www.finnfacts.com/english/economy/ indicators/trade.html (accessed 6 January 2006); Jari Parviainen, "Forests and Forestry," web site of Virtual Finland, http://virtual.finland.fi/netcomm/news/ showarticle.asp?intNWSAID = 25854 (accessed 6 January 2006).

14. "World Economic Forum's Information Technology Report 2004–05," http://www.weforum.org/site/homepublic.nsf/Content/Global + Competitive ness + Programme% CGlobal + Information + Technology + Report (accessed 6 January 2006); "World Economic Forum's Global Competitiveness Report 2005–06," http://www.weforum.org/site/homepublic.nsf/Content/Global + Comp etitiveness + Programme%5CGlobal + Competitiveness + Report (accessed 6 January 2006).

15. Web site of Luxembourg Income Study, http://www.lisproject.org/ keyfigures/ineqtable.htm (accessed 6 January 2006); "Women's Empowerment: Measuring the Global Gender Gap," web site of World Economic Forum, http:// www.weforum.org/site/homepublic.nsf/Content/Global + Competitiveness + Programe5CWomen%27s + Empowerment%3A + Measuring + the + Global + Gender + Gap (accessed 6 January 2006).

16. "The Constitution of Finland," web site of Finnish Ministry of Justice, http://www.om.fi/74.htm (accessed 6 January 2006).

17. "The Judicial System in Finland," web site of Finnish Ministry of Justice, http://www.oikeus.fi/8108.htm (accessed 6 January 2006); Byron Nordstorm, *The History of Sweden* (Westport and London: Greenwood Press, 2002), xi. Pertti Pesonen and Olavi Riihinen, *Dynamic Finland: The Political System and the Welfare State* (Helsinki: Suomalaisen Kirjallisuuden Seura, 2002), 213.

18. Finnish Ministry of Defense, *Taskutietoja puolustusvoimista 2003* (Helsinki: Pääesikunnan tiedotusosasto, 2003); "Suomen rauhanturvaajat," web site of Finnish Minsitry of Defense http://tietokannat.mil.fi/rauhanturvaajat/ main.php3 (accessed 6 January 2006).

2

Finland's Origins:
Prehistoric and Historic

In attempting to understand the history of any people or place, one encounters questions of origins. The interest in Finland's origins has not been just a scholarly pursuit. The creation of a national identity relies, in part, on establishing a strong sense of tradition: the longer a nation can prove its existence, the more securely people seem to uphold their national identity. Unlike their larger neighbors, the Swedes and Russians, Finns cannot build a national identity based on hundreds of years of visibility as an independent polity on the map of Europe. As Finland entered the twenty-first century, there were still thousands of Finns born before their country had become an independent nation-state. The lack of a long, visible past has provided fertile ground for the creation of fanciful myths about the Finns' prehistoric origins. These concocted pasts have proclaimed the Finns as the founders of civilizations ranging from ancient Egypt to Renaissance Venice. For generations, Finnish schoolchildren were taught that their ancestors came to Finland in a great migration from the Urals at about the time of Christ. Outside of Finland, people have learned that the Finns have descended from the Turks or Mongols. These myths are not just products of an ignorant past—new ones appear regularly.[1]

Prehistory is simply that part of the past for which no or very few written records exist. In the case of Finland, prehistory ends in the twelfth century A.D., a time when more southern parts of Europe had been in the historic Middle

Ages for centuries. The division of any prehistory into periods or ages is relative rather than absolute. A scarcity of data often makes demarcation between periods very difficult. Prehistory consists of long-term developments that do not always have clear beginnings and ends. As a result, presentations of the prehistoric often use varying chronologies. Any periodization is a scholarly construct based on available information and the researcher's perspective.

Three groups of researchers—archaeologists, linguists, and geneticists—have investigated and argued over Finland's prehistoric origins. Each group has its own methods of analysis, areas of emphasis, and explanatory power. All of them suffer, to varying degrees, from a scarcity of evidence. Archaeologists seek to understand the past by focusing on physical remains, such as ruins of ancient monuments, pots, weapons, and jewelry. Archaeologists gather material culture from such places as settlement sites, garbage pits, burial sites, and fortresses. Since the late 1800s, archaeologists have adopted methodologies from the natural sciences, including paleobotany, zoology, and geology. The best-known of these is the dating of certain types of organic matter (burned wood, for example) by measuring the decay of its carbon-14 atoms.

The anomalous position of Finnish in Europe's linguistic geography has drawn linguists to Finland's prehistoric development. The origins of Finland's Swedish-speaking and Sámi populations similarly have attracted linguists. Linguists have examined Finnish and Sámi by comparing the development of these languages to other Finno-Ugric languages, using the methods of historical or comparative linguistics. The establishment of Swedish and Sámi settlements has been identified, in part, through a study of place-names, a narrow form of historical linguistic examination.

The third and newest group of scholars of prehistoric Finland consists of geneticists. Whereas archaeologists examine pots and linguists examine words, geneticists compare the genes of Finland's population to other neighboring populations as a means of finding patterns concerning the settlement of the Finnish Peninsula. The genetic background of a people does not determine its culture or language. There is no "Finnish gene"; cultures are learned.

The very fact that archaeologists, linguists, and geneticists do not examine the same body of data means that they will probably never agree on the details concerning the settlement and development of prehistoric Finland. Nonetheless, there are some broad points of agreement. The Finns as we know them today are the result of thousands of years of habitation in Finland. They did not arrive on the Finnish Peninsula as a ready people. Thus, scholars have discarded the widespread belief that Finland was populated in one great migration from central Russia at the time of Christ. There are few reliable connections between the development of language, material culture, and ethnicity in prehistoric Finland. At times, these three defining aspects of a civilization probably developed independently of each other. In other words, separate groups of people provided the genetic, material, and linguistic heritage of Finland's population. Scholars see prehistoric Finland as a place of great diversity. Archaeologists conceptualize prehistoric Finland in terms of layers of migration and culture. Linguists point to influences from several languages on the development of Finnish. Geneticists see the Finns' genetic makeup not as a pine tree with one main root but, rather, as a fir tree with several roots radiating out in various directions. All scholarly approaches uphold Finland's position as a borderland between Western and Eastern Europe.[2]

FROM THE ICE AGE INTO THE STONE AGE

More than 11,000 years ago, Finland emerged from under a retreating sheet of ice that had covered northern Europe for some 60,000 years. What the ice left behind bore little resemblance to Finland today: only the eastern and northern fifths of today's Finland lay above water. The land that had been pushed under water by the ice began to rise, closing off coastal inlets. This process created thousands of lakes. Although it reached its current shape at around 3000 B.C., Finland is still rising from the sea at rates ranging from 80 centimeters (31.4 inches) per century near the city of Vaasa on the west coast to 20 centimeters (7.9 inches) per century on the southeast coast.[3]

With the melting of the ice, Finland left the Ice Age and entered the Stone Age. Research is continually discovering new and reevaluating old clues concerning the date of the first settlement after the Ice Age. Based on the most recent evidence, one can safely date the first traces of post-Ice Age human habitation in Finland to approximately 10,500 years ago.[4] Migrants from the south and east created a body of settlements known as the Suomusjärvi culture, named after the locale in southwestern Finland where the first settlement of this type was found. Finds of ball-shaped hammerheads and slate adzes characterize the early Suomusjärvi culture. Later finds consist of chisels and quartz arrowheads. Settlements of the Suomusjärvi culture predominate in the western and southern parts of the peninsula, although pioneer migration seems to have spread all over Finland.[5] This differentiation between the south and west (a region that runs west of a line drawn roughly from a bit north of Kokkola on the west coast southeast to the end of the Finnish-Russian border at the Gulf of Finland) and the north and east serves as a template for many historical developments in Finland.

Finland's earliest inhabitants lived by hunting, fishing, and gathering berries, roots, and other plants. People lived in small-scale societies of roughly 15 to 50 people. Groups probably distinguished themselves from other groups in the same way that nations separate themselves from each other today. No clues exist that would unambiguously illuminate these earliest inhabitants' ethnic and or linguistic backgrounds. The people of the Suomusjärvi civilization were probably ethnically and linguistically diverse.[6]

Chronology of Prehistoric Finland

Chronology (Based on calibrated 14-C datings)	Western Finland	Eastern Finland
circa 8500–5100 B.C.	Suomusjärvi Culture	Suomusjärvi Culture
c. 5100–4000 B.C.	Early Combed Ceramics	Early Combed Ceramics
c. 4000–3600 B.C.	Typical Combed Ware	Typical Combed Ware
c. 3600–2800 B.C.	Late Combed Ware	Asbestos Ceramics
c. 3200–2300 B.C.	Battle-Axe Culture	Asbestos Ceramics
c. 2300–1700 B.C.	Kiukainen Ceramics	Asbestos Ceramics
c. 1800–500 B.C.	Bronze Age	Bronze Age/Early Metal Age
c. 500 B.C.–1050/ 1155 A.D.	Iron Age	Early Metal Age/ Iron Age
c. 1050/1155–1300 A.D.	The Age of Crusades	The Age of Crusades

Sources: Christian Carpelan, "Käännekohtia Suomen esihistoriassa aikavälillä 5100–100 eKr.," in *Pohjan polulla: Suomalaisten juuret nykytutkimuksen mukaan*, ed. Paul Fogelberg, Bidrag till kännedom av Finlands natur och folk 153 (Ekenäs: Eckenäs tryckeri, 1999), 273; Torsten Edgren, "Om Arkeologin," in Torsten Edgren and Lena Törnblom, *Finlands historia*, vol. 1 (Esbo: Schildts, 1993), 19; Matti Huurre, "Maatalouden alku," in *Suomen maataloushistoria*, vol. 1, ed. Viljo Rasila (Helsinki: WSOY, 2003), 23; Mika Lavento, *Textile Ceramics in Finland the on the Karelian Isthmus: Nine Variations and a Fugue on a Theme of C. F. Meinander*, Suomen muinaisyhdistyksen aikakauskirja, vol. 109 (Vammala: Vammalan kirjapaino, 2001).

CERAMICS AND AXES

By 5000 B.C., a new civilization had emerged—the Combed Ceramic Culture. This culture derives its name from the characteristic combed design on its ceramic pots. A major technological development in the Stone Age, ceramic pots allowed for the cooking of food. Covering an area from the Baltic Sea into central Russia, this new culture spread out over Finland with the exception of the extreme northwest. Traders and migrants from the east and south probably brought this culture to Finland.[7]

As a result of the migrations, most scholars believe that by the middle (or typical) phase of the Combed Ceramic Culture the population was speaking very remote versions of the Finnish language (often called proto-Finnic). This conclusion is drawn from the correspondence of the Combed Ceramic Culture's area to the maximum geographical spread of Finno-Ugric languages. Two factors are important to keep in mind concerning the transformation of Finland during the Combed Ceramic Age. First, prehistoric migrations probably were not large in number. Migrants numbering in the hundreds could have a major impact on an indigenous population of a few thousand. Second, the introduction of proto-Finnic did not mean the arrival or creation of the Finns. For most of European history, language has been a mode of communication and not a basis of group identity. Society still remained small-scale.[8]

For decades, linguists and some archaeologists maintained that the first home of the Finns lay at the bend of the Volga River in southern Russia. In recent years, the search for a prehistoric single first home has yielded to an acceptance of several first homes. Recent genetic research indicates that the population of Finland is genetically closer to populations west of Finland than to those east of it. Finnish is related to languages that cover parts of Eastern Europe. Archaeological research reveals that Finland's prehistoric material culture comes from East and West. Most linguists now accept that although the Volga bend is the point of origin of Finno-Ugric languages, the genetic and cultural origins of the Finns lay primarily elsewhere. This variety of influences has prompted many to conclude that the first home of the Finns is actually Finland.[9]

Around 3200 b.c., another migration changed prehistoric Finland's material culture, economy, and languages. These new inhabitants brought the Battle-Axe Culture into Finland. This culture spread across much of the northern half of Europe, from the Rhine River into western Russia, including prehistoric Finland's south and west. In Finland, hammer-shaped axes and ceramics impressed with cord before firing characterize this culture. This corded ware differed from combed ceramics in that they tended to be smaller and had flat bottoms. This new decoration did not completely eliminate combed ceramics. Rather, the two cultures coexisted.[10]

In addition to enriching the material culture, the Battle-Axe people may have introduced animal husbandry and agriculture. The introduction of agriculture was sporadic and experimental for the next two millennia. Climate and an inability to find suitable forms of grain probably were the biggest barriers to the development of agriculture. Even when agriculture was consistently practiced in a particular area, it still often had a transient element in that land was farmed using various methods of slash-and-burn agriculture. A forested area would be burned down and the ground, fertilized by the ash, would then be planted with crops, mostly various types of grains. This type of agriculture (along with more settled forms) as well as nomadic hunting and gathering coexisted on the Finnish Peninsula into the nineteenth century.[11]

The people of the Battle-Axe Culture made a significant impact on the development of Finland's languages. Their language has been the topic of some debate. Scholars of the Finnish language believe that those Battle-Axe people who reached the eastern Baltic spoke a language belonging to the Indo-European family. The Battle-Axe people in southern and western Finland adopted the language of the original inhabitants but infused early

Indo-European words into it. As a result, they turned proto-Finnic into an early version of the Finnish language (or proto-Finnish).[12] This and later influences from Germanic languages have led linguists to conclude that Finnish has "its roots in the East, its branches in the West."[13] In the north and west, the area outside of the Battle-Axe Culture's strong influence, proto-Finnic developed into proto-Sámi.[14] The spread of Finnish and the contraction of the Sámi-speaking area over the subsequent millennia largely stemmed from a victory of agriculture over hunting and gathering. Agriculture was spread not only by Finnish-speaking settlers, but also by Sámi who adopted agriculture. In doing so, the Sámi adopted the language of Finnish-speaking farmers.[15]

By about 2300 B.C., the two cultures of Finland's south and west, the Battle-Axe and the Combed Ceramic, merged into the Kiukainen Culture. A factor in this fusion may have been a cooling of the weather, which heightened conflict as well as cooperation between the two cultures. The ceramics of the Kiukainen settlements have the traits of both combed and corded ware. In the north and east, the culture of Asbestos Ceramics that had existed for some 2,000 years was coming to an end. Throughout the Finnish Peninsula, the period from about 2500–1500 B.C. was one in which the people were slowly exposed to metals and their potential uses.[16]

THE BRONZE AGE

By 1500 B.C., metals had begun to come into common use in Finland. As in other parts of Europe, the first of these was bronze, an alloy of copper and tin. Traders from the West introduced bronze, possibly in exchange for furs and seal blubber. Bronze artifacts consist of daggers, some swords, jewelry, even combs and razor blades. A cooling of the weather aided trade from the West. Colder and longer winters facilitated easier travel across the ice to and from the Scandinavian Peninsula. An increase of trade with central Europe was necessary for all of Scandinavia to enter the Bronze Age, since it lacked the resources for making bronze. This trade brought southern and western Finland into a Bronze Age civilization stretching from southern Scandinavia to southwestern Finland.

The traders from the West had more than an economic impact on Finland's south and west; it is believed that some of them settled there. Contacts with the West brought an increase of Germanic loan words into Finnish, and the interchange with the West is also seen in the adaptation of Scandinavian burial mounds in Finland. These mounds, usually made of stones, mostly range from 3 to 20 meters (about 3 to 20 yards) in diameter and 1 to 2 meters high. Mounds as large as 36 meters in diameter and 5 meters high have been discovered. The deceased's cremated remains and valuables were often buried in the mound. It is assumed that the introduction of the burial mound reflected a change in religious rituals.[17]

As had happened during the Stone Age, Finland's metal ages had influences from East and West. Northern and eastern parts of the peninsula joined the Bronze Age people through trade and small amounts of migration from the east. In addition to receiving bronze goods, the people of northern and eastern Finland adopted the use of textile ceramics. This ceramic is characterized by the imprint of loosely-woven fabric. Textile ceramics originated in the region of the upper Volga and Oka Rivers in Russia and succeeded the combed ceramic and corded ware in that area.[18]

During the Bronze Age, the sporadic practice of agriculture spread into places in Finland's north and east. In the south and west, evidence suggests that agriculture began to take an equal position to hunting, fishing, and gathering in food production, at least in some places. The institution of the farm with specific plots for farming, stables for animals, and buildings for the storage of grains begins to appear.[19]

THE IRON AGE

From about 500 B.C. onward, iron came into use in northern Europe. While bronze had to be imported, low-grade iron was available basically everywhere in Finland's swamps and lakes. Following a larger prehistoric pattern, the people of the Finnish Peninsula imported iron-making skills and iron goods from their eastern and western neighbors. Growth in population and economic activity, as well as diversification in spiritual practices and changes in social structure, characterize Finland's Iron Age.

Evidence suggests slow but steady population growth during the Iron Age. Small numbers of people from the west, mostly traders, continued to settle in Finland. Many factors limited population growth, even under the best of conditions. Average life expectancy, about 30 years, was much shorter than today's standards. Infant mortality was high and most live births resulted in death by age 10, if not within the first year. The difficulties of having several small children at the same time further limited population growth. People who lived off of hunting and gathering needed to stay as mobile as possible. In many cases, breastfeeding was necessary even up to age 5 because of a lack of appropriate food for young children. Growth could easily turn into decline with the smallest of natural disasters, diseases, or violent conflicts. As a result, the population, probably a few thousand at the time of the Suomusjärvi culture, probably increased only a tenth of a percent annually during the entire prehistoric era. Scholars have estimated that by the end of the Iron Age, Finland had a population between 20,000 and 40,000. More reliable population figures from later periods suggest that the Iron Age population might have been even higher.[20]

Interestingly, Finland's population growth was little affected by the most significant migration out of the Scandinavian Peninsula in the Iron Age—the

Viking expansion across northern Europe during the ninth and tenth centuries. The Vikings did not colonize Finland but did leave a record of activity in the country. The Sagas (early Scandinavian poems) tell of Viking attacks on the western Finnish region of Ostrobothnia from Norway and northern Sweden in the eleventh century. On their journeys between the Scandinavian Peninsula and points east, the Vikings in southern Finland left artifacts ranging from swords to Arab coins.[21]

As is often the case in pre-industrial societies, economic growth paralleled population growth. An increase in internal trade and a vibrant foreign trade significantly improved the quality and quantity of material possessions. The cultivation of grain continued to expand. Agriculture surpassed hunting and gathering as the major economic activity in the south and west, and it made significant inroads in the interior. Evidence suggests that the expansion of agriculture satisfied both a demand for food and alcoholic brews. Cultivated grains and hops produced better beer than did wild plants.[22]

Belief systems and spiritual practices in prehistoric Finland were very diverse. A variety of burial practices suggests an increased diversity during the Iron Age, especially during the Merovingian and Viking eras (600–1050 A.D.). There were various types of burial mounds and burial grounds. In some cases, the deceased was buried with valuables, or even his boat if he was a merchant. In other cases, the deceased was buried in a casket with no valuables. Both inhumation (burial) and cremation were used to usher the dead into the next life. Belief systems included animism, a belief system based on personalized, supernatural beings that inhabit animals and objects. At least some prehistoric people seemed to have believed that gods influence the world through natural forces such as thunder, lightning, or wind. There is also evidence of ancestor worship, a practice of seeking supernatural help through gifts to dead relatives at their burial site. Shamanism was one widespread way of reaching the supernatural realm. Shamanism centers on the shaman, a person believed able to influence the course of natural events on Earth (such as the curing of an illness) through a special connection to the spirit world. A shaman reaches spirits through rituals, dreams, and herb-induced hallucinations.[23]

At the end of the Iron Age, the spread of Christianity across northern Europe reached Finland. In Denmark, King Harald Bluetooth baptized himself in the 960s; Norway's King Olav Trygvasson converted to the new faith in the 990s; and King Olof Skötkonung of Sweden adopted Christianity around the year 995. To the east of Finland, Grand Duke Vladimir of Kiev adopted Christianity in 988. These rulers' embrace of Christianity gave the new religion a firm foothold in northern Europe, even though paganism or fragments of pagan belief and ritual endured for centuries.[24]

Before prehistoric Finns adopted Christian beliefs, they adopted Christian material culture. From the ninth century onward, Christian objects, such as crosses, were imported from both Eastern and Western Europe. Most Christian artifacts, however, are dated from the eleventh century onward. At first, many wore Christian crosses for purely decorative purposes; others wore the cross as a means of gaining access to the Christian world. In the early phase of Christian expansion into northern Europe, pagans who wore the cross were allowed to enter shrines and participate in masses without formal baptism. They could also more easily conduct trade with Christian merchants. At the same time, Christian inhumation became more common. Finland's first stone churches were built on the Åland Islands in the late thirteenth century. Wooden churches that have not survived might have preceded these buildings.[25]

At the same time as religious practices were becoming more diverse, social structures were becoming more complex. The construction of hillforts during the last centuries of the Iron Age suggests a growth in social hierarchy and organization of labor. Meanwhile, some of the small-scale societies of prehistoric Finland created larger tribal affiliations, such as the Karelians in the southeast and the Tavastians in the central regions. The unity of these tribes probably did not go beyond a loose association of traditional small-scale societies.[26]

During the Iron Age, the first written sources concerning Finland were produced. These earliest written references are anything but reliable or comprehensive. The Roman geographer and historian Tacitus made the first significant written mention of Finland. In his work *Germania* (published circa 98 A.D.), Tacitus describes a people that he calls the *Fenni.* For a long time it was believed that this was the first written confirmation of the existence of a Finnish people, but scholars now agree that Tacitus's term *Fenni* corresponds more closely to the Sámi than the Finns.[27] In an account of his voyages, the ninth-century Viking explorer Ohthere tells of a people, the *Cwenas,* the inhabitants of *Cwenaland,* a region that lay roughly along the northern coast of the Gulf of Bothnia. The *Cwenas* were in frequent conflict with the populations of northern Norway.[28] From the words *Cwenas* and *Cwenaland* comes the modern name for the region of Kainuu along Finland's east-central border with Russia. The eleventh-century geographer Adam of Bremen wrote the most fanciful description of the Finnish Peninsula's inhabitants. In his work on northern Europe, he described the inhabitants of Finland as Cyclops, Amazons, and humans with the heads of dogs![29]

THE AGE OF THE CRUSADES

The last of the prehistoric periods, the Age of the Crusades (circa 1050/1155–1300 A.D.), is often considered Finland's first historic period. The increased number of written sources concerning Finland from the eleventh century onward has led some scholars to consider the eleventh, twelfth, and even thirteenth centuries Finland's early historical phase.

As in the case of previous periods, the Age of the Crusades was molded by influences from the East and West. From both directions came the two types of power that had held sway over most other parts of Europe. One was temporal power, that is, the power of kings and princes. The other was ecclesiastical power, or the power of the church. By the end of the eleventh century, there was a formal split in European Christianity. The Roman Catholic Church, led by the pope in Rome, held the allegiances of Europeans in the western two-thirds of the continent, while Christian communities in the Balkans, Asia Minor, and in the area of today's Russia and Ukraine belonged to the Orthodox Church, led by the patriarch of Constantinople. Finland would not only be subject to competing forms of temporal power from the East and West, but both competing forms of Christianity as well.

The traditional starting point of Finland's history has been the year 1155, when King Erik of Sweden and Bishop Henry of Uppsala, the head of the Catholic Church in Sweden, led a crusade across the Gulf of Bothnia to convert the heathen Finns. In recent years, scholars have heavily scrutinized the event's significance and even its very occurrence. According to the current scholarly consensus, the event most likely occurred in the second half of the 1150s (probably 1157), but on a much smaller scale than had been commonly believed. The flotilla of crusaders probably consisted of some small ships that landed somewhere on the southwestern coast of Finland. Representatives of the Swedish Crown and the Catholic Church probably led the operation. No sources exist from the time of the event that verify Erik's participation or even the existence of a Bishop Henry; their roles became visible only in later accounts and legends. In any case, the crusaders encountered a population that for centuries had been dealing with visitors from the other side of the Gulf of Bothnia. Evidence suggests that already in the eleventh century the Swedish Crown was collecting taxes from the eastern side of the Gulf of Bothnia. Christian influences had existed in Finland long before Erik or Henry. This mission aimed not so much at the conversion of the people as at the formal organization of Rome's ecclesiastical and Sweden's temporal control over the eastern half of the Gulf of Bothnia.[30]

The assertion of Swedish authority occurred in the face of a wider competition among various temporal and ecclesiastical powers in the Baltic Sea region. Pope Eugene III encouraged the spread of ecclesiastical power from the West. In 1147, he announced an absolution of sins for participants in crusades against pagans in the Baltic. The Roman Church's encouragement of crusades in the north occurred at the same time that the Church was sponsoring better-known crusades to the Holy Land. Also at this time, Orthodox Christianity was spreading into Finland's east. The two most important centers for Orthodoxy in Karelia were the monasteries of Valamo (*Valaam* in Russian) and Konevitsa (*Konevets* in Russian). In terms of temporal power, the principality of Novgorod was expanding its political and economic influence westward among the Tavastians and Karelians. The cities of the German Hanse (the Hanseatic League) sought to expand their commercial reach all over the Baltic Sea. In the early thirteenth century another German force, the Teutonic Knights, moved into the eastern Baltic coast in order to bring the pagan populations into the Roman Catholic fold. The Danes were making moves, as well, taking northern Estonia in 1219.[31]

According to legend, the first Swedish crusade ended in the murder of Bishop Henry by a local peasant named Lalli at Lake Köyliöjärvi near the village of Kokemäki in the southwest region of Finland. Contrary to popular understanding of the legend, Lalli probably did not kill Henry for religious reasons. The legend itself suggests that Lalli was already a Christian and that he acted out of anger about new Church taxes. The Catholic Church in Finland would later honor the legendary bishop's work by proclaiming him Finland's patron saint. King Erik, himself murdered in Uppsala in 1160, became Sweden's patron saint. The lack of strong temporal and ecclesiastical leadership for the rest of the twelfth century diminished the immediate significance of this crusade. In 1171 or 1172, Pope Alexander III issued a bull, or papal decree, complaining that the people of Finland were loyal Christians only in the presence of the Swedish troops. According to the pope, priests frequently were subject to physical harm.[32]

The strengthening of the Catholic Church's and the Swedish Crown's grip on Finland would increase in three spasms of activity during the thirteenth century. The first occurred during the tenure of Bishop Thomas (circa 1225–1245). Although a separate office of bishop for Finland (under the archbishop of Uppsala) had been established some years earlier, Thomas was the first bishop credited with strengthening the Church's institutions in Finland. Thomas used armed force to establish the Church's control over the people of Tavastland (in Finnish, Häme). Thomas's army reached deep into Karelia before Novgorod's army under Prince Alexander Nevski crushed it at the Neva River in 1240.[33] The next important step came in the year 1249 or even later, when Birger Jarl, the brother-in-law of King Erik Eriksson, led another foray into Tavastland. Until the end of the 1250s, Birger's military operations were the first to place the region more firmly under the Swedish Crown's control and then protect it from Novgorod. With Tavastland in hand, the battle between Sweden and Novgorod again would shift to Karelia.[34]

In 1293, Marshal Tyrgils Knutsson and Bishop Benottenrici Korp of Västerås in Sweden led the last of Sweden's crusades. The invasion of Karelia went well at first, resulting in conquest of the Karelian Isthmus by the year 1300. Then, for the next quarter-century the front would oscillate radically, with Novgorod's forces plundering Turku (Åbo) in 1318.[35] In 1323, the war between Sweden and Novgorod ended with the Peace of Nöteborg. The treaty not only ended hostilities but also drew a line dividing Sweden's and Novgorod's interests on the Finnish Peninsula. Historians have long understood the treaty as

drawing a border from the southern end of the Karelian isthmus, roughly dividing the land bridge into western and eastern halves. The border then continued to follow a roughly northwestern route, eventually following the
Pyhäjoki River to the Gulf of Bothnia. A more recent interpretation asserts that
the border actually forked off in the Savolax region, with one border running
west to the Gulf of Bothnia and another running north to the White Sea. The
land in between was actually an area of joint jurisdiction. Political borders in
this and many later periods were rough and porous approximations. For the
two parties to the treaty, the crucial border zone ran through the Karelian isthmus northward toward approximately the modern-day town of Varkaus. This
part of the border was actually marked with posts, and maps defined it.[36] Neither side, especially the Swedish Crown, was interested in having the rest of
the border well-defined.

The Finnish Peninsula during its prehistoric and early historic phases was
a place of great diversity. Cultures and populations settled there from all possible directions. It is from this diversity that a people later known as the Finns
would emerge. Political and cultural borders between East and West were
drawn several times during the period in question. Finland at the end of the
early historic period was still a collection of tribes and small communities.
Neither a sense of national unity nor a central political force existed. Attempts
at placing the people of Finland under a single authority brought the country
into the historical age and made it a battleground between Eastern and Western princes, and Eastern and Western Christianity. These conquests, while
ending prehistoric Finland, would mold the country into an independent
historical entity.

NOTES

1. Derek Fewster, "The Invention of the Finnish Stone Age," in Matti Huurre
et al., *Dig it All: Papers Dedicated to Ari Siiriäinen* (Helsinki: Finnish Antiquarian
Society, 1999), 13–20; Aira Kemiläinen, *Suomalaiset, outo Pohjolan kansa: Rotu-
teoriat ja kansallinen identiteetti* (Helsinki: Suomen Historiallinen Seura, 1993);
Aira Kemiläinen et al., *Mongoleja vai germaaneja? Rotuteorioiden suomalaiset*
(Helsinki: Suomen Historiallinen Seura, 1985); Sigurd Wettenhovi-Aspan, *Suomen kultainen kirja*, vol. 2 (Helsinki: K. F. Puromiehen Kirjapaino, 1935).

2. Reijo Norio, "Mitä geenitutkimus voi kertoa suomalaisista," in *Pohjan
polulla: Suomalaisten juuret nykytutkimuksen mukaan*, ed. Paul Fogelberg, Bidrag
till kännedom av Finlands natur och folk 153 (Ekenäs: Ekenäs tryckeri, 1999),
305.

3. Matti Huurre, *9000 vuotta Suomen esihistoriaa* (Helsinki: Otava, 1995), 9;
"Maihinnousu mm/vuosi," web site of Finnish Geodetic Institute, www.fgi.fi/
osastot/geodesia/projektit/tarkkavaaitus/maannousu.html (accessed 6 March
2006).

4. Huurre, *9000 vuotta*, 234–36; Timo Jusslia, "Joutsenon Kuurmanpohjan kivikautisten asuinpaikkojen koekaivaus v. 2000," Web site of Mikroliitti Oy, http://www.mikroliitti.fi/kuurmanp/esipuhe.htm (accessed 3 January 2006); Hannu Takala, *The Ristola Site in Lahti and the Earliest Postglacial Settlement of South Finland* (Jyväskylä: Gummerus, 2004).

5. Huurre, *9000 vuotta*, 13–23, 234–236, 259–260.

6. Turkka Aaltonen and Martti Arkko, *Lallin pidot: Elämyksiä ja ruokamatka Suomen esihistoriaan* (Helsinki: Edita, 2001), 18; Huurre, *9000 vuotta*, 13–23, 234–236, 259–260; Kari Pitkänen, "Suomen väestön historialliset kehityslinjat," in *Suomen väestö*, ed. Seppo Koskinen (Helsinki: Gaudeamus, 1994), 23.

7. Huurre, *9000 vuotta*, 24–32, 237–240.

8. Christian Carpelan, "Käännekohtia Suomen esihistoriassa aikavälillä 5100–1000 ekr.," in *Pohjan polulla: Suomalaisten juuret nykytutkimuksen mukaan*, ed. Paul Fogelberg, Bidrag till kännedom av Finlands natur och folk 153 (Ekenäs: Ekenäs tryckeri, 1999), 249–256; Kaisa Häkkinen, *Suomalaisten esihistoria kielitieteen valossa* (Helsinki: Suomen Historiallinen Seura, 1996), 15–22; Huurre, *9000 vuotta*, 24–32, 237–240.

9. These perspectives are presented in several collections of articles, the most recent of which is in *Ennen, muinoin: Miten menneisyyttämme tutkitaan*, ed. Riho Grünthal (Helsinki: Suomalaisen Kirjallisuuden Seura, 2002).

10. Huurre, *9000 vuotta*, 71–84.

11. Huurre, *9000 vuotta*, 256–258; Matti Huurre, "Viljaviljelyn varhaisvaiheet," in *Suomen maatalouden historia*, vol. 1, ed. Viljo Rasila et al. (Helsinki: Suomalaisen Kirjallisuuden Seura, 2003); 26–54; Milton Nuñez, "Role of Food Production in Stone Age Finland," in *Pohjan polulla: Suomalaisten juuret nykytutkimuksen mukaan*, ed. Paul Fogelberg, Bidrag till kännedom av Finlands natur och folk 153 (Ekenäs: Ekenäs tryckeri, 1999), 135–142; Irmeli Vuorela, "Viljelytoiminnan alku paleoekologisen tutkimuksen kohteena," in *Pohjan polulla: Suomalaisten juuret nykytutkimuksen mukaan*, ed. Paul Fogelberg, Bidrag till kännedom av Finlands natur och folk 153 (Ekenäs: Ekenäs tryckeri, 1999), 143–151.

12. Häkkinen, *Suomalaisten esihistoria*, 144–147.

13. Ulla-Maija Kulonen, "Kielitiede ja Suomen väestön juuret," in *Ennen, muinoin: Miten menneisyyttämme tutkitaan*, ed. Riho Grünthal (Helsinki: Suomalaisen Kirjallisuuden Seura, 2002), 114.

14. Christian Carpelan, "Katsaus saamelaistumisen vaiheisiin," in *Johdatus saamentutkimukseen*, ed. Ulla-Maija Kulonen et al. (Helsinki: Suomen Historiallinen Seura, 1994), 13–42; Huurre, *9000 vuotta*, 260–264; Ulla-Maija Kulonen, "Saame kielikunnassaan," in *Johdatus saamentutkimukseen*, ed. Ulla-Maija Kulonen et al. (Helsinki: Suomen Historiallinen Seura, 1994), 87–100.

15. Huurre, 151–54; Veli-Pekka Lehtola, *Saamelaiset: Historia, yhteiskunta, taide* (Jyväskylä: Gummerus, 1997), 20, 31–32.

16. Ari Siiriäinen, "Suomen esihistoria," in *Suomen historian pikkujättiläinen*, ed. Seppo Zetterberg (Porvoo: WSOY, 1987), 20–21.

17. Huurre, *9000 vuotta*, 91–94, 103–107; Siiriäinen, "Suomen esihistoria," 21–24.

18. Huurre, *9000 vuotta,* 110–115; Siiriäinen, "Suomen esihistoria," 24.

19. Huurre, "Viljaviljelyn varhaisvaiheet," 34–37; Siiriäinen, "Suomen esihistoria," 23.

20. Aaltonen and Arkko, *Lallin pidot,* 18; Huurre, *9000 vuotta,* 13–23, 234–236, 259–260; Pitkänen, "Suomen väestön historialliset kehityslinjat," 23.

21. Huurre, *9000 vuotta,* 217–222; Siiriäinen, "Suomen esihistoria," 27–39.

22. Huurre, *9000 vuotta,* 256–258.

23. Veikko Anttonen, "Elämä esihistoriallisessa Suomessa," *Suomen kulttuurihistoria,* vol. 1, ed. Tuomas M. S. Lehtonen and Timo Joutsivuo (Helsinki: Tammi, 2002), 52–60; Thomas A. Dubois, *Nordic Religions in the Viking Age,* (Philadelphia: University of Pennsylvania Press, 1999), 46–61;

24. Jouko Vahtola, "Keskiaika," in *Suomen historian pikkujättiläinen,* 47.

25. Anttonen, "Elämä esihistoriallisessa Suomessa," 61–80; Heikki Kirkkinen and Viktor Railas, *Ortodoksisen kirkon historia* (Pieksämäki: Sisälähetysseuran Raamattutalon kirjapaino, 1976), 155–157.

26. Huurre, *9000 vuotta,* 218; Siiriäinen, "Suomen esihistoria," 35–37; Vahtola, "Keskiaika," 41–46.

27. Anttonen, "Elämä esihistoriallisessa Suomessa," 64; Häkkinen, *Suomalaisten esihistoria,* 25; Tuomo Pekkanen, "Suomi ja sen asukkaat latinan- ja kreikankielisessä kirjallisuudessa 1000-luvulle asti," in *Suomen väestön esihistorialliset juuret,* ed. Jarl Gallén, Bidrag till kännedom av Finlands natur och folk 131 (Helsinki: Societas Scientarum Fennica, 1980), 227–247.

28. Vahtola, "Keskiaika," 42; "The Voyages of Ohthere and Wulfstan," in *Sweet's Anglo-Saxon Reader,* ed. Dorothy Whitelock (Oxford: Clarendon, 1967), 17–22.

29. Häkkinen, *Suomalaisten esihistoria,* 29; Pekkanen, "Suomi," 227–247.

30. Tuomas Heikkilä, *Heikkilä, Tuomas: Pyhän Henrikin legenda* (Helsinki: Suomalaisen Kirjallisuuden Seura, 2005); Tuomas Heikkilä and Samu Niskanen, *Europan synty: Keskiajan historia* (Helsinki: Edita, 2004), 192; Simo Heininen and Markku Heikkilä, *Suomen kirkkohistoria* (Helsinki: Edita, 1996), 16–17; Vahtola, "Keskiaika," 48–52; *Suomen historia jääkaudesta Euroopan unioniin* (Keuruu: Otava, 2003), 35–39; Pentti Virrankoski, *Suomen taloushistoria kaskikaudesta atomiaikaan* (Helsinki: Otava, 1975), 14.

31. Vahtola, "Keskiaika," 48–54.

32. Heininen and Heikkilä, *Suomen kirkkohistoria,* 15–17; Vahtola, *Suomen historia,* 37–38.

33. Heininen and Heikkilä, *Suomen kirkkohistoria,* 18–19; Markus Hiekkanen, "Vipuri lääni—rautakaudesta keskiaikaan," in *Viipurin läänin historia I: Karjalan synty,* ed. Matti Saarnisto (Jyväskylä: Gummerus, 2003), 496–504; Tapani Kärkkäinen, *Kirkon historia: Ortodoksin käsikirja* (Jyväskylä: Gummerus, 1999) 174–176; Vahtola, "Keskiaika," 55.

34. Heininen and Heikkilä, *Suomen kirkkohistoria,* 18–19; Vahtola, "Keskiaika," 55.

35. Heininen and Heikkilä, *Suomen kirkkohistoria,* 20.

36. Vahtola, *Suomen historia,* 45–46.

3

Finland as Part of the Swedish Realm (circa 1157–1809)

For more than six centuries, most if not all of the Finnish Peninsula was an integral part of the kingdom of Sweden. This association with the Swedish realm left a lasting mark on Finland, especially in terms of religion, language, political institutions, culture, and economy. Historians structure this long epoch into somewhat smaller periods of time. From about 1157 until about 1500, Finland and the rest of Europe were in the medieval period or the Middle Ages. Then Europe entered the early modern period, which historians see as ending in the late eighteenth or early nineteenth century. Scholars of Sweden's and Finland's history divide the early modern era into a variety of phases. In this work, the era will be divided into the Age of Gustav Vasa (1523–1560), the Age of Expansion (1560–1721), the Age of Liberty (1718–72), and the Gustavian period (1772–1809).

FINLAND IN THE SWEDISH KINGDOM

As has been previously mentioned, one of the challenges in understanding Finland's past is to think outside the constraints of modern nationalism. Applying the model of a modern nation-state does little to illuminate Finland's place in the kingdom of Sweden. The historian Nils Erik Villstrand has given the best explanation of Finland in the Swedish realm: "There was no Finland, there was a Finland, there were two [Finlands], and there were many [Finlands]."[1]

No Finland existed as a separate sovereign entity within the Swedish realm. The kingdom of Sweden did not consist of one monarch ruling two states. The frequently used term *Sweden-Finland* is thus misleading. Instead, the terms *Swedish kingdom* and *Swedish realm* will be applied to those areas under the control of the Swedish monarch, including Finland. The term *Sweden* will describe those areas west of the Gulf of Bothnia that encompass today's Sweden. With respect to the medieval and early modern eras, Finland is identified as the vast part of the Finnish Peninsula under the control of the kingdom of Sweden. Similarly, the terms Finnish and Finn refers to people born and living primarily in Finland. It is a geographic rather than an ethnic term. It applies to all language groups.

A Finland did exist as a geographic expression applied to the kingdom's areas east of the Gulf of Bothnia. Like many geographic expressions, its boundaries often were vague and changed over time. Sometimes a Finland existed as a distinct administrative unit within the kingdom of Sweden. In any case, Finland as a geographic or administrative expression was a creation of kings and local elites, not an expression of the common people.

There were two Finlands in that the southwestern part of the Finnish Peninsula formed the eastern half of the political, cultural, and economic center of the Swedish realm, with the area around the kingdom's capital Stockholm as the western half. The rest of Finland belonged to the peripheral areas of the Swedish kingdom that included areas on the western side of the Gulf of Bothnia. There were also two Finlands in that although most of the Finnish Peninsula was under the Swedish Crown, smaller areas were under the rule of Russia and its predecessors.

There were also many Finlands. The medieval and early modern periods preceded the triumph of the centralized, modern nation-state, in which people see their nation as their primary and often only loyalty in society. In those earlier periods, regions and communities had a greater significance for people than they do today. Moreover, language served as a mode of communication and not a basis for group identity. One could say with only a bit of exaggeration that most medieval and early modern polities consisted merely of collections of culturally, economically, and politically autonomous regions—or even states—under a common ruler.[2]

THE MEDIEVAL CHURCH

The establishment of the Roman Catholic Church on the Finnish Peninsula during the medieval period had three long-term impacts in addition to the obvious changes in religious belief. First, the Church facilitated the establishment of Swedish power. The Swedish Crown followed the Church in establishing a bureaucracy, a judiciary, and tax collection. Like elsewhere in Europe, the Crown and the Church influenced each other. The kingdom's bishops had permanent seats on the Council of the Realm, the king's chief advisory body. Rulers would often have a say or the only say in the naming of high Church officials. Unlike elsewhere in medieval Europe, however, the relationship between the Crown and the Church was largely harmonious.[3]

Second, while the Church integrated the Finnish Peninsula with the Swedish kingdom, the Church in Finland at the same time developed a very local identity. During the Middle Ages, native-born Finns came to dominate the clergy. Magnus, the first Finnish-born bishop of Turku, assumed the position in 1291. After the consecration of Bero II Balk in 1385, all bishops of Turku would be born in Finland until well into the seventeenth century. The

Finland's Eastern Borders. Adapted from Helge Pohjolan-Pihonen, *Suomen historia 1523–1617*, vol. 7, *Suomen historia* (Porvoo: WSOY, 1960), 565. Adapted with permission.

medieval Church's visibility and the strength were buttressed by the fact that the bishop of Turku governed all parishes on the Finnish Peninsula.

Third, the Church connected Finland with medieval European culture. Medieval Finland lacked the wealthy cities and royalty that supported cultural development elsewhere in Europe. Only the Church had the financial and intellectual resources to bring Finland into the fold of European civilization. The Church provided most of the formal education. The most prestigious school, the cathedral school in Turku, educated young boys seeking both religious and secular vocations. The kingdom of Sweden did not have a university until a small and often-moribund one was established in Uppsala in 1477, whereas in Finland a university was founded in Turku in 1640. During the Middle Ages, students from Finland studied in foreign universities, (primarily in Paris) and, later in the sixteenth century, in German universities. In the medieval and early modern periods, formal education was available for only a handful of boys and young men of means. Only a small percent of the population was even literate.[4]

THE CROWN'S AUTHORITY

The establishment of the Swedish Crown's power over Finland was slower than the Church's but no less successful in integrating the eastern half of the Gulf of Bothnia with the western half. Although the Roman Catholic Church had a monopoly over ecclesiastical power, temporal or civil power, that is, the power of kings and other temporal leaders, was much more widely diffused. Kings did not have standing armies or large bureaucracies at their disposal. The king shared political power with the major social groups in society—the nobility, clergy, urban burghers, and peasantry. Because these groups elected the Swedish king, the monarch depended on cooperation with these groups in order to rule at all. Those who elected the king had the right to remove their ruler. Of the Swedish kingdom's 15 rulers between 1290 and 1520, 12 were overthrown.

The indirect and limited nature of royal power can be seen in how Swedish kings extended their authority into Finland. Kings ruled Finland through local officials who had a great deal of autonomy. A further devolution of royal authority lay in the founding of Finland's cities. In receiving a royal charter, cities gained internal autonomy and special commercial privileges. The most important of these privileges allowed trade with foreign merchants. Finland's first city, Turku, received its privileges by 1309 at the latest. By 1500, there were six cities: Ulvila (Ulvsby), Rauma (Raumo), Naantali (Nådendal), and Turku on the west coast, as well as Porvoo (Borgå) and Viipuri (today known as Vyborg in Russian) on the southern coast. Nonetheless, by the fifteenth century Finland had become fully integrated in the Swedish kingdom's bureaucracy and politics. Finnish representatives not only had seats on the

Council of the Realm, but also, starting in 1362, electors from Finland participated in the election of a new king.[5]

Finland's integration with Sweden occurred in a wider context of Scandinavian unification. During most of the fourteenth century, each of the three Scandinavian kingdoms combined with one or both into some type of union. The most durable of the unions, the Kalmar Union, the Union of the Three Crowns, was constituted in 1397 and lasted, at least formally, until Gustav Vasa's election to the Swedish throne in 1523. The union was essentially under the Danish Crown. The creation of the Kalmar Union stemmed from the internal weaknesses of each of the three Scandinavian kingdoms in the face of growing German influence. The association of German commercial cities known as the German Hanse (the Hanseatic League) dominated the foreign trade and influenced the internal politics of the Scandinavian kingdoms. The Hanse's leading city, Lübeck, was particularly powerful in Scandinavia. Many northern German princes were active in the region as well.[6] The Kalmar Union was fractious and unable to curb German influence. In the long term, however, it did contribute to the creation of Finland's identity as a member of the Scandinavian or Nordic community.

Despite closer integration with the West, Finland still remained a place of contention between East and West. Both the Swedish Crown and Novgorod sought to expand their influence in northern and eastern Finland by ignoring the border drawn in 1323. Short border skirmishes aside, neither side wanted formally to go to war. In 1471, the Swedish kingdom's Eastern antagonist was no longer Novgorod but, rather, the Grand Duchy of Muscovy (known by the sixteenth century as Russia). In that year, Grand Duke Ivan III of Muscovy conquered Novgorod. In the medieval era, the only sustained conflict with Russia came in the years 1495–1497. King Hans of Denmark encouraged the Russians to invade Finland as a means of pressuring the Swedish kingdom's elites into formally accepting him as the king of the Kalmar Union. The war ended in Hans achieving his goal without ceding the Russians anything.[7]

POPULATION, SOCIETY, AND ECONOMY

The steady population increase of the prehistoric era continued into the sixteenth century. By 1570, Finland's population had reached at least 300,000. Several factors contributed to this population increase. An abundance of unsettled arable land allowed for a growing population to feed itself. The country avoided the common causes of catastrophic population loss: protracted wars, widespread crop failures, and epidemics. For the most part, Finland seems to have been spared from the most devastating epidemic in European history—the Black Death that spread over Europe in the years 1347–1351. However, in the seventeenth and eighteenth centuries, years of consistent population growth were interrupted by episodes of population decline, such as those caused by wars and famine. In the years 1695–1697, crop failures and epidemics decimated Finland's population by a third. Life expectancy by the beginning of eighteenth century had remained pretty much the same as it had been in prehistoric times.

Until the outbreak of the Black Death, immigration significantly contributed to Finland's population growth. Swedes first migrated to Finland's south-western regions. From the late twelfth century onward, they colonized the south-central coastal region of Uusimaa (Nyland). Most Swedish settlements were built in uninhabited areas. Swedish as well as German merchants migrated to Finland's cities in the medieval era. The Germans' preponderance led King Magnus Eriksson in 1350 to decree that Germans could hold no more than half of a city council's seats.[8]

No reliable numbers exist concerning the total number of immigrants or the linguistic makeup of Finland's medieval or early modern population. Probably less than 20 percent spoke Swedish as its first language. German speakers comprised about two percent of the population and the rest spoke Finnish as its first language. Even though Swedish was the language of the elites in Finland, no single official or national language existed in the medieval or early modern periods. Until the sixteenth century, Latin was the language of the Church. In the cities, German was sometimes spoken more frequently than Swedish. As the Swedish kingdom grew into a Baltic empire, German became an important *lingua franca* among the empire's various parts. Swedish was the main language of civil administration in Finland, but among the Crown's local servants proficiency in Finnish was common. Finnish was even used as a language of command in the Swedish kingdom's armies. In the eighteenth century, French became the language of the Swedish king's court, following a wider European fashion.[9]

Medieval and early modern European society was based on groups rather than individuals, privileges rather than rights. The society of the Swedish kingdom consisted of four major social groups, or estates: the peasantry, burghers, clergy, and nobles. In the Swedish kingdom, each of these estates participated in local as well as national decision making. The kingdom's parliament, the Estates-General (*riksdag* in Swedish) consisted of four chambers, one for each estate. In keeping with the corporate nature of the society, the Estates-General's decisions were made by each estate voting as a group. This society, which was more inclusive than most at the time, rested on inequality; it was certainly not democratic. One's estate determined the limits of an individual's life. With the exception of the clergy, one's membership in an estate was almost exclusively determined by birth. In their own right, women did not belong to any of the estates, and men without property—a large minority of the medieval population—enjoyed no estate privileges. Privileges made for wide social and economic differences. For example, some estates paid taxes—the peasantry and burghers—and others—the nobles and clergy—did not.

The most populous of the four estates consisted of the peasants—small, independent farmers. In the medieval era, the agrarian population comprised at least 95 percent of the population. Most of this population consisted of landowning small farmers. In Finland, the peasants owned more than 90 percent of the land, probably the highest ownership rate in Europe. In Sweden, for example, peasants owned only half of the land, although they were roughly as large a percentage of the population as they were in Finland. The high level of peasant land ownership stemmed from two reasons. First, land remained plentiful. Second, the king rather than the local elites or nobilities controlled unsettled lands. It was in the Crown's interest to encourage settlement, that is, to increase the number of farmers, as a way of increasing the number of taxpayers. The peasantry's widespread land ownership and political power, especially in local matters, created the impression of a free peasantry, but this impression requires qualification. Peasants paid more taxes as a percentage of income than did other groups. This burden became much heavier in the early modern period. Peasants had the lowest status of the four social groups, and few achieved upward mobility. Peasants did not occupy any of the kingdom's high offices; those positions were reserved for members of the other three higher estates that, combined, made up about three percent of the population.

The clergy constituted a second estate. This group included priests, high Church officials, and some teachers, a reflection of the Church's role in education. The clergy owned about 2.5 percent of the land in Finland but they comprised about 1 percent of the population. The clergy lived off their land holdings and Church tax revenues.

The burghers were a third estate. They were inhabitants of cities who had the right to vote for the town's council and had various commercial privileges. They made up only a small percentage of a city's total inhabitants and a few tenths of a percent of the total population. They were also politically the least influential of the four estates.

The nobility, comprising a few tenths of a percent of the population, was the most politically and economically powerful estate. In general, European nobles were characterized by their conduct of warfare for the king, their significant land holdings, and their legal authority over those who lived on their land. The Swedish kingdom's nobility developed these traits very slowly, if ever. Until the sixteenth century, it is even difficult to apply the term nobility to the Swedish kingdom. The group that eventually became the nobility was in the medieval era known as the *frälse* in Swedish (*rälssi* in Finnish), a word meaning those free from taxation. Those able to provide the king with a fully armed horseman received an exemption from taxation. Large landowning families as well, as some peasants, were able to buy this tax-exempt status.

Over the medieval period, the *frälse* were able to strengthen their tax-free privileges, regardless of service. By the beginning of the sixteenth century, the *frälse* began to look more like a European nobility. In 1569, the status of *frälse* was formally made hereditary. *Frälse* in the medieval era were not major land-owners in Finland, where they possessed about three percent of the land. This percentage increased among the nobility during the early modern era. Unlike in other parts of Europe, nobles exercised legal authority over the inhabitants of their land only in limited cases. Civil justice and administration largely belonged to the king.[10]

The family forms a central building block of any society. Finland's place as a borderland between Eastern and Western Europe is evident in family formation. Families west of the Kymi River valley were formed along Western European practices. Families here consisted of couples marrying in their mid-twenties and creating small nuclear families. In the West, the basic family unit consisted of a husband, wife, and children. Eastern parts of Finland followed the Eastern European pattern of family formation known as the multiple-family household. In the Eastern family, a household would consist of several conjugal pairs, who married much earlier than their Western counterparts. Instead of one son inheriting the father's land and younger sons setting up their own separate households, sons would remain in their parents' household even after marriage. Starting in the eighteenth century, changes in law concerning land ownership and population growth led to the decline of the extended family and the growth of the nuclear family in eastern Finland. This transformation was very slow and uneven. Traces of extended family structures existed in eastern Finland until the eve of World War II.[11]

THE REIGN OF GUSTAV VASA (1523–1560): STATEBUILDING AND RELIGIOUS REFORM

Finland entered the sixteenth century still a part of the Kalmar Union. Since the middle of the fifteenth century, the union had suffered deep divisions, because the Swedish kingdom's estates sometimes chose to recognize the existence of the Scandinavian union but not the authority of the Danish king. In 1517, King Christian II of Denmark began a sustained campaign to reassert his claim to authority over the Swedish realm, which climaxed in November 1520 in a massacre of Swedish nobles and leading personages known as the Stockholm bloodbath. Christian's tyrannical actions ignited a revolt in the Swedish kingdom, led by the nobleman Gustav Vasa, whom his countrymen proclaimed king in June, 1523.[12]

The reign of King Gustav Vasa (ruled from 1523 to 1560) brought the Swedish kingdom into the early modern age. Many of King Gustav's achievements fall under the rubric of statebuilding. A state is defined as an organized political community in which the powers of legal violence, that is, the conduct of war, as well as law enforcement and taxation are vested in a central authority. In medieval Europe, kings, the Church, nobles, and cities exercised the powers of legal violence and taxation. In the early modern era, Europe's monarchs made a determined effort to centralize legal violence and taxation into institutions that they could control.

In his drive to achieve a strong state, Gustav Vasa first eyed the wealth and privileges of the Church. At a meeting of the Estates-General in the Swedish town of Vesterås in 1527, Gustav argued that an appropriation of the Church's considerable wealth was the only way for the newly independent and nearly bankrupt Swedish kingdom to survive. The estates gave the king a mandate to confiscate the Church's wealth. Bishops were required to surrender their castles to the king. Fines levied in Church courts went to the Crown. The Crown confiscated Church lands. The Church lost its independent power of taxation to the king. King Gustav started deposing bishops and naming new ones without the approval of the pope. In 1540, the estates made the king the supreme head of the Church in the Swedish realm. Four years later, the estates made the monarchy hereditary.

Gustav's shakedown of the Church occurred in the wider context of religious reform in sixteenth-century Europe. The best-known of these reformers was the German monk Martin Luther (1483–1546). Luther's criticism of the Church centered on its emphasis on the performance of good works as a necessity for salvation. From this criticism, Luther developed a wider plan for reforming the Church. Luther, as well as other reformers, intended to reform the one Roman Catholic Church rather than create new churches. The ultimate fracturing of Christianity into Roman Catholic and various Protestant denominations, such as Lutheranism, stemmed to a great extent from the actions of Europe's rulers to impose one of the reform programs on their subjects as a means of strengthening their own power. A case in point is Gustav Vasa. At the Vesterås meeting, Gustav stated that he wanted the Church to proclaim "the pure word of God." Over the next couple of decades, Gustav Vasa placed Lutheran reformers in high Church offices without really understanding Lutheran theology. The promotion of Lutheranism furthered the separation of the kingdom's Church from Rome and thus enhanced the king's power over it.

By the time Gustav Vasa died in 1560, the Swedish Church was a decidedly royal but not an irrevocably Lutheran institution. The theology of the Church remained in flux until 1593, when the estates formally adopted the Augsburg Confession, the founding creed of Lutheranism. In any case, religion remained a communal rather than an individual matter. Those in charge of the community had the final say in how people worshiped God. The alliance between Crown and altar continued to develop in the seventeenth century, climaxing in the Church Law of 1686. This law made membership in the Lutheran

Church a condition for residing in the kingdom. Even before this law was proclaimed, there was pressure on religious dissidents to convert or leave. The best-known example of this was the decision of Queen Christina (r. 1632–1654) to abdicate the throne and exile herself upon converting to Roman Catholicism.

A central tenet of Lutheran reform called for the proclamation of Holy Scripture in the language of the people, not in Latin—long a dead language except among the clergy. This call had a particular impact on languages such as Finnish, which had little or no literary tradition. The pioneer in putting the Word of God into Finnish was the Finnish pastor Mikael Agricola (1510–1557). From 1536 to 1539, Agricola studied at Wittenberg University in Germany, the center of Lutheran scholarship at the time. In his time there, he became acquainted with Martin Luther, who wrote a letter of recommendation to Gustav Vasa for a scholarship for Agricola. The Swedish king, known for his stinginess, refused to give the young student money. Returning to Finland in 1539, Agricola published a spelling primer for the Finnish language in 1543. In the following year, he published a prayer book in Finnish. In 1548, he published what is widely considered the origin of Finnish as a written language—the New Testament in Finnish. Agricola's achievements helped him to win promotion in 1550 to the post of bishop of Turku. He later came to be known as the "Father of the Finnish language."[13]

The clergy's continued cultivation of the Finnish language fostered the language's survival. In the seventeenth century, members of the clergy collected folklore; in the eighteenth century, laws were passed that bound Lutheran pastors to ensure the literacy of their flocks. The ultimate responsibility for teaching literacy lay with parents, who either had to teach their children to read or find some form of outside instruction. Ministers tested the literacy of their parishioners on a yearly basis. Until the year 1910, those who failed literacy tests could not marry in the Lutheran Church. The tests were not comprehensive, usually consisting of reciting well-known (and often memorized) biblical passages. However, literacy improved over the course of the eighteenth century in both Finnish and Swedish.[14]

King Gustav was not only interested in tapping domestic sources of wealth, but also in broadening his kingdom's slice of trade in the Baltic Sea. The Baltic Sea region played an integral role in the early modern European economy. The region supplied the economies of Western Europe with grain, the very staff of life. Timber as well as other naval supplies such as hemp, flax, and tar were used to build the large navies of Western Europe. Finland became a major exporter of pitch and pine tar, necessary materials in shipbuilding. Sweden was a major supplier of copper and later iron. The eastern littoral of the Baltic (where Estonia, Latvia, and Lithuania are located today) as well as Russia produced the tallow and beeswax needed for church candles.[15]

Finland played an important role in Gustav's drive to enhance the Swedish kingdom's economic position in the Baltic. Gustav aimed to make his kingdom an intermediary in Western Europe's trade with Russia. His most ambitious enterprise in this respect was the founding of the city of Helsinki on Finland's southern coast in 1550. The city was supposed to compete with the Hanse city of Reval (Tallinn) as the Western outpost of trade with Russia. Helsinki never became a serious competitor to Reval. Only about 250 years after Gustav's death would Helsinki rise to a level of prominence.[16]

FINLAND AND THE SWEDISH KINGDOM'S EXPANSION

The death of Gustav Vasa in 1560 ended a period of intense internal transformation. The king's successors for the next century and a half would place the Swedish kingdom on a path of external expansion and almost constant warfare. By the mid-seventeenth century, the kingdom of Sweden had become the dominant power in the Baltic. It had conquered territory from Denmark, Poland, Germany, and Russia. It had even established a short-lived colony at the mouth of the Delaware River in North America, New Sweden (1638–1655), with colonists from both sides of the Gulf of Bothnia.

The Swedish imperial experience had a considerable impact on Finland's development. Wars with Russia moved the kingdom's borders eastward, encompassing new Finnish-speaking populations that were Orthodox, not Lutheran. In the Peace of Stolbova (1617), the Swedish Crown gained the province of Käkisalmi (Kexholm) around Lake Ladoga and the area along the Gulf of Finland's southeastern coast known as Ingria. In both places, the majority Orthodox population would became majority Lutheran by the end of the seventeenth century. Despite the religious protections offered by the Peace of Stolbova for the conquered Orthodox communities, many Orthodox fled in into Russia rather than live under the Lutheran Swedish Crown. Lutheran Finns moved into those areas.[17]

As a whole, the Swedish kingdom succeeded in expanding by squeezing every bit of tax revenue and manpower available. Taxes were raised greatly throughout the kingdom. At the beginning of the sixteenth century, Finland provided about 20 to 30 percent of the Crown's revenue. At the end of the century, Finland's share was about 60 percent. This rise in taxes stemmed, to a great extent, from a war against Russia, 1570–1595. Since taxes during this time were paid in kind rather than money, the Crown would often focus tax collection on an area where the most-needed resources were.

In the 1590s, the campaign of eastern expansion made Finland an important stage in the Swedish kingdom's internal political struggles. When King Johan III died in 1592, he left the throne to his son Sigismund. The new king was the offspring of Johan's marriage to Polish princess Katarina Jagiellonica. It was these Polish roots that facilitated Sigismund's election to the Polish throne in 1587. Sigismund's accession to the Swedish throne pleased those in Finland charged with the war effort against Russia, since it meant a stronger Swedish–Polish alliance against Russia. King Johan's brother, Duke Charles of Söder-manland, also sought the throne. Charles built support by claiming that Sigismund, a Catholic, was going to reimpose Catholicism in the Swedish kingdom. With respect to Finland, Charles sought to stir up trouble against Sigismund's supporters by calling on disgruntled peasants to rise up against the military leadership. Even though the war with Russia ended in 1595, the heavy burdens placed on the peasantry did not end. In 1596, peasants, mostly from Ostrobothnia, rose up in rebellion in a conflict known as the War of the Clubs. Sigismund's supporters crushed the rebellion in the following year. In the meantime, Charles was more successful in pursuing his ambitions on the western side of the Gulf of Bothnia. In 1597, a rump meeting of the Estates-General declared Charles regent of the kingdom, effectively replacing Sigismund. Supporters of Sigismund in Finland sought to coordinate an attack on Charles's stronghold with soldiers from Poland. The two armies on two occasions failed to synchronize their movements. On the later occasion, Charles's army defeated Sigismund's army, while forces from Finland withdrew for the second time across the gulf. In 1599, a full meeting of the estates proclaimed him "hereditary prince" of Sweden. Later, he would formally adopt the title King Charles IX.

Rulers of the Early Modern Swedish Kingdom

Gustav I Vasa	1523–1560
Erik XIV	1560–1568
Johan III	1568–1592
Sigismund	1592–1599
Charles IX	1599–1611
Gustav II Adolf	1611–1632
Kristina	1632–1654 (regency 1632–1644)
Charles X Gustav	1654–1660
Charles XI	1660–1697 (regency 1660–1672)
Charles XII	1697–1718
Ulrika Eleonora	1719–1720
Frederik I	1720–1751

Adolf Frederik	1751–1771
Gustav III	1771–1792
Gustav IV	1792–1809

In the seventeenth century, the Swedish King Gustavus Adolphus (also known by his Swedish name, Gustav Adolf) (r. 1611–1632) decided to intervene in the biggest conflict of the early modern period, the Thirty Years' War (1618–1648). This war took the armies of the Swedish realm into central Europe against the armies of Habsburg Holy Roman emperors and their allies. During the seventeenth century, for every 100 men born in the Swedish kingdom, 30 died in war. During the Thirty Years' War, Finland provided as much as one-third of the recruits for the Crown's war effort. Finland's population during the Thirty Years' War comprised only about a fifth of the kingdom's population. This mobilization of manpower for warfare kept Finland's population growth stagnant during most of the seventeenth century. The best-known Finnish troops were the cavalrymen, known as the *hakkapeliitat* because of their battle cry "hakkaa päälle [strike them]!" Today, Finnish spectators at international sporting events use this battle cry to spur on their countrymen.[18]

Swedish power declined steadily in the second half of the seventeenth century in the face of the rise of France, Prussia, and, above all, Russia. In 1699, Russian Emperor Peter I (Peter The Great) and two of Sweden's other neighbors, Denmark and Poland, signed an alliance aimed against Swedish power. The time seemed favorable to the Russians. The Swedish kingdom had a new monarch—the 19-year-old Charles XII (r. 1697–1718). Charles did not wait for war but, rather preemptively, attacked the enemy coalition. In doing so, he sparked a conflict known as The Great Northern War (1700–1721). The Swedish army quickly subdued Denmark; the Russians were defeated in November 1700 at the battle of Narva on the Gulf of Finland; and Poland was quickly neutralized and surrendered in 1706. Charles had won battles but not the war. The king's hesitation to build on his victory at Narva allowed Emperor Peter to regroup his forces. In 1708, when Charles decided to invade Russia, he met an enemy more than his match. The Swedish monarch's army advanced deep into Emperor Peter's realm until the Battle of Poltava in June 1709, when the Russians handed the Swedish king a crushing defeat. The king fled to the protection of the Ottoman Turkish Empire, where he stayed for five years as an uninvited guest. The king's armies retreated out of Russia. Between 1713 and 1721, Russian armies occupied Finland.

With the signing of the Peace of Nystad (Uusikaupunki) in 1721, the Swedish realm was relegated to the second-tier powers in Europe. Russia annexed the kingdom's eastern Baltic provinces and took southeastern Finland, drawing a new border that corresponds to Finland's current southeastern border with Russia. The defeat in war changed the political system of the Swedish kingdom.

The four estates that had agreed to the creation of a strong absolutist monarchy in 1680 assumed greater power than ever after the war.[19] For Finland, an important tide had turned. Ever since the Peace of Nöteborg (1323), the struggle between East and West on the Finnish Peninsula had gone in favor of the Swedish kingdom. For the next two centuries, Russia would hold the momentum. In this growth of Russian power, various expressions of a separate Finnish identity would develop.

FINLAND EMERGES

After the Great Northern War, Finland developed a more distinct and separate profile as a part of the Swedish kingdom. Officials in Stockholm began to treat Finland as a place with special economic and military needs. Actions to rebuild Finland after the Russian occupation included tax abatements for rebuilding communities, as well as various agrarian, commercial, and industrial reforms. Many of these measures were inspired by the physiocrats, a group of economists throughout Europe that sought to liberate economic activity from regulations and special privileges that hindered free trade. The leading physiocrat of the Swedish kingdom was a Finnish clergyman and member of the Estates-General, Anders Chydenius (1729–1803). His book, *The National Gain* (in Swedish, *Den nationale vinsten*), published in 1765, argues for free trade for all individuals, regardless of their social standing or place of residence. In many respects Chydenius anticipated the theses of free trade that were more widely associated with Adam Smith more than a decade later.[20]

Finland's profile in the Swedish realm grew for demographic reasons as well. The loss of the eastern Baltic provinces after the Great Northern War made the Swedish kingdom much smaller, and Finland's proportion of the kingdom's total population accordingly increased. In addition, Finland underwent a population explosion of its own. At the beginning of the 1720s, Finland (including areas ceded to Russia in 1721) had a population estimated at about 400,000. The number of inhabitants more than doubled by 1800. For a century after 1750, Finland led Europe in population growth, at an annual rate estimated between 1.2 percent and 1.5 percent. The only other country with growth over 1 percent during the same period was England at 1.1 percent. The major reason for the growth was a lack of wars, epidemics, and crop failures. In 1720, Finland comprised about 17 percent of the Swedish kingdom's population; by 1809, it accounted for one-quarter, even though Finland had lost land and population to Russia during the previous decades. The population growth mirrored a similarly strong economic expansion.[21]

Continued tension between the Swedish kingdom and Russia furthered Finland's emergence as a distinct entity. Unable to face Russia alone, the Swedish kingdom's political leaders sought useful opportunities in the conflicts between the great powers to reconquer land from its eastern neighbor. Taking advantage of the diplomatic upheavals caused by the deaths of Holy Roman Emperor Charles VI and Empress Anne of Russia, the Swedish kingdom attacked Russia in 1741, in what is known as the Hats' War, after the party that dominated the Swedish kingdom's politics at the time. The war resulted in another Russian occupation of Finland. Before the occupation, however, Empress Elizabeth of Russia opened up the possibility of a different future for Finland. She offered the people of Finland help to create an independent Finland if they turned their weapons against Sweden. Otherwise, her army would occupy the country. Elizabeth's manifesto was not embraced and Russian troops rolled over Finland. The Peace of Turku of 1743 gave Russia another slice of Finland—the southeastern border was now pushed west to the Kymi River. Elizabeth's offer of independence, although understood as probably only bargaining chip in peace negotiations, did present the possibility of an alternative future for Finland.[22]

The outcome of the Hats' War led many to conclude that the Swedish kingdom could no longer conduct offensive war against Russia. Rather, the realm had to dig in against growing Russian power. A permanent naval force was stationed on Finland's south coast. Fortifications were built, the most impressive of which was a redoubt built on islands at the approaches to Helsinki. This fortress was christened Sveaborg, or Fortress of Sweden. It is known today as Suomenlinna, or Fortress of Finland. Construction of this so-called Gibraltar of the North was started in 1748 and building continued for the rest of the century. This concern about Finland's defenses was a part of the greater concern about the defense of the whole kingdom. In this wider context, some of the kingdom's military planners saw Finland as a place that could be sacrificed to save the rest of the kingdom in the event of a Russian attack.[23]

However, the dream of territorial gain did not completely die out among the kingdom's leaders. In 1771, Gustav III ascended to the Swedish throne. In the next year, the ambitious king usurped the estates' power and restored the absolutist monarchy. Most legislative as well as all executive power now rested with the king. Gustav's absolutist constitution would remain in force in Finland until 1919—a century longer than in Sweden. Gustav then looked east for territorial gain. In 1788, with Russia at war with Turkey, Gustav decided to attack his eastern neighbor.

The so-called Gustav's War (1788–1790) quickly proved to be a losing enterprise. The king gained no territory and ignited long-brewing opposition to his rule. In Finland, some Finnish officers acted on their conviction that the Swedish Crown no longer protected Finland's interests. On August 9, 1788, seven officers met in the eastern border village of Liikkala. In a letter to Empress Catherine the Great of Russia, the officers expressed a desire for peace. They believed that a Russian cession of territory to Finland would foster a desire among Finland's people for peace. This letter is sometimes misinterpreted as a declaration of separation from Sweden, since the man who carried the letter to Empress Catherine, Jan Anders Jägerhorn (1757–1825), himself advocated independence for Finland at the Russian court. In any case, the Russian empress rejected the officers' overture. In the meantime, the authors of the Liikkala letter joined a larger protest meeting of officers both from Sweden and Finland at the Finnish town of Anjala. The officers appealed to their king to make peace with Russia and to restore the estates' privileges in deciding the kingdom's affairs. Facing an attack from Denmark, Gustav sued for peace with Russia. The Swedish kingdom suffered no territorial losses, but the feeling grew among Finland's elites that their country was just a military stage for the Swedish Crown's misguided expansionist ambitions. In 1792, the opposition to Gustav climaxed in his assassination at a masquerade ball in Stockholm, an event Giuseppe Verdi made into an opera, *Un ballo in Maschera*.[24]

For the most part, the rebels of Liikkala and Anjala were not interested in separating Finland from Sweden. A Finnish aristocrat, Göran Magnus Sprengtporten (1740–1819), did develop a plan in the late 1770s and early 1780s for an independent Finland with close ties to Russia. Sprengtporten believed that cutting ties with Sweden would ensure peace for Finland. In expressing his views, he fell into the bad graces of Gustav III. He left Finland in order to find fame and fortune elsewhere. He even sought to move to America in order to help the revolutionaries against the British. Sprengtporten then entered Russian service in 1786, where he shared his plans with the Russian court and led Russian troops during Gustav's War. Sprengtporten was a lone wolf in the eighteenth century, but his plans and influence at the Russian court would make him a key person for Finland in the nineteenth century.[25]

THE RISE OF FENNOPHILIA

Over the course of the eighteenth century, Fennophilia—the appreciation of Finnish language and culture—grew among Finland's educated elites. Fennophilia was inspired by the two major European intellectual movements of the eighteenth century, the Enlightenment and Romanticism. Enlightenment thought championed the use of reason as the means for an individual to improve one's own condition. The Enlightenment ignited the transformation of European society from one based on groups and privileges to one of individuals and universal rights. The Enlightenment influenced some Fennophiles to study the Finnish language and folklore as a science, with the larger goal of advancing human progress. Romanticism reacted to the Enlightenment by emphasizing the subjective, irrational, spiritual, and emotional in the life of the individual. In short, the Enlightenment emphasized reason whereas Romanticism emphasized feeling. Romanticism influenced Fennophilia in its focus on the common people as the basis of culture. Instead of advancing human progress, romantic Fennophiles saw their mission as the restoration of a lost higher culture.[26]

Two scholars stand out in the Fennophile movement. One is the clergyman and scholar Daniel Juslenius (1676–1752). As a student, Juslenius collected stories from Finland's folklore and, in a history he wrote of Turku, *Aboa vetus et nova* (*Turku Old and New*) (1700), Juslenius argues—from a modern standpoint, fanticizes—that Finland had a highly developed ancient culture of its own, destroyed by the arrival of the Swedes. According to Juslenius, Noah's grandson Magog led the ancient Finns to the Finnish Peninsula and the Amazons of Greek mythology had lived in Finland. Drawing on his impressive knowledge of languages, Juslenius draws connections between Finnish, on one hand, and Greek and Hebrew on the other. He maintains that Finnish begat languages such as Russian, Polish, and Hungarian. Juslenius's work is a totally fanciful understanding of Finland's prehistory, but it helped propel a tradition of finding that great prehistoric Finnish civilization that would last into the twenty-first century. In his next book, *Vindiciae Fennorum* (*The Defense of the Finns*) (1703) Juslenius makes an even more impassioned statement for a separate identity for Finland's people. For Juslenius, Finns were all people who inhabited Finland, regardless of language.[27]

The other pioneering scholar was a professor of Latin, Henrik Gabriel Porthan (1739–1804). Porthan is recognized as the father of both scientific historical and literary scholarship in Finland. In his best-known work, *De poësi Fennica* (1766–1778), he clarifies the rules of Finnish-language poetry. His scholarship refuted longstanding beliefs about the origins of the Finnish language, such as its alleged kinship to Hebrew and Greek. In his historical studies, Porthan cast doubt on the veracity of certain folklore stories but, in keeping with the Romantic notions of his time, he did see folklore as a reflection of a lost great civilization. For Porthan, there was a difference between population and ethnicity regarding Finland. Finns were those who spoke Finnish, whereas the inhabitants of Finland, whether, Finns, Swedes, or Sámi, shared a common country, a common past, and a larger kingdom. In making these distinctions, Porthan grasped the complex web of loyalties and communities created by language, territory, history, and political power in which early modern Europeans lived. Porthan shared his views beyond his ivory tower. He was a founding and leading member of the Aurora Society, which sought to cultivate an interest in Finland's culture. Members of this society included men from various elite groups. The society published Finland's first newspaper, the Swedish-language *Tidningar utgifne af et sällskap i Åbo.*[28]

Virtually all expressions of Finnish separateness were made with the understanding, whether implicit or explicit, of Finland's place in the Swedish kingdom. Separateness did not mean separatism from Sweden. Furthermore, the elites held these understandings of Finland's distinctness but they were not consciously shared by the masses. Finnish separateness was a necessary but not the only ingredient for the growth of nationalism in the nineteenth century.

As it entered the nineteenth century, Finland seemingly faced several possible futures. The most likely one was continued association with the Swedish kingdom, although as a more visible part of it. There was also the possibility of Finland joining the Russian Empire, and there was even the distant possibility of independence. In the years 1808–1809, Russian troops occupied Finland for the third time in less than a century. This occupation ended differently than the previous two: Russia returned none of Finland to the Swedish kingdom.

NOTES

1. Nils Erik Villstrand, "Stormaktstiden 1617–1721," in *Finlands historia*, vol. 2, ed. Rainer Fagerlund, Kurt Jern, and Nils Erik Villstrand (Esbo: Schildts, 1996), 130.

2. Torbjörn Eng, *Det svenska väldet: Ett konglomerat av uttrycksformer och begrepp från Vasa till Bernadotte* (Uppsala: Acta Universitatis Upsaliensis, 2001), 440–441; Villstrand, "Stormaktstiden 1617–1721," 130–139.

3. Tuomas M.S. Lehtonen, "Kirkko ja kruunu," in *Suomen kulttuurihistoria*, vol. 1, ed. Tuomas M. S. Lehtonen and Timo Joutsivuo (Helsinki: Tammi, 2002), 104–111.

4. Jouko Vahtola, "Keskiaika," in *Suomen historian pikkujättiläinen*, ed. Seppo Zetterberg (Porvoo: WSOY, 1987), 120–124.

5. Vahtola, "Keskiaika," 50, 72–74, 114–116; Vahtola, *Suomen historia jääkaudesta Euroopan unioniin* (Keuruu: Otava, 2003), 381.

6. Philippe Dollinger, *The German Hansa* (London: Macmillian, 1970), 284; Jason Lavery, *Germany's Northern Challenge: The Holy Roman Empire and the Scandinavian Struggle for Baltic Hegemony 1563–1576* (Boston and Leiden: Brill, 2002), 6–12; Michael Roberts, *The Early Vasas: A History of Sweden* (Cambridge, UK: Cambridge University Press, 1986), 5–10.

7. Vahtola, *Suomen historia*, 48–49, 97–99.

8. Kari Pitkänen, "Suomen väestön historialliset kehityslinjat," in *Suomen väestö*, ed. Seppo Koskinen (Helsinki: Gaudeamus, 1994), 48; Vahtola, *Suomen historia*, 60.

9. Sulo Huovinen, "Finska språkets ställlning i det svenska riket," in *Finland i det svenska riket*, ed. Sulo Huovinen (Stockholm: Kulturfonden för Sverige och Finland, 1986), 66–67.

10. Vahtola, *Suomen historia*, 58–59; Vahtola, "Keskiaika," 114–116.

11. Tapani Hämynen, "History of the Karelian Orthodox Families in Suojärvi 1500–1939," in *Family Life on the Northwest Margins of Imperial Russia*, ed. Tapani Hämynen et al. (Joensuu: Joensuu University Press, 2004), 93–133; Kirsi Sirén, *Suuresta suvusta pieneen perheeseen: Itäsuomalainen perhe 1700-luvulla* (Helsinki: Suomen Historiallinen Seura, 1999), 250–254.

12. Roberts, *Early Vasas*, 5–24.

13. Simo Heininen and Markku Heikkilä, *Suomen kirkkohistoria* (Helsinki: Edita, 1996), 61–77.

14. Esko Laine, "Papisto kulttuurin välittäjänä," in *Suomen kulttuurihistoria*, vol. 2, ed. Rainer Knapas and Nils Erik Forsgård (Helsinki: Tammi, 2002), 209–216.

15. Harry A. Miskimin, *The Economy of Later Renaissance Europe 1460–1600* (Cambridge, UK: Cambridge University Press, 1977), 136–139.

16. Jorma Keränen, "Kustaa Vaasa ja uskonpuhdistuksen aika," in *Suomen historian pikkujättiläinen*, ed. Seppo Zetterberg (Porvoo: WSOY, 1987), 139–141.

17. Markus Hiekkanen, "Vipuri lääni—rautakaudesta keskiaikaan," in *Viipurin läänin historia I: Karjalan synty*, ed. Matti Saarnisto, (Jyväskylä: Gummerus, 2003), 496–504; Tapani Kärkkäinen, *Kirkon historia: Ortodoksin käsikirja* (Jyväskylä: Gummerus, 1999), 174–176; Erkki K. Osmonsalo, "Kreikkalaiskatolinen kirkko Suomessa 1800-luvulla: Eräitä piirteitä," *Suomen kirkkohistoriallisen seuran vuosikirja* 31–32 (1941–1942): 267–276; Vahtola, "Keskiaika," 55.

18. Keränen, "Kustaa Vaasa," 138; Vahtola, *Suomen historia*, 93, 113–116, 132–133, 152, 218–228.

19. Byron Nordstrom, *The History of Sweden* (Westport, CT: Greenwood Press, 2002), 48–49.

20. Vahtola, *Suomen historia*, 181–188.

21. Vahtola, *Suomen historia*, 208–209.

22. Ilkka Mäntylä, "Vapauden aika," in *Suomen historian pikkujättiläinen*, ed. Seppo Zetterberg (Porvoo: WSOY, 1987), 289–291.

23. Erik Lönnroth, "Kustaa III:n tie Anjalaan," in *Kahden kruunun alla: Kymijoki rajana 1743–1811*, ed. Eeva-Liisa Oksanen (Kouvola: Kouvolan kirjapaino, 1992), 22; Jonas Nordin, "Suomi Ruotsin valtakunnassa," in *Suomen kulttuurihistoria*, vol. 2, ed. Rainer Knapas and Nils Erik Forsgård (Helsinki: Tammi, 2002), 44–47; Vahtola, *Suomen historia*, 192.

24. Aulis J. Alanen, *Suomen historia kustavilaisella ajalla* (Porvoo: WSOY, 1964), 375–380, 412; Yrjö Blomstedt, "Anjalan liitto–ihanteita ja propagandaa," in *Kahden kruunun alla: Kymijoki rajana 1743–1811*, ed. Eeva-Liisa Oksanen (Kouvola: Kouvolan kirjapaino, 1992), 38–42; Lönnroth, "Kustaa III:n tie Anjalaan," 26–32; Mäntylä, "Vapauden aika," 321–333.

25. Blomstedt, "Anjalan liitto," 34–36; Yrjö Blomstedt, "Suomen itsenäisyys: Aateita ja hankkeita 1700-luvulta 1900-luvulle," in *Näkökulmia menneisyyteen: Eino Jutikkalan juhlakirja*, ed. Sven-Erik Åström, Yrjö Blomstedt, and Ilkka Hakalehto (Porvoo: WSOY, 1967), 226–229; Kaisu-Maija Nenonen and Ilkka Teerijoki, *Historian suursanakirja* (Helsinki: WSOY, 1998), 478–479.

26. William A. Wilson, *Folklore and Nationalism in Modern Finland* (Bloomington, IN: Indiana University Press, 1976), 16–19.

27. Juha Manninen, *Valistus ja kansallinen identiteetti: Aatehistoriallinen tutkimus 1700-luvun Pohjolasta* (Helsinki: Suomalaisen Kirjallisuuden Seura, 2000), 76–85; Wilson, *Folklore* 12–15.

28. Manninen, *Valistus*, 158, 207–240; Wilson, *Folklore*, 20–21.

4

The Creation of Autonomous Finland (1809–1890)

Traditionally, the period of Russian rule over Finland (1809–1917) has been known as the Age of Autonomy. More recently, some historians have employed the term the Imperial Era. These two terms connote different but complementary perspectives. On one hand, a separate, well-defined, and autonomous Finland did originate in terms of political institutions, nationhood, economy, and civil society. On the other hand, imperial Russian power helped advance these developments. During the years 1809–1890, Finnish autonomy and Russian power worked harmoniously together. Only afterwards did they collide.

THE RUSSIAN CONQUEST OF FINLAND

Until the nineteenth century, the bilateral struggle between Sweden and Russia drew the line between East and West that ran through Finland. Subsequently, wider European conflicts would demarcate the line. In the nineteenth century, the wars of the French Emperor Napoleon Bonaparte determined Finland's place in Europe. After suffering years of defeats as a member of the anti-Napoleonic alliance, Emperor Alexander I of Russia (r. 1801–1825) signed the Treaty of Tilsit with Napoleon in July 1807. In exchange for peace with the French emperor, Alexander agreed to join the Continental System, Napoleon's blockade of his most implacable enemy, Great Britain.

Alexander also agreed to bring Sweden, one of the last holdouts against Napoleon, into the blockade.

Unable to persuade King Gustav IV (r. 1792–1809) of Sweden to join the blockade, Alexander I ordered an invasion of Finland in February 1808. In spite of a spirited defense, Russian forces quickly spread out over the country. In a final example of the Swedish Crown's reluctance to defend Finland's interests, Gustav refrained from sending reinforcements to Finland due to his fear of a French attack from central Europe.

Alexander originally had sought to occupy Finland as a means of pressuring Gustav to join the Continental System. At the end of March 1808, he instead decided to annex Finland to the Russian Empire. Defensive considerations prevailed in Alexander's decision. Finland provided an added layer of defense around the capital, St. Petersburg, against future foreign aggression. This understanding of Finland in defensive terms has framed Russian policy toward Finland ever since. On September 17, 1809, the Swedish Crown signed the Peace of Fredrikshamn (Hamina in Finnish) with Russia. The treaty recognized Russian conquests east of the Gulf of Bothnia. Finland legally now belonged to the Russian Empire.

THE GRAND DUCHY OF FINLAND

Even before reaching a settlement with the Swedish Crown, Emperor Alexander I had achieved peace with his new subjects. At the emperor's request, representatives of Finland's four estates met in the city of Porvoo between March 25 and July 19, 1809. During this meeting, the estates pledged allegiance to their new ruler, who would bear the title of Grand Duke of Finland. For his part, the emperor-grand duke promised to uphold Finland's "constitution," estate privileges, as well as the Lutheran religion. In doing so, Alexander made Finland legally autonomous from the rest of his empire.[1]

Why did Alexander create a separate Finnish entity? Why did he not just impose Russian laws and institutions on this new dominion? Scholars point to several reasons. Among them, Alexander was continuing a tradition in Russian westward conquests by maintaining local political institutions, laws, and elites. The preservation of the status quo kept the country peaceful, thus serving Russia's defensive interest in Finland. Moreover, Alexander's pledge at Porvoo did not constitute a concession to his new subjects. During the last decades of Swedish rule, absolute monarchs, such as Alexander, had ruled Finland. In his pledge at Porvoo, Alexander upheld himself as an absolute ruler. The emperor gave himself and his successors even more maneuvering room by leaving the term "constitution" undefined. In Finland and most European countries at the time, a constitution was not a single document but, rather, the whole of those documents, laws, and customs upon which political rule rested. Many at Porvoo assumed that Alexander shared their view of

Finland's constitution as consisting of the Swedish Law Code of 1734, as well as King Gustav III's constitutional acts of 1772 and 1789. This mutual reluctance to explicitly define the constitution would lead to conflict at the end of the century.[2]

In maintaining laws, privileges, and religion, Emperor Alexander launched a transformation of Finland. Geographically, Finland became larger and more unified. The Peace of Fredrikshamn (1809) pushed the traditional border between Sweden and Finland westward from the Kemi River to the Tornio River. In 1812, the Russians appended to the new grand duchy the territories of southeastern Finland that they took in the eighteenth century, areas known collectively as Old Finland. This amalgamation made practical sense from the emperor's standpoint, since both the grand duchy and Old Finland shared the same Swedish legal system. In 1826, a border agreement between Russia and Norway resulted in Finland gaining the its eastern arm of Lapland, the area around Lake Inari. A larger grand duchy contributed toward winning the people of Finland over to the new order.[3]

Finland's legal autonomy precipitated the need for autonomous state institutions to enforce the country's laws. The understanding of this period as an age of autonomy has been primarily based on the existence of a separate, although not independent, Finnish state. At its founding, this state had three major components. First and foremost stood the Russian emperor, or Finland's grand duke. All other state institutions were extensions of his power. The second component was the governor-general. He served as the emperor's personal, permanent representative and commander of Russian forces in Finland. The first governor-general was the eighteenth-century visionary of an independent Finland, Göran Magnus Sprengtporten.

Russian Emperors/Grand Dukes of Finland

Alexander I	(r. 1809–1825)
Nicholas I	(r. 1825–1855)
Alexander II	(r. 1855–1881)
Alexander III	(r. 1881–1894)
Nicholas II	(r. 1894–1917)

The third component, the Senate, conducted the daily administration of country in the emperor's name. The body originally consisted of 14 members born in Finland, half noble and half non-noble. This number of senators and their social status fluctuated over time. A senator served for a three-year term, renewable at the emperor's pleasure. The Senate's work was divided into two sections. The judicial section acted as Finland's supreme court. The economic section assumed other aspects of administration, such as finance, infrastructure, and education. Although the governor-general was supposed to lead meetings of the Senate, the use of Swedish as the language of business reduced the governor-general's daily role in the Senate. The vice-chairs of the two sections often ran the Senate's meetings. Over time, the Senate's economic section would begin to resemble a cabinet of ministers. The economic section's importance is underscored by scholars' reference to the Senate as the economic section unless otherwise stated. Although an administrative body for Russian imperial power, the Senate was, in the words of one expert, "a strong symbol of the governmental existence of Finland."[4] In addition, entities based in St. Petersburg, such as the Finnish Affairs Committee (1809–1826, 1857–1891) and the office of State Secretary for Finnish Affairs, assisted the emperor in administration.[5]

This new Finnish state received a new capital city. During the Swedish era, Finland's administrative center was Turku. In 1812, Helsinki, a small fledgling port town on the country's southern coast, became Finland's new capital. The Russians wanted an administrative center closer to St. Petersburg than to Stockholm. They placed the job of transforming Helsinki into the hands of a German-born architect, Carl Ludwig Engel (1778–1840). He designed buildings in the neoclassical style popular at the time. Engel's most significant achievement was Senate Square (the new center of Helsinki) and the buildings that surrounded it. From the eastern end of the square rose the Senate building, now called the Palace of the Council of State, the main wing of which was completed in 1822. At the square's north end, Engel designed Helsinki's Lutheran cathedral, which was completed in 1852. Although this new church became the most visible symbol of Finnish Lutheranism, the Church's headquarters remained in Turku. At the square's western end, the main building of the Imperial Alexander University (Helsinki University) was completed in 1832. Based in Turku since its founding in 1640, the university was moved to Helsinki after fire destroyed much of Turku in 1827. Buildings that housed three major authorities of the new grand duchy thus surrounded the Senate Square: the Senate, the Church, and the university.[6]

These new autonomous state institutions were the products of Russian imperial power, not the popular will of Finland's people. The new order was anything but democratic. The new state institutions gave bureaucrats unprecedented power over the people. The country's elites supported the new order because, no matter how authoritarian, the new regime gave Finland a separate identity and gave its elites new opportunities. Meetings of the estates, called with some regularity even under absolutist Swedish kings, did not convene for more than half a century after 1809. The power to convene Finland's Estates-General rested solely with the monarch. The emperor-grand duke needed the estates' approval for proposals concerning certain taxes, constitutional laws, the Lutheran Church, and estate privileges. Even in these limited instances, the emperor could often legislate without the estates' consent.[7]

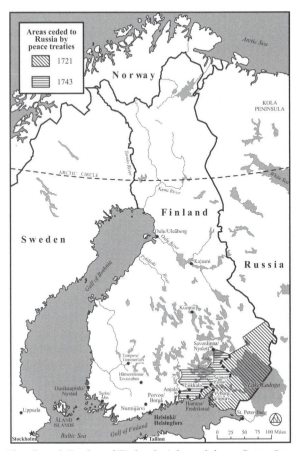

The Grand Duchy of Finland. Adapted from Osmo Jussila, Seppo Hentilä, and Jukka Nevakivi, *From Grand Duchy to Modern State: A Political History of Finland since 1809* (London: Hurst, 1999), 2. Adapted with permission.

Russia's defeat in the Crimean War (1853–1856) to the Ottoman Empire, France, and Britain shook the empire's whole political system. During the war, Emperor Nicholas I (r. 1825–1855) died. His son and successor, Alexander II (r. 1855–1881), concluded that Russia's defeat stemmed from its backwardness compared to other European powers. Among his modernizing reforms, the best-known is the emancipation of Russia's serfs in 1861. Alexander II believed he could best reform his empire by opening up the political process, although he would keep the final say. Against this backdrop, Alexander II called Finland's Estates-General to meet in 1863. In 1869, Alexander II issued a new law that called for the Estates-General to meet at least every five years. Elsewhere in Europe, legislatures were gaining more powers and the right to vote was expanding to include more of the population. However, this law did neither. The Estates-General remained a body with few powers elected by a small minority of men with estate privileges—less than two percent of the population.[8] The real reforms came in the form of imperial decrees, not votes in the legislature. Nonetheless, the reformed Estates-General facilitated more open discussion of public affairs. Finland's growing nationalist movements seized the opportunity.

THE RISE OF NATIONALISM

At Porvoo, Alexander I proclaimed that he had "raised Finland into the family of nations." His action did not immediately create a Finnish nation but, rather, separate Finnish state institutions. This new situation challenged Finland's people to consider their group identity, their sense of nationhood, or, in other words, their sense of autonomy from other peoples. At first, Finns could only identify themselves as no longer belonging to Sweden and not really belonging to Russia. This feeling of separateness is best described by the slogan attributed to a professor of philosophy at the University of Turku, A. J. Lagus: "Swedes we are not, Russians we will never be, so let us be Finns."[9]

The nineteenth century was a time of nationbuilding in Europe. A nation is, to quote the scholar Benedict Anderson, "an imagined political community." A nation exists to the extent that people believe it exists. Such things as a common language, culture, history, religion, and geographic space form national imagination. In many parts of Europe, people long had identified themselves with these imagined communities along with other, less abstract groupings: a village, social group, church, or state. By the nineteenth century, Europeans were pledging their highest political allegiance to their nations over all other communities. This belief in the primacy of the nation as the primary source of political allegiance and state power is known as nationalism.

In a comparative sense, Finland was fertile ground for the growth of nationalism. There was no religious divide that stymied nationbuilding in places such as Germany and Ireland. Regional differences did not fuel conflict. Finland had its own state institutions, an important instrument of nationbuilding in Western Europe. As in Eastern Europe, Finland had a strong literary movement behind nationbuilding.

The literary roots of nationalism in Finland reach back to the Fennophiles of the eighteenth century. In the nineteenth century, the mission of Fennophilia changed from the purely academic to one with a broader public agenda. The vanguard of this change was a group known as the Turku Romantics. These scholars, who were most active around the years 1818 to 1822, pursued a three-point program. First, they wanted to build national pride by exalting Finland's past. Second, they encouraged Swedish speakers to learn and use

Finnish. Third, they encouraged the development of Finnish-language literature. The Turku Romantics did not remain together for long. One of the group's leaders, A. I. Arwidsson, fled to Sweden in 1823 after running afoul of the authorities. Many relocated to Helsinki with the university. In 1830, the Saturday Society continued the romantics' work. This group in the following year founded the Finnish Literature Society. This organization set as its goals the cultivation of the Finnish language and literature, as well as the dissemination of information about Finland's history.

In 1822, three young men entered the university in Turku who would have the greatest impact on the development of Finnish nationalism in the nineteenth century. The first of these students, Elias Lönnrot (1802–1884) was a student of philosophy and medicine. After graduating in 1832, he moved to the northeastern city of Kajaani. When not practicing medicine, Lönnrot collected folk poetry with the support of the Finnish Literature Society. The young doctor traveled through Finland, Russian Karelia, Estonia, and Ingria to collect poems recited by ordinary people. Incorporation into the Russian Empire opened Finland's eastern border, on the other side of which lived speakers of Finnish and related languages. In 1835, Lönnrot published his collected poems as *The Kalevala*, an epic poem. A second, more extensive edition, was published in 1849. The widespread celebration of this work stemmed from the understanding of *The Kalevala* not as a work of literature but, rather, as a chronicle of Finland's lost past. *The Kalevala* sparked an interest in finding the country's roots from the East, rather than from the West. For example, during the 1840s the linguist M. A. Castrén (1813–1852) made several trips to northern Russia; his work identified the relationship between Finnish and the Finno-Uralic several languages spoken there.[10]

The second in the trio of 1822 was Johan Ludvig Runeberg (1804–1877), Finland's national poet. Runeberg's poetry painted the landscape of agrarian Finland. His collection of poems, *The Tales of Ensign Stål* (1848), is an account of the war of 1808–1809. The first of these poems, "Our Land," provided the lyrics for Finland's national anthem of the same name. Runeberg's contribution to the national cause did not lie in his cultivation of the Finnish language. Runeberg wrote his poems in Swedish, and is recognized as one of (if not the greatest) poet to write in Swedish. Instead, his contribution lay in giving the people of Finland a sense of uniqueness. His poetic creation of the peasant Paavo of Saarijärvi became the archetypal Finnish peasant: a diligent man confronting and eventually overcoming the difficulties of living on the land. Similarly, later in the century the writer and historian Zachris Topelius (1818–1898) wrote about the common past and current place that united Finland's people.[11]

Possessing many ingredients for nationhood, the people of Finland lacked what many considered the most important component—a common language. At the beginning of the nineteenth century, about 15 percent of Finland's population spoke Swedish as its first language. Nonetheless, Swedish was the language of government, education, and the elites. Virtually the rest of the population spoke Finnish as its first language. According to the precepts of nineteenth-century European nationalism, a common language constituted an essential basis for nationhood. The existence of two languages posed difficult questions: Was there a Finnish nation? Who was a Finn? What was the role of language in nationhood? These questions engendered a long struggle that would last until the eve of World War II.

J. V. SNELLMAN AND THE RISE OF FENNOMANIA

The third man of the trio of 1822, Johan Vilhelm Snellman (1806–1881) was the most influential figure of Finland's nineteenth century. Like his contemporary, Karl Marx, Snellman was heavily influenced by the German philosopher Georg Wilhelm Friedrich Hegel (1770–1831). Similar to Marx, Snellman sought to apply philosophy to social action. Snellman moved the basis of nationalism in Finland from literary to linguistic. Snellman's Finnish-language nationalist ideology consisted of three basic elements. First, one Finnish-speaking nation inhabited Finland. This assertion rested on the idea of the German philosopher Johann Friedrich von Herder (1744–1803) that the language of the masses expressed a nation's spirit (*Volksgeist*). In the case of Finland, the Swedish-speaking population had to accept this premise and adopt the Finnish language. Like many of his supporters, Snellman articulated this view almost exclusively in Swedish. Second, the Finnish nation could survive only through an improvement of Finnish-language education. Third, the survival of the Finnish nation depended upon loyalty to the emperor. Russian authorities openly encouraged Fennophilia and Fennomania as a means of distancing Finland from Sweden. Snellman's program consisted of a cultural, not a political liberation movement.

Snellman pursued his agenda as a student, journalist, and professor. In 1863, Emperor Alexander II recognized Snellman's work by naming him to the Senate. This appointment started a transformation of the Senate from a board of nonparty civil servants to a council of the country's leading political figures. In the same year, Snellman's influence with the emperor resulted in the promulgation of the Language Rescript. This decree placed the Finnish language on a path to becoming co-official with Swedish as the country's official language by 1883. This measure had been preceded in the 1850s by a series of decrees that required Finnish language skills from local officials in Finnish-speaking areas.[12]

Fennomania in the 1860s developed into a political organization known as the Finnish Party. Many in the party expanded their interest beyond language to social issues. The many faces and phases of Fennomania would eventually break apart into several parties. As a result, many of modern Finland's political parties claim Fennomane roots.

OTHER NATIONAL VISIONS: LIBERALISM AND SVECOMANE

In pursuit of its agenda, the Fennomane movement had to contend with competing visions of nationhood. As was occurring elsewhere in Western Europe, a significant Liberal movement had established itself in Finland by the 1860s. In the nineteenth century, Liberalism emphasized the individual as the building block of society. Liberals believed in a society based on individual rights rather than group privilege. They advocated free-enterprise economics and representative, although not always democratic, government. Liberalism had supporters among the growing middle classes. The Liberal agenda appealed to many people seeking solutions for the new Europe of industrial economies and nation-states.

Liberals saw Finland's legal autonomy, rather than language, as the basis of the nation. Finland would remain a nation only as long as its eastern neighbor did not swallow up the Finnish state. Liberals believed that any change to the status of Finland's two languages should come as a result of natural changes in the society, not government mandate. The Liberals succeeded in influencing political and economic reforms, particularly in the 1860s. However, their alternative to nationbuilding failed to garner widespread support. The advance of the Fennomanes split the Liberals, with many joining a national movement based on the Swedish language. This so-called Svecomane movement, whose founding ideologue was Professor Axel Olof Freudenthal (1836–1911), agreed with Snellman that language indeed constituted the basis for nationhood. Freudenthal concluded that the presence of two main language groups meant the existence of not one, but two, nations in Finland— a Swedish one and a Finnish one. The two groups did share Finland as a common fatherland. Like the Fennomanes, the Svecomanes focused their activities on education. They upheld Swedish as the language of education; Finnish, the Svecomanes argued, was unsuitable as a language of culture and learning. However, the Svecomanes accepted the creation of a Finnish-language educational infrastructure as long as resources were not diverted from Swedish-language schools. In other words, they opposed the use of public funds for Finnish-language education. In 1882, adherents of the Svecomane cause formed a political organization, the Swedish Party. Like the Fennomanes and the liberals, the Svecomanes did not envision a politically independent Finland.[13]

THE EMERGENCE OF FINNISH

The development of the Finnish language into a complete means of communication aided the Fennomane cause. At the beginning of the nineteenth century, Finnish was so underdeveloped that, after some first attempts to use Finnish, the protocols of the Finnish Literature Society were written in Swedish until 1858. Finnish lacked the vocabulary and unified rules of written expression necessary for a language of science, the arts, and public affairs. Over the course of the nineteenth century, however, scholars and writers worked to cultivate the language. The rise of a vibrant Finnish-language press, in particular, expanded the language's vocabulary and standardized usage. The publication of Finnish-language books grew at a fast rate. In the years 1543 to 1808, 174 works were published in Finnish; between 1809 and 1855, 425 Finnish books were published; and in the following decade, 481 Finnish works appeared.[14]

In the years after 1860, Finnish-language literature developed beyond religious writings and collections of ancient folk poems, into novels, modern poetry, and drama. The father of modern Finnish-language literature is Aleksis Kivi (1834–1872). Originally named Aleksis Stenvall, Kivi was not born into circumstances conducive for a career as Finland's national writer. He was not born in an urban center but, rather, in Nurmijärvi, today a bedroom community for Helsinki but at that time a small, isolated village in southern Finland. Between 1821 and 1868, only seven people from Nurmijärvi completed university preparatory school; Kivi was the only commoner among them. Kivi, whose first language was Finnish, had to attend Swedish-language schools in order to receive any education. Like many Finnish speakers, Kivi received poor grades in school.

Kivi entered university in 1857. He never earned a degree, deciding instead to become a writer. Like many who embraced the cause of the Finnish language, he Finnicized his Swedish surname Stenvall to the Finnish Kivi. In 1860, he won a competition sponsored by the Finnish Literature Society for his first play, *Kullervo*, inspired by the tragic figure of *The Kalevala* of the same name. Over the course of a decade, Kivi produced several other works. His crowning achievement was his last novel, *The Seven Brothers*, published in 1870. This novel describes the flight of seven delinquent brothers from their village and their triumphant return as good citizens. Kivi did not live long enough to enjoy the acclaim his works engendered. Long suffering from mental illness, he died in 1872. After his death, Kivi would be recognized as the founder of Finnish-language literature, in a way similar to Shakespeare for English.[15]

Over the course of the nineteenth century, Finnish became a language of education on a par with Swedish. In the 1840s, some elementary schools began to offer instruction in Finnish for Finnish-speaking pupils in the first few grades. It was not until 1856 that a decree allowed for schools to offer instruction solely in Finnish. The Swedish speakers who dominated state administration were reluctant to fund Finnish-language schools until the 1880s. In response, a network of privately funded Finnish schools sprang up across the country. In 1860, only 5.5 percent of the new students entering Helsinki University spoke Finnish as a first language. By 1889, Finnish speakers represented a majority of freshmen, a majority that would continue to grow during the next century. The university had made accommodations in anticipation of this new reality. By the 1850s, Finnish was well-enough developed that Helsinki University allowed Finnish-language doctoral dissertations, the first of which was defended in 1858. In 1863, the university permitted the use of Finnish as a language of instruction. In 1865, Emperor Alexander II decreed that all new instructors in law, theology, and pedagogy must have fluent command of Finnish as of 1872. Despite these changes, instruction in Finnish at the university would only predominate after Finland's independence.[16]

POPULATION AND ECONOMY

In 1811, Finland had a population of one million; by 1879, this number had doubled. This unprecedented growth occurred despite one of the greatest catastrophes in the country's history. In the years 1866–1868, poor harvests and epidemics killed about 138,000 people, more than seven percent of the population. Another source of population loss came in the form of emigration. In the years 1881–1914, some 280,000 Finns emigrated to the United States and Canada. By the end of the nineteenth century, almost 40,000 immigrants from Finland lived in St. Petersburg. Finland's population growth in the nineteenth century stemmed, to a great extent, from the same factors that contributed to eighteenth-century growth. With the exception of some British attacks on Finland's coast during the Crimean War, Finland experienced no military conflict on its soil after the War of Finland (1808–1809). After the 1860s, the country suffered no significant natural catastrophes. Fertility remained high, with women giving birth to about five to six children, on average. In addition, a public health infrastructure slowly developed throughout the country so that by the end of the nineteenth century life expectancy began to lengthen noticeably, further contributing to population growth.[17]

A small but important contribution to population growth came in the form of immigration. Germans played a significant role in the commercial growth of Helsinki. An immigrant from the German principality of Holstein, Franz Georg Stockmann (1825–1906), bought a glassware shop from his employer, the Nuutajärvi Glass Works, in 1862. By the 1870s, Stockmann had transformed the shop into the city's leading department store and a national institution. Another north German, Gustav Paulig (1850–1907), started a coffee company in Helsinki in 1876, which grew into the country's largest such company.[18] Russian immigrants contributed to economic growth as well. In 1821 Nikolai Sinebrychoff, whose father had settled in Old Finland in the late eighteenth century, established a brewery in Helsinki. The Sinebrychoff brewery still produces many of Finland's best-selling beers. Another Russian, Feodor Kiseleff, founded a major sugar factory in 1812. The first location of that factory, a building at the edge of Senate Square, still stands today as a market hall. Both Kiseleff and Sinebrychoff participated in the significant Russian activity in Helsinki's construction industry. Russian immigrants were instrumental in the growth of restaurants and food stores in nineteenth-century Helsinki. Another Russian entrepreneur, Sergei Nikolaeff, Jr. (1878–1920), founded a company that imported the first automobiles seen in Finland.[19]

Population growth had several widespread impacts on society. In the countryside, there was a growing shortage of arable land for the increasing population. In the far north, the Sámi found themselves increasingly hemmed in by an even faster-growing Finnish-speaking population. The urban population also grew. For example, the population of Helsinki, which was about 4,000 at the beginning of Russian rule, had grown to about 140,000 by 1910. Nonetheless, by 1890, only 10 percent of the population lived in the country's cities. The Estates-General and municipal councils became increasingly unrepresentative, since a growing part of the population had neither the wealth nor privileges necessary for political participation.

The population growth had an impact on the country's language groups. The number of Finnish speakers grew at a greater rate than the Swedish speakers. In 1870, about three-quarters of the population of Helsinki spoke Swedish as its first language. By 1910, this number decreased to about half, with a greater number of Swedish speakers possessing a good command of Finnish. Some Swedish-speaking families followed Snellman's call and began to use Finnish in their homes. Some Finnicized their Swedish surnames. For example, a leader of the Finnish Party, Professor and Senator Georg Zachris Forsman changed his name to Yrjö Sakari Yrjö-Koskinen in 1882 when the emperor ennobled him. The Finnicization of surnames reached its height in the years 1906–07, during which some 32,500 households, or about 100,000 people, changed their last names.[20]

In creating the Grand Duchy of Finland, the Russians sought to create a politically as well as economically autonomous polity. Finland's state finances were separate from those of the empire; taxes paid in Finland stayed in the country. Already in 1811, a central bank, later known as the Bank of Finland, was founded to facilitate the introduction of a new currency to replace Swedish money. Despite attempts to introduce the Russian ruble or a Finnish ruble, a stable, lasting alternative currency to Swedish money was not established until 1860 when, at the initiative of J. V. Snellman and the Senate, Alexander II decreed for Finland a new currency, the mark.[21] With respect to trade, Russian authorities separated Finland from Sweden by gradually lowering tariffs between Finland and Russia while raising them between Sweden and Finland. An abrupt end to Finland's economic dependence on Sweden would have resulted in the type of instability the Russians wanted to avoid in the new grand duchy. By the 1840s, the Russian Empire had replaced Sweden as Finland's biggest trading partner. While Finland had exported mostly grain to Sweden, the Russian market demanded higher-value industrial and agricultural goods: iron products, butter, and, later, textiles and paper products.[22]

In the nineteenth century, industrialization transformed Europe's economy. Europeans, who had made their livelihoods on farms and in their own homes, in increasing numbers sought work in factories away from their ancestral lands. Although Finland industrialized later and more slowly than did much of Europe, it followed the typical European pattern. Increased agricultural productivity produced excess capital and labor; investors placed spare capital into machines and factories. The excess labor force on the farms migrated to the factories in search of work. As in many other parts of Europe, textiles spearheaded Finland's industrial revolution. A Scot, James Finlayson, built the country's first textile factory in Tampere. Finlayson, who had founded textile plants in Russia, sold his firm to St. Petersburg investors in 1835. By 1860, the factory had about 1,600 employees.[23]

Economic change is as often a function of law as it is of money. Industrialization benefited from the deregulation of domestic economies and international trade. These changes had their greatest impact on the development of Finland's wood and forest products industries. In the 1860s, the heavy regulation of the cutting of forests was ended. Great Britain, the engine of the nineteenth-century European economy, reduced its protective tariffs on non-Canadian wood, making Finnish wood more competitive in this important market. New technologies made it easier to turn wood pulp into paper, and Finnish paper products found plenty of buyers in Russia. Moreover, greater demand for wood and paper products grew as Europe industrialized and entered a consumer economy in the second half of the nineteenth century. The growth of the forest products industry spread wealth throughout the country. Peasants, who owned most of the forestland, received new wealth from selling or renting their forests to wood companies; they used this new capital to further modernize agriculture. Landless agricultural workers found work during the winter months cutting wood.[24]

The improvement of the transportation infrastructure further facilitated Finland's industrialization. Public investments in canals connected Finland's extensive inland waterways with the sea. The most important of these, the Saimaa Canal, was completed in 1856. Still in use, the canal connects Lake Saimaa with the Gulf of Finland. In 1862, the first railroad was built between Helsinki and Hämeenlinna. In the years 1868–1870, another line connected Helsinki to the Finland Station in St. Petersburg. By century's end, rail lines reached as far north as Oulu and Kuopio. Railroads moved goods more quickly and cheaply, thus increasing access to foreign markets. Although institutionally separate from Russia, Finland's rail network used the same rail gauge as the rest of the empire—a gauge wider than elsewhere in Europe. To this day, rail traffic going from Finland to Sweden must change trains at the border.[25]

Between 1860 and 1890 Finland's economy grew at an unprecedented average rate of 2.2 percent annually. Still, Finland's industrialization, while transformative, does need to be placed into a broader European perspective. Finland by 1890 was still an overwhelmingly agrarian country with only eight percent of the workforce in industry. In terms of national wealth, Finland ranked well below the Western European average, although the gap narrowed in the years after 1860.[26]

CHANGES IN THE CHURCH AND RELIGION

A separate state and economy, as well as the various national movements, gave the people of Finland a collective sense of autonomy. At the same time, individuals were gaining greater autonomy from larger groups and institutions, such as the Lutheran Church. The rise of revivalist movements challenged the Church's virtual monopoly on religious expression. These groups had their roots in the wider tradition of pietism. Beginning in Germany in the late seventeenth century and spreading later throughout the Protestant world, pietism arose out of dissatisfaction with the perceived bureaucratic, academic, and rational nature of institutional Protestantism. Pietists emphasized a personal, emotional relationship with God, as well as personal acts of piety and a strict moral code. The belief in a personal relationship with God is pietism's contribution to modern Christianity.

Pietism's spread to Finland in the eighteenth century was limited to some elites and to isolated small communities. In the nineteenth century, pietist (more frequently called revivalist) movements had the leadership to appeal to a broader public. The first of the revivalist movements, the Awakened, spread from Ostrobothnia to Savolax and Karelia. In the 1830s, Paavo Ruotsalainen (1777–1852) became the leading figure of the Awakened. An uneducated peasant, Ruotsalainen attracted a substantial following by appealing to the poor and the oppressed through his emphasis on the inability of people to save themselves. Only God can save people, he said. A parish minister in Swedish Lapland, Lars Levi Laestadius (1800–1861), launched a campaign in the 1840s against what he considered sinful activities, above all the consumption of alcohol. Support for Laestadius's campaign spread into Finnish Lapland and other northern regions. Laestadianism emphasizes the importance of confession of sins and the absolution of sins by someone of uncorrupted faith. Laestadianism is characterized by its specific application of teaching to everyday activities. Laestadians abstain from alcohol and condemn the use of contraception. Today's observant conservative Laestadian avoids television. Two other smaller pietist groups arose in western Finland. An offshoot of the Awakened, the Evangelicals emphasize the Lutheran teaching of salvation by faith and the importance of baptism. Supplicationism is characterized by long kneeling prayers and adherence to certain song books, hymnals, and devotional books.

For the Lutheran Church, open religious expression outside of its purview obviously threatened its authority. Civil authorities feared that the revivalists, who appealed to the masses, could endanger the world order. Both the Church and state took legal measures against these movements. Paavo Ruotsalainen found himself in court several times. Over the second half of the nineteenth century, the revivalists reached an accommodation with religious and civil authorities. The movements became integrated into the Lutheran Church, where they exist today. The revivalists proved to be as obedient to civil authority as were mainline Lutherans. At the same time, the tight alliance between the Church and the Crown was ending. In 1865, the state established self-governing municipalities to replace the Church's civil administration of rural areas. In 1869, the state assumed the supervision of education, taking this responsibility away from the Church. New opportunities offered by a growing economy and state bureaucracy made careers in the Church less lucrative. As a result, the Lutheran clergy became increasingly of Finnish-speaking, peasant, and working-class origin.[27]

While the Church broadened the boundaries of religious activity for individual Lutherans, it also had to accept individual religious activity outside of the Church. Much of the diversification of religious life came from the East, not the West. Soldiers of the Russian army brought Judaism and Islam to Finland. Russian emperors ensured that the country's Orthodox minority enjoyed unhindered freedom of worship and, in practice, the same civil rights as Lutherans. Practitioners of the Orthodox faith, who numbered only about 2,500 before the Russian conquest, grew to 25,000 after 1809. This increase stemmed, to a great extent, from the incorporation of Old Finland into the grand duchy. The presence of Russian officials, soldiers, and immigrants later added to the Orthodox population. The return of Roman Catholicism to Finland also came through Russia. In the eighteenth century, Russian authorities allowed for the founding of a Roman Catholic parish for Polish soldiers in Viipuri (Vyborg). In Helsinki, a Catholic parish was founded in 1855 to serve civil servants and soldiers from the Russian Empire's western parts.

In 1889, the estates approved a new law pertaining to religion, which allowed Lutherans to join other Protestant churches and gave legal protection to other Protestant communities. Starting in the 1860s, Protestant denominations such as Methodism and Baptism had gained a foothold. Nonmembership in a church was not accepted, nor was conversion to a non-Protestant community. Roman Catholics and non-Christians were not given any legal status as communities and, as a result, they did not enjoy citizenship as individuals. Full individual freedom of religion and citizenship without a religious basis would not occur until after independence. Nonetheless, over the course of the nineteenth century, religious activity in Finland, as elsewhere in Europe, became more a function of personal conscience and less a function of communal values and norms.[28]

THE BREAKDOWN OF ESTATE SOCIETY

Individual autonomy was furthered by the breakdown of the estates' power. Before the nineteenth century, groups largely structured European societies. In Finland, the main social groupings were the four estates: the clerics, nobles, burghers, and peasants. In this social structure, one's estate determined an individual's interests, privileges, and activities. In the nineteenth century, a civil society replaced the estate-based society. Four broad traits define a civil society. First, it is based on individuals rather than groups. Second, civil societies emphasize individual rights over group privileges. Third, participants in public affairs aim to benefit society, not just one social group. Fourth, all individuals are entitled to partake in public affairs. Moreover, individual rights are understood, in principle, to apply to all people. The existence of a civil society is a necessary step toward more democratic forms of government.

Three primary agents contributed to the creation of this new society in Finland. The first was the revivalist movements, which emphasized the importance of individual rather than corporate religious experience. Although drawing primarily from the peasantry, the revivalists attracted followers from all estates. In confronting social problems ranging from alcoholism to poor relief, revivalists believed that they were working to benefit all of society. The second agent was the nationalist movements: the Fennomanes, Liberals, and Svecomanes. They all sought to appeal to people regardless of estate. Language, whether Swedish or Finnish, cut across social lines. As a basic article of faith, liberals believed in a society based on individuals. The third agent was demographic change. Finland's estate-based society represented the interests of most people in the medieval and early modern eras. By the middle of the nineteenth century the estate society did not recognize many large segments of the population, such as those involved in the industrial economy and the landless rural population. A new social model was needed. Evidence of the civil society's rise in the second half of the nineteenth century is the explosion of associations that sought to cross social boundaries and enrich society as a whole: temperance associations, educational foundations, volunteer fire departments, and sports clubs.[29]

AUTONOMY FOR WOMEN

At the middle of the nineteenth century, Finland's women enjoyed none of the rights and equality that they enjoy today. Most had no legal autonomy until 1864, when a new law made unmarried women legally independent individuals after age 21. Married women still were still legally dependent upon their husbands until the twentieth century. In the second half of the nineteenth century, women became more visible outside of the home as industrialization and economic expansion drew women into the paid workforce. Women were visible in the rise of a civil society. The temperance movement, as in other countries at the time, was heavily female.[30]

The real improvement in freedom for women, however, came as a result of increased educational opportunities. In 1843, schools for girls were permitted throughout the grand duchy. Before then, the only schools for girls were those founded in Old Finland under Russian rule before 1809. In the 1860s, schools were founded for the education of women as schoolteachers, but women still had great difficulty in reaching university; schools that provided university preparation often refused to admit girls. Until 1901, a woman needed to appeal to the emperor in order to take the matriculation examination for the university! Those women who managed to complete the education needed for university admission found university officials reluctant to admit women. In 1871, university officials decided that women could study at the university—but only medicine. Rules were gradually loosened to allow women to enter other fields. The university's first female graduate in 1882, Irene Åström, went on to have a career as an instructor in pedagogy. In 1901, all discriminatory legal barriers against women entering university were removed. By the beginning of World War I, women represented almost 40 percent of all graduates of university preparatory schools.[31]

In describing Finland's experience between 1809 and 1890, the word autonomy, in terms of self-governance, is quite appropriate. State institutions and an economy autonomous from Russia were formed. Movements arose that sought to establish a national identity autonomous from Russia and Sweden. The rise of a civil society emphasized the autonomy of all individuals.

Autonomy also can imply something short of complete independence. In this sense, too, the word is useful in describing Finland's experience. None of these developments toward autonomy occurred without the approval, support, or at least acquiescence of Russian imperial power. Until about 1890, Russian imperial power and Finland's autonomy were two sides of the same coin that separated Finland from Sweden and made it a peaceful part of the Russian Empire. In the last decade of the nineteenth century, Russian imperial power began to see its autonomous creation not as an achievement but, rather, as a threat.

NOTES

1. Seppo Zetterberg, "Suomen sota," in *Suomen historian pikkujättiläinen*, ed. Seppo Zetterberg (Porvoo: WSOY, 1987), 359–371.

2. Osmo Jussila, *Maakunnasta valtioksi: Suomen valtion synty* (Porvoo: WSOY, 1987), 13–58.

3. Panu Pulma, "Rauhoituspolitiikan kausi," in *Suomen historian pikkujättiläinen*, ed. Seppo Zetterberg (Porvoo: WSOY, 1987), 374–375.

4. Raimo Savolainen, *Suosikkisenaattorit: Venäjän keisarin suosio suomalaisten senaattoreiden menestyksen perustana 1809–1892,* Hallintohistoriallisia tutkimuksia 14 (Helsinki: VAPK, 1994), 345.

5. Seppo Tiihonen and Paula Tiihonen, *Suomen hallintohistoria* (Helsinki: VAPK, 1984), 99–114.

6. George C. Schoolfield, *Helsinki of the Czars* (Columbia, SC: Camden House, 1996), 7–13.

7. Matti Klinge, "Sensuuri ja mielipiteet," in *Suomen kulttuurihistoria*, vol. 2, ed. Rainer Knapas and Nils Erik Forsgård (Helsinki: Tammi, 2002), 247–250; Tuomo Olkkonen, "Modernisoituva suuriruhtinaskunta," in *Suomen historian pikkujättiläinen*, ed. Seppo Zetterberg (Porvoo: WSOY, 1987), 402; Tiihonen, *Suomen hallintohistoria*, 150.

8. Olkkonen, "Modernisoituva" 408–409, 493; Tiihonen, *Suomen hallintohistoria*, 98–99, 101–102 114–115, 118; Jouko Vahtola, *Suomen historia jääkaudesta Euroopan unioniin* (Helsinki: WSOY, 2003), 259–261.

9. Matti Klinge, *Finlands historia*, vol. 3 (Esbo: Schildts, 1996), 38; Päiviö Tommila, "Valtiollisen identiteetin synty," in *Herää Suomi: Suomalaisuusliikkeen historia*, ed. Päiviö Tommila and Maritta Pohls (Jyväskylä: Gummerus, 1989), 52.

10. Lauri Honko, "Kansallisten juurien löytäminen," in *Suomen kulttuurihistoria*, vol. 2, ed. Päiviö Tommila, Aimo Reitala, and Veikko Kallio (Helsinki: WSOY, 1980), 47; Kai Laitinen, *Suomen kirjallisuuden historia* (Helsinki: Otava, 1997), 176–185; Raija Majamaa, "Elias Lönnrot–kulttuurivaikuttajana," in *Suomen kulttuurihistoria*, vol. 2, ed. Rainer Knapas and Nils Erik Forsgård (Helsinki: Tammi, 2002), 441–444; William A. Wilson, *Folklore and Nationalism in Modern Finland* (Bloomington, IN: Indiana University Press, 1976), 33–44.

11. Nils Erik Forsgård, "Johan Ludvig Runeberg" and "Zachris Topelius," in *Suomen Kulttuurihistoria*, vol. 2, ed. Rainer Knapas and Nils Erik Forsgård (Helsinki: Tammi, 2002), 460–470; Laitinen, *Suomen kirjallisuuden historia*, 166–173, 185–188.

12. Marja Jalava, "J.V. Snellmanin kirjallisuuskäsitys," in *Suomen kulttuurihistoria*, vol. 2, ed. Rainer Knapas and Nils Erik Forsgård (Helsinki: Tammi, 2002), 446–455; Kai Laitinen, *Suomen kirjallisuuden historia*, 173–176; Erkki Lehtinen, "Suomalainen patriotismi ja kansallistunne Ruotsin kaudella," in in *Herää Suomi: Suomalaisuusliikkeen historia*, ed. Päiviö Tommila and Maritta Pohls (Jyväskylä: Gummerus, 1989), 13–47; Tiihonen, *Suomen hallintohistoria*, 113; Päiviö Tommila, "Mitä oli olla suomalainen 1800-luvun alkupuolella," in *Herää Suomi: Suomalaisuusliikkeen historia*, ed. Päiviö Tommila and Maritta Pohls

(Jyväskylä: Gummerus, 1989), 60–62; Pirjo Rommi and Maritta Pohls, "Poliittisen fennomanian synty ja nousu," in *Herää Suomi: Suomalaisuusliikkeen historia*, ed. Päiviö Tommila and Maritta Pohls (Jyväskylä: Gummerus, 1989), 71–80, 119; Wilson, *Folklore and Nationalism*, 28–30.

13. Martti Ruutu, "Kulttuurikehtiyksen yleislinjat," in *Suomen kulttuurihistoria*, vol. 2, ed. Päiviö Tommila, Aimo Reitala, and Veikko Kallio (Helsinki: WSOY, 1980), 102–108.

14. Pirkko Leino-Kaukiainen, "Suomen kielen käytön yleistyminen," in *Herää Suomi: Suomalaisuusliikkeen historia*, ed. Päiviö Tommila and Maritta Pohls (Jyväskylä: Gummerus, 1989), 339–340; Paavo Pulkkinen, "Suomen kielestä täyspainioinen sivistyskieli," in *Herää Suomi: Suomalaisuusliikkeen historia*, ed. Päiviö Tommila and Maritta Pohls (Jyväskylä: Gummerus, 1989), 307–337.

15. Laitinen, *Suomen kirjallisuuden historia*, 198–207; Pirjo Lyytikäinen, "Impivaaraan ja takaisin," in *Suomen kirjallisuushistoria*, vol. 1, ed. Yrjö Varpio and Liisi Huhtala (Helsinki: Suomalaisen Kirjallisuuden Seura, 1999), 341–347; Yrjö Varpio, "Aleksis Kivi," in *Suomen kulttuurihistoria*, vol. 2, ed. Rainer Knapas and Nils Erik Forsgård (Helsinki: Tammi, 2002), 416–418.

16. Kaisa Häkkinen, *Agricolasta nykykieleen: Suomen kirjakielen historia* (Helsinki: WSOY, 1994), 64–65; Riitta Hjerppe, *Kasvun vuosisata*, (Helsinki: VAPK-kustannus, 1990), 94; Laura Kolbe, "Yliopisto, ylioppilaat ja kansallinen omakuva," in *Suomen kulttuurihistoria*, vol. 3, ed. Anja Kervanto Nevanlinna and Laura Kolbe, (Helsinki: Tammi, 2003), 129–131; Antti Lappalainen, *Suomi kouluttajana*, (Helsinki: WSOY, 1991), 57–80; Olkkonen, "Modernisoituva," 484–485, 498–500, 527; Vahtola, *Suomen historia*, 330–331; Heikki Waris, *Muuttuva suomalainen yhteiskunta* (Helsinki: WSOY, 1974), 35.

17. Max Engman, "Ulkosuomalaisuuden synty," in *Kansa liikkeessä*, ed. Risto Alapuro et al. (Helsinki: Kirjayhtymä, 1987), 109.

18. Schoolfield, *Helsinki of the Czars*, 128.

19. Kenneth Danielsen, "Maamme moottoriliikenteen alkumetirt kolmen perheen vauhdittamana"; Igor Kurkimies, "Kauppasliikemiesten F. P. Kiseleffin ja F. F. Kiseleffin—isän ja pojan—merkittävä osuus Helsingin talouselämän kasvuun 1800-luvulla"; and Arja Pullinen, "Sinebrychoffit—marketentistä kauppiassuvuksi" in *Venäläiset kauppiaat Helsingin historiassa*, ed. Konstantin Svante Kuhlberg (Helsinki: Helsingin Venäläinen Kauppayhdistys ry, 2002), 240–285, 210–239,137–199.

20. Kari Pitkänen, "Väestörakenteen muuttuminen," in *Suomen väestö*, ed. Seppo Koskinen (Helsinki: Gaudeamus, 1994), 368–369; Aleksandra Ramsay, "Kansa ja sen kaksi kieltä," in *Suomen kulttuurihistoria*, vol. 3, ed. Anja Kervanto Nevanlinna and Laura Kolbe, (Helsinki: Tammi, 2003), 151; Vilja Rasila, "Väestönkehitys ja sosiaaliset ongelmat," in *Suomen taloushistoria*, vol. 2, ed. Jorma Ahvenainen et al. (Helsinki: Tammi, 1982), 138; Vahtola, *Suomen historia*, 212, 300–304.

21. Timo Myllyntaus, "Suomen talouspolitiikka," in *Suomen taloushistoria*, vol. 2, ed. Jorma Ahvenainen et al. (Helsinki: Tammi, 1982), 340–342; Viljo Rasila, "Kauppa ja rahaliike," in *Suomen taloushistoria*, vol. 2, ed. Jorma Ahvenainen et al. (Helsinki: Tammi, 1982), 103–104.

22. Pulma, "Rauhoituspolitiikan kausi," 422–426.

23. Per Schybergson, "Teollisuus ja kasityö," in *Suomen taloushistoria*, vol. 1, ed. Eino Jutikkala et al. (Helsinki: Tammi, 1980), 414; Pentti Virrankoski, *Suomen taloushistoria kaskikaudesta atomiaikaan* (Helsinki: Otava, 1975), 147–150.

24. Sakari Heikkinen and Kai Hoffman, "Teollisuus ja käsityo," in *Suomen taloushistoria*, vol. 2, ed. Jorma Ahvenainen et al. (Helsinki: Tammi, 1982), 67–70; Viljo Rasila, "Liberalismin aika," in *Suomen taloushistoria*, vol. 2, ed. Jorma Ahvenainen et al. (Helsinki: Tammi, 1982), 22–23; Arvo M. Soininen, "Maa ja metsatalous," in *Suomen taloushistoria*, vol. 2, ed. Jorma Ahvenainen et al. (Helsinki: Tammi, 1982), 29, 47–48; Virrankoski, *Suomen taloushistoria*, 129–132;

25. Rasila, "Liberalismin aika," 15; Viljo Rasila, "Liikenne," in *Suomen taloushistoria*, vol. 2, ed. Jorma Ahvenainen et al. (Helsinki: Tammi, 1982), 122–125; Virrankoski, *Suomen taloushistoria*, 157–160.

26. Riitta Hjerppe, *Kasvun vuosisata*, 22–35; Olkkonen, "Modernisoituva," 474–477; Kari Pitkänen, "Väestönkehitys," in *Suomen taloushistoria*, vol. 2, ed. Jorma Ahvenainen et al. (Helsinki: Tammi, 1982, 138–140; Virrankoski, *Suomen taloushistoria*, 186.

27. Simo Heininen and Markku Heikkilä, *Suomen kirkkohistoria* (Helsinki: Edita, 1996), 170–179, 195; Matti Klinge, "Sensuuri ja mielipiteet," 247–250; Kari Salonen, Kimmo Kääriäinen, and Kati Niemelä, "The Church at the Turn of the Millenium—The Evangelical Lutheran Church of Finland from 1996 to 1999," web site of the Church Research Institute of Finland, http://www.evl.fi/kkh/ktk/publication96–99/index.shtml (accessed 3 January 2006).

28. Heininen and Heikkilä, *Suomen kirkkohistoria*, 204–206; Heikki Kirkkinen and Viktor Railas, *Ortodoksisen kirkon historia* (Pieksämäki: Sisälähetysseuran Raamattutalon kirjapaino, 1976), 194–205; Olkkonen, "Modernisoituva," 495; Hannu Rautkallio, *Suomen juutalaisten aseveljeys* (Helsinki: Tammi, 1989), 15–34; Kalevi Vuorela, *Finlandia Catholica: Katolinen kirkko Suomessa 1700-luvulta 1980-luvulle* (Helsinki: Studia Catholicum), 30–37.

29. Risto Alapuro and Henrik Stenius, "Kansanliikkeet loivat kansakunnan, in *Kansa liikkeessä*, ed. Risto Alapuro et al. (Helsinki: Kirjayhtymä, 1987), 9–22; Olkkonen, "Modernisoituva," 535–541; Pulma, "Rauhoituspolitiikan kausi," 468–471.

30. Olkkonen, "Modernisoituva," 535–541.

31. Matti Klinge, *Helsingin Yliopisto 1640–1990*, vol. 2, *Keisarillinen Aleksananterin Yliopisto 1808–1917* (Helsinki: Otava, 1989), 590–592, 647–648; Laura Kolbe, "Yliopisto, ylioppilaat, ja kansallinen omakuva,"126–129; Lappalainen, *Suomi kouluttajana*, 57–61; Saara Tuomaala, "Katekismuksesta päästötodistukseen," in *Suomen kulttuurihistoria*, vol. 3, ed. Anja Kervanto Nevanlinna and Laura Kolbe, (Helsinki: Tammi, 2003), 332–334; Pulma, "Rauhoituspolitiikan kausi," 468–471.

5

Oppression, Independence, and Civil War (1890–1918)

The years of Russian rule after 1890 are often referred to as the Age of Oppression. This term refers to the growing political oppression that the people of Finland were experiencing at the hands of Russian authorities. At the same time, however, there was social and economic oppression. A growing segment of the country's population felt increasingly exploited by both an antiquated agricultural economy and new industry. The twin issues of Russian policy and growing social inequality dominated the country's political discussions. They would provide an explosive compound that would result in independence and then civil war. These crises occurred against a backdrop of antagonisms among the great powers that highlighted Finland's place between East and West.

THE BACKGROUND TO IMPERIALIZATION

The relationship established between Finland and Russia in 1808–1809 had proven mutually beneficial. Russia enhanced its security in northern Europe and the Finns gained wide-ranging autonomy. Even Emperor Nicholas I, who reluctantly accepted Finland's special status, eventually advised his and future generations to "Leave the Finns alone. It is my large empire's only province that has not caused me a minute of worry or dismay during my reign." The Russian decision to change the terms of Finland's autonomy had nothing to do with problems in the bilateral relationship. Throughout the nineteenth century, Russia and other European powers sought to centralize state power. This centralization process was driven by the desire to modernize state institutions and unify ethnically diverse populations into a common sense of nationhood. Over the course of the nineteenth century, those parts of the Russian Empire that had some form of autonomy, such as Bessarabia, Poland, and the Baltic provinces, lost it. By 1890, Finland stood as the last place in the Russian Empire with its local administrative institutions intact.[1]

Already in the 1880s, concrete plans were being laid to reduce Finland's autonomy, a policy known as imperialization. In 1881, Emperor Alexander III named a new governor-general, F. L. Heiden. The governor-general made many proposals to his superiors for reducing Finland's autonomy, such as increasing the use of the Russian language in Finland's administrative institutions, merging Finland's small army with the imperial armed forces, and tightening economic ties. The most important goal was to subjugate Finland's laws and lawmaking to that of the empire as a whole. All of Finland's laws deemed to have an impact on the whole empire would go through the imperial rather than the separate Finnish legislative process. An example of Finland's legal autonomy from the rest of the empire is that the Russian Empire had extradition treaties with every European country except Finland! By the early twentieth century, this fact would become well-known to Russian revolutionaries seeking protection from Russian police.

Heiden and his boss, Alexander III, believed in introducing these initiatives very slowly, perhaps even over generations. The challenge in changing Finland's status lay not only in overcoming Finnish opposition, but also in bridging divisions among Russia's elites. The major proponents of narrowing Finland's autonomy consisted of the Russian nationalist press and the military. Wealthy Russians who owned villas on the Karelian Isthmus resented being treated as aliens in their own empire. At the same time, some Russians involved directly in Finland's governance were reluctant to eliminate their own sources of power. Others in the emperor's administration questioned the need to disturb a peaceful quarter of the empire. Certain Russian economic interests feared the increased competition of Finnish firms that would result from a removal of economic barriers.[2]

Although nationalism and modernization provided the long-term impetus for changes in Finland's status, the accelerating factor behind Russian policy was the growing need for security after 1890. During most of the nineteenth century, Russia sought to keep Finland peaceful as it fought wars elsewhere in southeastern Europe, such as the Crimean War (1853–1856) and the Turkish War (1877–1878). By 1890, Russian security concerns shifted to central and northern Europe because of the rise of a new, unified nation-state in Europe, Germany. In 1894, Russia signed a military alliance with Germany's archenemy, France. In 1907, France and Russia joined Great Britain in a military alliance, the Triple Entente. This alliance was targeted against the Triple Alliance, a coalition consisting of Germany and its allies, the Austro-Hungarian Empire and Italy. Like other European powers, Russia significantly increased spending on its military establishment. The security concerns motivated Alexander III's Postal Manifesto in 1890. This decree placed the Finnish postal service under the control of the Russian Ministry of the Interior. In Finland, as in most European countries of the time, the postal service delivered the mail as well as ran the telephones and telegraphs—important infrastructures in wartime.[3]

In 1894, Alexander III died. His son and successor, Nicholas II, was a much weaker ruler who fell under the spell of those who wanted to narrow Finland's autonomy more quickly. In 1898, Nicholas appointed a new governor-general for Finland, Nikolai Bobrikov. The new governor-general's understanding of Finland was formed during his time as chief of staff of the St. Petersburg military district. In that position, Bobrikov was charged with the defense of Russia's capital, which lay some 20 miles (32 kilometers) from Finland. For Bobrikov, Finland represented a front line in the defense of Russia's capital.

The first major act of Bobrikov's tenure was the February Manifesto of 1899. This imperial decree addressed the autonomy of Finnish state institutions to make their own laws. According to the manifesto, any proposed Finnish law that had an impact on the rest of the empire had to go through the Russian imperial legislative process. Finnish institutions, such as the Senate, the Estates-General, and the office of governor-general, would have only an advisory role in developing such laws. The determination of which laws would go through the Russian legislative process lay with the emperor. Despite the widespread outrage that the February Manifesto provoked, it was based on precedent and not extralegal or arbitrary whole cloth. In the decades of Russian rule before 1899, about 200 laws pertaining to Finland had gone through the Russian legislative process. From the Russian standpoint, the manifesto was meant to clarify existing legislative procedures.[4]

In 1900, at Bobrikov's initiative, Emperor Nicholas promulgated the Language Manifesto. According to this order, Russian would become the language of administration and the judiciary within 10 years. The people of Finland could still use Finnish or Swedish in their dealings with authorities, but the authorities would have to communicate in Russian among themselves. So that the position of the Russian language would improve, the teaching of Russian was increased in schools. The introduction of the Russian language was primarily meant to unify Finland's administration with the rest of the empire, and not to Russify the Finns. Moreover, Russian authorities continued to support the use of Finnish at the expense of Swedish in public institutions. In the Bobrikov era, Finnish displaced Swedish in the Senate. By 1905 the protocols of both sections of the Senate were kept in Finnish and Russian.

The Russians aimed for a situation in which Russian would serve as the language of administration, Finnish the language of the people, and Swedish would be reduced to having some geographically localized rights.[5]

In 1901, Russian officials instituted a new military conscription law. This law had been the primary goal of Bobrikov and his supporters at Nicholas's court. Since 1878 Finland had had military conscription; draftees served in Finland in units separate from the Russian army. Now, Finnish draftees could be stationed anywhere in the empire. To meet the widespread opposition to all of these measures, Bobrikov used his authority to restrict public expressions of opposition. In 1903, the emperor empowered him to place Finland under martial law.[6]

THE OPPOSITION ORGANIZES

The ensuing conflict fundamentally stemmed from divergent understandings of events in 1808–1809. From the Russian standpoint, Finland was conquered in the name of security, and the new Russian policy was consistent with this longstanding security concern. Although Emperor Alexander I pledged to uphold Finland's laws, he and his successors, as absolute rulers, could unilaterally change the terms of the Finnish–Russian relationship. For the Finns, their grand duchy was founded on an agreement between a ruler and his new subjects. Alexander I had promised to uphold Finland's constitution and religion in exchange for loyalty. The Finns justifiably believed that they had upheld their end of the bargain. In short, the Russians viewed Finland in terms of security, while the Finns understood their relationship with Russia in terms of law and morality. Moreover, by 1899, the Finnish–Russian dialogue had revealed that the Russian side saw Finland as an autonomous province within the Russian Empire. For the Finns, there was a growing conviction that Finland was a separate state united with the empire only through the emperor.[7]

The promulgation of the February Manifesto provoked a widespread belief that the emperor's new policy stemmed from bad advice from advisors. As a means of persuading the emperor to change course, 523,000 Finns within a matter of a few weeks signed a petition in which they proclaimed their loyalty to their grand duke and politely called for a change in policy. This address carried the signature of one in six Finns (one in three Finnish adults). A delegation took the so-called Great Address to St. Petersburg in March, 1899. Emperor Nicholas refused to see his Finnish subjects. Historians have considered the emperor's action a serious mistake in that, by meeting the delegation, he could have taken steam out of the protest.[8]

The national unity evidenced by the Great Address could not paper-over the growing divisions about how to confront Russia. Until the 1890s, political divisions concerned language and nationhood; now the Russian question recast the political spectrum. The country's political establishment split into so-called constitutionalists and appeasers. These two divergent approaches toward Russian power would take turns guiding Finland until the end of the twentieth century. The Russian question split the Finnish Party into Old Finn and Young Finn parties. The Old Finns, the appeasers, remained loyal to the ideals and traditions of the Fennomane movement as established by J. V. Snellman. In particular, they emphasized Snellman's thesis of loyalty to Russia as the key to Finland's prosperity and survival. The most important leaders of the Old Finn Party were Yrjö Sakari Yrjö-Koskinen (1830–1903) and Johan Richard Danielson-Kalmari (1853–1933). They and their fellow Old Finns called for concessions to the Russians with respect to Finland's state autonomy, in the hope that the Russians would leave Finnish culture and language alone. Old Finns sought to keep the civil service as much as possible in Finnish hands. They believed that it was better for Finns to do Russian bidding than leave Finland's governing structures in Russian hands. The Old Finns made a distinction between state and nation: a separate Finnish state was not a prerequisite for the survival of the Finnish nation.

The constitutionalists offered an opposing program. They argued for the defense of Finland's state autonomy and the constitutional framework at all costs. The creation of an autonomous Finnish state, argued the constitutionalists, provided the basis for the creation of a Finnish nation. State and nation were inextricably linked. If the Russians succeeded in destroying the Finnish state, the people of Finland would run the risk of being culturally Russianized.

In contrast to the appeasers, the constitutionalists did not belong to one, but rather to three political parties. The first and most visible constitutionalist party was the Young Finn Party. Over time, the party adopted more of a socially and economically liberal agenda, as well as a diminished interest in the language question. A majority in the Swedish Party supported Young Finn constitutionalism. A third party that backed the constitutionalist stance was the Social Democratic Party. Founded in 1899 as the Finnish Workers' Party, this party quickly gained support among the country's industrial and agricultural workers. The party program approved in Forssa in 1903 called for universal suffrage, compulsory school education, free health care, a separation of church and state, an eight-hour workday, and prohibition of the sale, production, and importation of alcohol. The Forssa program established the party on the foundations of Marxist Socialism and changed the party's name to the Social Democratic Party.

The constitutionalist movement exercised opposition in two ways. Peaceful civil disobedience was the more prevalent approach. The most visible example of civil disobedience consisted of the evasion of military conscription by many young Finnish men. In the first year after the promulgation of the 1901 Military Conscription Law, some 45 percent of drafted Finnish men refused to answer the call to the Russian army. These men received help from the constitutionalist opposition, particularly the constitutionalist civil servants. A minority known as the Activists chose to explore more violent alternatives to opposition. Shooting clubs sprang up throughout Finland. In addition to fostering good marksmanship, these clubs served as the basis for organized armed opposition. One member of a shooting club was a civil servant named Eugen Schauman. On June 16, 1904, Schauman entered the Senate Building (the building that today houses Finland's Cabinet), walked up to Governor-General Bobrikov, and shot three bullets into him. Then Schauman shot himself twice, dying instantly. Bobrikov expired the next day. Schauman left a suicide note listing Bobrikov's illegal actions. He emphasized that he acted alone and did not belong to any conspiracy. Technically, Schauman told the truth about acting alone, although the Activists knew about his plans.[9]

THE TURN OF THE TIDE

Bobrikov's murder foreshadowed further setbacks for the policy of imperialization. In the fall of 1905, news spread throughout the empire of Russia's shocking defeat to Japan in the Russo-Japanese war of 1904–1905. In this moment of defeat, dissatisfied elements throughout the empire demonstrated for political reform. A general strike engulfed Finland in November 1905. Nicholas II responded by making concessions to his subjects. He replaced the Old Finn majority in the Senate with constitutionalists. Nicholas did this for two reasons. First, the success of the constitutionalist opposition had discredited the Old Finns' appeasement to the point that the Old Finn Senate could not govern. Second, in this chaotic environment the emperor appreciated the constitutionalists' emphasis on law and order. Then, in his November Manifesto of 1905, the emperor suspended the February Manifesto and subsequent legislation. In addition, he promised Finland a new, more representative legislature.

By the beginning of the twentieth century, Finland's four-chamber legislature, the Estates-General, had begun to appear undemocratic on several counts. Voting was done by groups and not by individual legislators, and the voting power of the three eligible groups bore no relationship to their proportion in the population. The nobility had 25 percent of the vote at the Estates-General but represented one-tenth of one percent of the population. The Estates-General excluded new social groups, such as industrial workers. Combined, the four estates represented only about 30 percent of the population; only about 8 percent of the whole population had a vote in the Estates-General. Common throughout Europe before the nineteenth century, this type of legislature was being replaced by legislative bodies in which each individual legislator had a vote. Legislators were being elected by a growing segment of the male population, if not by universal male suffrage. By 1900, Finland's Estates-General was the last legislature of its kind in Europe.

In the transition from the Estates-General to the new Parliament, Finland went from having the most antiquated to the most innovative legislature on the continent. Finland's Parliament was (and still is) a single-chamber, 200-seat body. The right to vote was extended to all men and women 24 years of age and older, making Finland the first country in Europe to extend the right to vote to women. This universal franchise applied only to parliamentary elections. The franchise for municipal elections was still based on property qualifications. Moreover, women did not yet enjoy full legal equality. Married women were not recognized as legally equal to their husbands until 1930.

About 1.2 million people voted in the first election for Parliament in 1907, approximately 10 times as many as had voted in the last election for the Estates-General. These new voters recast the political spectrum to include parties not only based on language and the Russian question, but on social and economic interests as well. The biggest winner of the election (with 80 seats) was a party that had no representation in the old Estates-General—the Social Democratic Party. The level of support for the party reflected the widespread discontent among the country's agrarian and industrial workers. Another new party that had a social agenda was the Agrarian League. This party was founded to defend the interests of medium-sized farmers in the country that predominated in northern and eastern Finland. These farmers saw themselves as caught between the interests of large estate landowners and Finland's growing landless peasantry. The party followed the ideas of Snellman on the language question and the constitutionalists on the Russian question.

Although the legislature was democratically elected, Finland had not become a democracy. On two critical counts the new Parliament did not exercise the powers associated with a legislature in a democracy. First, it had the same few legislative powers that the Estates-General had; most legislative power still rested in the hands of an unelected emperor-grand duke. Parliament could pass laws on its own initiative but the emperor had an absolute veto over anything that the legislature passed. For example, Parliament passed a law prohibiting the production, sale, and importation of alcoholic beverages in October 1907. The approval of this law reflected the strength of the temperance movement, particularly in the Social Democratic Party. The law's opponents inside Finland encouraged the emperor to reject the law. In a second respect, Finland's new Parliament still could not hold the executive to account. It could not remove the emperor, the governor general, or members of the Senate.[10]

The new Parliament's weakness was evident in the face of renewed imperialization after 1907. The concessions of 1905 consisted of nothing more than a tactical retreat. In 1910, Nicholas II signed legislation requiring certain laws passed by the Finnish Parliament deemed to have an impact on the entire empire to be submitted to the new Russian Parliament (Duma) for approval. This action was obviously a thinly veiled attempt to reimpose the February Manifesto. In 1912, the emperor signed the so-called Equality Law that gave all Russian subjects in Finland rights equal to those of Finnish citizens. Before the promulgation of this law, Russian subjects coming to Finland from other parts of the empire had a status corresponding to that of an alien. They could not hold political office or vote, and their ability to live and make a living in Finland was limited. On the basis of this new law, in 1913 the emperor began to fill the Senate with non-native-born Finns, mostly Russian military officers with varying levels of experience in Finland. Already in 1909, Nicholas had radically changed the composition of the Senate by naming to it military officers who were born in Finland. This new so-called Saber Senate or Admiral Senate aided Nicholas's efforts to make Finland contribute more to the empire's defense. Instead of reinstituting conscription, the emperor called for Finland to make monetary contributions for the empire's defense. In 1909, some 10 million Finnish marks were transferred to Russian coffers. This sum rose by a million each year, reaching 17 million in 1916.[11] Historian Osmo Jussila argues for placing the significance of these Russian actions in two larger contexts. First, they were part of a larger attempt to harmonize governance throughout the entire empire. Second, Russian authorities realized that Finland was different enough from the rest of the empire that even the most extensive vision of imperialization would have to concede Finland some legislative, administrative, and cultural autonomy in order to govern the grand duchy effectively.[12]

THE GOLDEN AGE OF FINLAND'S CULTURE

During this period of national struggle, Finland entered a cultural Golden Age. Artists ranging from authors to sculptors created monuments of nationhood. At the same time, these artists redeemed their place in a greater European creative community. They felt comfortable both in the salons of Paris and the forests of Karelia. The achievements of Finland's artists made their country more visible throughout the world at a time of national struggle.

One of the pioneers in creating art that was both national and European was the painter Albert Edelfelt (1854–1905). A child prodigy, he originally wanted to paint scenes out of Finland's past. In 1877, Edelfelt went to Antwerp, the center of historical painting, for further training. There he embraced the realist movement that had broad appeal in European painting at the time. Realism aims to depict nature or contemporary life in an accurate, detailed, and unembellished fashion. By 1879, Edelfelt had moved to Paris for training more in line with his interests. For the rest of his life, Edelfelt shuttled between France and Finland. His best-known contribution to the national mission of Golden Age art is his 1879 painting, *A Child's Funeral*. In the following year, he finished *The Luxembourg Gardens,* a painting of mothers observing their children at play in a Paris park. During the 1880s, Edelfelt became a well-known portrait artist in Paris. In 1886, he finished his most famous portrait, that of the French scientist Louis Pasteur.

The best-known painter of the Golden Age is Akseli Gallen-Kallela (1865–1931). In the course of his studies in Paris in the 1880s, Gallen-Kallela broke with realism and dedicated himself to portraying *The Kalevala.* Helsinki's Ateneum Art Museum houses Gallen-Kallela's most famous *Kalevala* paintings, such as *The Aino Myth* (1891) and *Lemminkäinen's Mother* (1897).

By the beginning of the twentieth century, many painters began to distance themselves from the national agenda by associating themselves with the European movements of symbolism and expressionism. Symbolists sought to create art that hinted at rather than portrayed reality. Expressionists sought to communicate the emotions of the subjects they painted. Nonetheless, national motifs are still evident in the best-known works of these genres. The symbolist painter Magnus Enckell's (1870–1925) work *Fantasy* (1895) depicts a human figure rising transfigured out of a lake. Although Enckell rejected a conscious national agenda, one sees aspects of the Finnish countryside both in the lake and the swans surrounding the figure. The expressionist Tyko Sallinen's painting, *The Fanatics* (1918), portrays the rapture felt by the faithful in a revivalist meeting. The painting reflects Sallinen's own religious upbringing.

Women's contributions to Golden Age Finland have only begun to be uncovered. Much of the focus has been placed on Helene Schjerfbeck (1862–1946). Like many of the Golden Age painters, she started her career as a historical painter. She lived most of her life as recluse, battling a variety of illnesses. Her best-known painting, *A Recovering Girl* (1888), reflects the mysteriousness and challenges of Schjerfbeck's life. The painting portrays a young girl recovering from an illness, sitting at a table holding a small vase with a green tree branch in it. Art historians agree that the branch symbolizes the girl's eventual recovery. They speculate on whether Schjerfbeck meant the painting as an autobiographical work. Historical paintings aside, Schjerfbeck's paintings defy easy placement into any genre.[13]

When walking through the streets of central Helsinki today, one encounters the omnipresence of Golden Age architecture. Much of this architecture was inspired by the European *Jugendstil* or *art nouveau* movement that was characterized by an emphasis on curving, free-flowing, asymmetrical lines. As in other aspects of Golden Age art, this European movement was adapted to the mission of creating a national art and monuments for Finland. One only needs to go to the central railroad station in Helsinki to witness an example of *Jugendtsil* architecture. The architect of the station, Eliel Saarinen, joined two other architects, Armas Lindgren and Herman Gesellius, to plan Finland's

National Museum, completed in 1910. Akseli Gallen-Kallela painted the museum's *Kalevala*-inspired ceiling murals.[14]

The merging of national mission and European impulse appears in sculpture as well. In 1908, the sculptor Ville Vallgren completed the task of creating a statue that was supposed to symbolize Helsinki. The city fathers expected that Vallgren would create a Finnish-looking feminine figure. Vallgren's final product, *Havis Amanda,* shocked the people of Helsinki. It was a nude statue that did not look like the maiden Aino from *The Kalevala,* but more like the Greek goddess Aphroditie rising from the sea. This reaction eventually subsided into an acceptance of the statue as the city's chief symbol of its claim as "daughter of the Baltic."[15]

In literature, writers turned from Aleksis Kivi's national idealism to national realism. The playwright Minna Canth (1844–1897) focused on the sufferings of ordinary people. Her stories take place not in Finland's ancient forests, but in its new urban environments. Her contemporary, Juhani Aho (1861–1921), wrote about the erosion of agrarian life at the hands of industrialization and modernization. His best-known work, the novel *Rautatie* (*The Railroad*) (1884), describes the confusions of a couple, Matti and Liisa, when the railroad is brought through their village. The shadow of *The Kalevala* did not diminish; it was extended by the most prolific writer of the Golden Age, the poet Eino Leino (1878–1926). Leino is recognized as the most versatile writer in Finnish, writing in almost every genre from poetry to literary criticism. He also translated many classics of foreign literature into Finnish.[16]

The Golden Age witnessed the rise of Finland's best-known cultural figure, the composer Jean Sibelius (1865–1957). Sibelius's music embodies the mixture of Finnish national and European influences typical of Golden Age art. His first significant composition, the symphony *Kullervo,* was based on the story in *The Kalevala* of a man who seduces a woman only to discover that she is a long-lost sister. The premier of this presentation in Helsinki in 1892 was hailed as the beginning of Finnish classical music. Sibelius wrote much of the symphony as a student in Vienna. After *Kullervo,* Sibelius returned to central Europe to become a composer of operas. His failure to produce operas resulted in well-known orchestral pieces, such as *The Swans of Tuonela* (1896), another *Kalevala*-inspired piece. In 1899, he completed the first of his seven symphonies (*Kullervo,* although a symphony, is counted separately). In 1904, he conducted his violin concerto for the first time. It would become Sibelius's most-recorded piece of music—a consolation to a man whose first musical ambition to become a violin virtuoso was dashed by stage fright. The mixture of national and international impulses in Sibelius's music survived long after his death in 1957. The last section of Sibelius's composition *Finlandia* (1899) was adopted as the melody for national anthem of Biafra. In the years 1967–1970, this secessionist western African state fought a losing war to break away from Nigeria.[17]

ECONOMIC GROWTH AND SOCIAL CRISES

Finland's population grew from 2.38 million in 1890 to around 3 million in 1918. In the period 1890–1913, the gross domestic product grew at a strong rate of three percent annually. Economic growth, however, was not widespread enough to resolve significant social problems. Finland's agrarian economy had fallen into a crisis of landlessness by the beginning of the twentieth century. The doubling of the country's population between 1820 and 1890 left a large segment of the country's agrarian population without land. Most had to scrape a living through tenant farming, that is, renting land from landowners. Tenant farmers most commonly paid rent in the form of labor to the landowner, but sometimes in the form of money as well. In 1815, 57 percent of agricultural production came from those who worked the land they owned; in 1901, 65 percent of Finland's agrarian output came from tenant farmers. This development was most visible in Finland's southern third.

Structural changes in European agriculture in the second half of the nineteenth century exacerbated the problem of landlessness. Greater productivity across the continent lowered the price of grain, the main product of Finnish agriculture. The attempt to compensate for this by increasing production of dairy products was short-lived, however. By the beginning of the twentieth century, refrigeration made butter and cheese subject to international rather than local competition. In order to maintain their own prosperity, landowners increased demands on their tenant farmers. With a surplus of willing tenants and few legal protections for tenant farmers, landowners had great latitude in changing the terms of tenancy. Public policy made the problem worse. For example, laws imposing longer-term tenancy agreements resulted in widespread evictions of tenant farmers by landowners who refused to make such commitments.

A well-known example of the weakness of the landless population is in Väinö Linna's novel *Here Under the Northern Star*. The main character of the book, a tenant farmer named Jussi, enters into an agreement with a Lutheran minister who, as part of his compensation, could rent out the church's agricultural land in his parish. The minister permits Jussi to drain and cultivate the swampland that he rented. The minister's successor grows jealous of Jussi's prosperity. He gradually changes the terms of the original agreement to eventually include service by Jussi and his wife in the household of the minister. Jussi, who had made a major investment in his swamp in a country where land is scarce, feels compelled to concede to the minister's wishes.[18]

In most parts of Europe, industrialization, despite the problems it caused, resolved the problems of agrarian overpopulation and land shortages. People left the land for industrial centers in search of work. In Finland, as elsewhere in the Russian Empire, industrialization was not extensive enough to absorb the unused agrarian labor force but was significant enough to create a new group of socially disadvantaged people—industrial workers. In factories, people worked 10- to 14-hour days, six days a week. Workers had few legal protections and labor by women and children was common.

WORLD WAR I AND NATIONAL INDEPENDENCE

In August 1914, World War I erupted. As armies mobilized, Europeans invested their hopes in the war. Disenfranchised groups ranging from women to national minorities saw the war as an opportunity for expanding democracy. Victory would force rulers to make concessions to the disenfranchised who helped fight and win the war. Finns widely believed that with victory over its enemies, Germany in particular, Russia would restore Finland's autonomy.

The widespread optimism and support for the war effort turned sour by 1916. Russia had suffered several defeats at the hands of the Germans. Shortages of food were spreading throughout the empire. These shortages hit Finland particularly hard, since it was dependent upon imported grain from Russia. Consumption of rye, a staple grain among the masses, decreased from 157.6 kilograms per capita in 1916 to 61 kilograms in 1917. At the same time, unemployment began to rise. Many Finns employed in building fortifications were let go as the Russian government ran out of money. These new wartime crises exacerbated longer-standing social problems.[19]

In 1916, Finland's oppressed industrial and agrarian workers expressed their discontent at the polls. The Social Democratic Party won an absolute majority (103 seats) in Parliament. This victory would remain hollow as long as the emperor refused to recognize the results by changing policy. The logjam broke when the Russian monarchy collapsed under the weight of military defeat and social unrest. On March 15, 1917 (old style March 2, 1917), Emperor Nicholas II abdicated his throne in favor of his brother, Michael. On the next day, Michael relinquished power in favor of a provisional government. As its name implied, this regime would govern until a constitutional convention created Russia's new form of government. This convention would also resolve the question of Finland's relationship with the new Russia. Until then, the provisional government aimed to keep Finland in the empire.

For Finland, the change of rulers in Russia meant an end to imperialization. Many members of the provisional government had expressed support for Finland's autonomy. The provisional government replaced many Russian officials, including the governor-general, and named a new Senate. This new Senate was significant for three reasons. First, although named by the Russian Government, the Senate was formed at the initiative of Finnish political parties, not the Russian authorities. Under the leadership of Social Democrat Oskari Tokoi, the Senate's economic section consisted of six Social Democrats and six from the main non-Socialist parties: the Young Finns, the Old Finns, the Agrarian League, and the Swedish People's Party. With broad parliamentary backing, the Senate began to resemble a Cabinet or Government, with the economic section's vice chair, Tokoi, acting as a prime minister. The terms *Government* and *Senate* begin to be used interchangeably. Second, this Senate was the first national Government in the world led by a Social Democrat. During the late nineteenth and early twentieth centuries, Social Democratic parties grew into major political movements throughout Europe. In spite of this widespread support, constitutional as well as political barriers had kept these parties from holding office. Third, this Senate embodied many key political divisions. Seemingly a Government of national unity, it was a Cabinet of national discord. With the collapse of the monarchy, all of the country's political parties wanted greater autonomy (if not total independence) for Finland. A division arose over the means to this end. Most members of the Young and Old Finn parties, as well as the Swedish People's Party, wanted to negotiate any new autonomy or independence with Russia's new rulers. This desire for a negotiated settlement rested on the understanding that the provisional government was the legal successor to the monarchy. For their part, the Social Democrats and the Agrarian League argued that the end of the monarchy ended the bond between Finland and Russia. Finland was free to determine its own future, either as an independent state or as a part of a new Russia.

In addition, the parties fought over whether the Senate or Parliament should exercise supreme authority. In July, 1917, the Social Democrats proposed an Enabling Act making Parliament the supreme body of state. It would have the final word on all matters except foreign and defense policy, which would be left to Russian authorities. This was not a vote over complete national independence. Parliament passed the measure by a wide margin of 136 to 66. The Social Democrats were encouraged to move by the provisional government's chief opponent in Russia, the radical Social Democrats, or Bolsheviks. Finland's Social Democratic Party believed that the Bolsheviks would take power in Russia soon after the Enabling Act was passed. The provisional government remained in power. It reacted the Finnish Parliament's action by dissolving Parliament and calling new elections. The Social Democrats tried to keep Parliament open but many non-Socialist members of Parliament, believing in the legality of the order for new elections, stayed away from Parliament. Senators began to resign.

The October elections resulted in the Social Democratic Party losing its majority in Parliament. The party entered the new Parliament still as the largest party with 92 seats. The non-Socialist parties won a majority by convincing voters that the Socialists bore the responsibility for the growing unrest in the country. The Russian threat had dissipated in the minds of many voters, while the threat of violent domestic revolution had risen. The end of the Tokoi Senate strengthened the hand of the Social Democratic Party's radicals who had argued against a coalition with non-Socialist parties. The Social Democratic Party, like its counterparts in other European countries, had become divided between reformist evolutionary and orthodox revolutionary wings. The reformists were willing to achieve the party's goals through a process of gradual, evolutionary change by participating in elections and sharing power with reform-minded parties. More orthodox Social Democrats believed that only a violent revolution could effect sustained social and political change. The Red Guards, a workers' militia formed in the spring of 1917, backed the Social Democratic Party's radical revolutionary wing.[20]

Before addressing a growing revolutionary situation at home, Finland's leaders had to confront another change of regime in Russia. On November 7, 1917, the Bolsheviks, led by Vladimir Illyich Lenin, overthrew the provisional government. The Bolshevik takeover transformed attitudes toward national independence. The country's non-Socialist parties immediately wanted to get out of a Russia run by radical Socialists, but the Social Democrats were now willing to wait and negotiate. On November 15, over Socialist opposition, Parliament passed a new Enabling Act similar to that passed in July. On November 27, the caretaker Senate under Eemil Nestor Setälä gave way to a non-Socialist Senate under Pehr Evind Svinhufvud, a Young Finn. On December 4, the Senate presented a declaration of independence to Parliament. Two days later Parliament approved the measure by a vote of 100 to 88. The opponents of the declaration, many of whom had backed the Enabling Act in July, were not opposed to independence but, rather, to the way the Senate was pursuing it.[21]

THE STRUGGLE FOR RECOGNITION

For a country to validate its claim to independence, it must have the recognition of foreign states. The Svinhufvud Government quickly learned that no foreign power was willing to recognize Finland's independence until Russia did so. As a result, a delegation of senators arrived on December 28 in Petrograd (St. Petersburg) to formally request that the Bolshevik government recognize Finland's independence. Finland's Senate was reluctant to seek recognition from the new Russian regime because it feared that the Bolsheviks would not remain in power very long. Dealing with the Bolsheviks might make it difficult to gain recognition from a successor regime in Russia. Nevertheless, the Council of People's Commissars recognized Finland's independence on December 31. Immediately thereafter, Finland received widespread diplomatic recognition; notable exceptions were Great Britain and the United States. Before granting recognition, both countries wanted to wait for the outcome of Russia's continuing domestic conflict. They were also concerned about the possible course of Finland's foreign policy, especially with respect to Germany.

For years, historians debated the motivations behind the Soviet recognition of Finland's independence. One must eliminate sentimental explanations, such as Lenin's desire to thank the Finns for sanctuary from Russian authorities. According to Lenin's doctrine of "unity through separation," the Bolsheviks believed that freeing Russia's national minorities would advance the revolution by changing the workers' focus from a national struggle to a class struggle against their own capitalist oppressors. The Bolsheviks believed that their revolution was the start of a worldwide wave of Socialist revolutions. After these national minorities underwent a proletarian revolution, they would lead their people back into the Soviet Russian fold. Given the social unrest at the time, the Bolsheviks could reasonably count on a revolution in Finland.[22]

THE CIVIL WAR: RED VERSUS WHITE

Even more challenging for the Svinhufvud Senate was gaining the approval of its own citizenry. Food shortages and unemployment continued to grow. Strikes both on the land and in industrial centers had been occurring with greater regularity since the spring of 1917. Finland's labor movement instigated a general strike during November 14–19, 1917. When the new Parliament convened at the beginning of November, the Social Democratic Party presented Parliament with its "We demand" program that called for a series of social reforms, including an eight-hour workday and the immediate end to tenant farming. Although Parliament's non-Socialist majority refused to debate the program, it understood the necessity of reform. By the end of 1917, Parliament legislated an eight-hour workday (the first country to do so) and universal suffrage in communal elections. Nonetheless, the Bolshevik takeover strengthened the conviction of Finland's radical Socialists to take their party and Finland onto the road of violent revolution. In a Social Democratic Party congress of January 19–21, 1918, the party's radical revolutionary wing succeeded in placing the party behind a revolutionary takeover of the government.[23]

In facing these challenges, the Svinhufvud Government lacked an armed police and military force. On January 12, the Senate, in anticipation of a civil war, named General Carl Gustav Emil Mannerheim head of its military forces. Born in Finland, Mannerheim had spent most of his adult life in the Russian army until the provisional government relieved him of his duties in October, 1917. A handful of other Finns whose careers in the Russian army had ended similarly offered their services to the Senate. On January 25, the Senate made the paramilitary Civil Guards (*Suojeluskunta* in Finnish, *Skyddskår* in Swedish) the Government's armed force. This organization was formed in the fall of 1917 in response to the Finnish Red Guards.

In reaction to the Senate's decision, on January 26 the Social Democratic Party's revolutionary executive committee gave the signal for the Red Guards to take action. Quickly, units of the Red Guards spread out over southern Finland. By the end of the month, they controlled the southern third of the country, including the country's four largest urban centers: Helsinki, Viipuri (Vyborg), Turku, and Tampere. On January 28, the Council of People's Commissars, led by former Speaker of Parliament Kullervo Manner, assumed the administration of the area under Red Guard control. This body became more commonly known as the Red Government. The Red regime sought to arrest the members of the Senate, but none were detained. P. E. Svinhufvud and another senator, Johan Arthur Castrén, fled to Estonia and from there to Berlin, where they sought aid from the Germans. Four senators managed to reach the city of Vaasa on the west coast. The rump Senate, or White Government, prepared to reassert its authority over the country.[24]

Neither side was ready for war. The Red Guards consisted of about 40,000 men at the end of February, a number that rose to about 65,000 at the end of April. Less than 40,000 were at the front at one time and many front-line soldiers were poorly armed. The White Government's troops consisted of drafted soldiers and Civil Guardsmen. At the beginning of March, the White army consisted of about 45,000 men, a number that rose to about 70,000 at the end of April.[25] In addition, there were some 40,000 Russian troops in Finland at the outset of the Civil War, most of whom just wanted to leave the country. For several reasons, the Red Government's attempts to get support from Russia resulted in only a few arms shipments. The Bolsheviks faced serious domestic challenges to their power. They doubted the Red Finns' desire and ability to stage a successful revolution. Lenin's regime also wanted to avoid any conflicts with Germany, with which it was negotiating a peace treaty.

As full hostilities erupted in February, the Whites had two advantages: military conscription and a trained officer corps. The White Government was recognized as the country's legal government in the northern two-thirds of the country that the Government controlled at the outset of the conflict. This recognition gave the Government the authority needed to institute military conscription. The Red Government's perceived illegitimacy among many in its area of control frustrated it from instituting conscription until the very end of the conflict. The White Government also had a trained military leadership, the larger segment of whom received their training in Germany, not Russia. In 1915–1916, roughly 2,000 young Finnish men had left for Germany for military training. These *Jääkärit* (the Finnish word comes from the German word for light infantrymen, *Jäger*) saw themselves as an army of liberation and, in the fall of 1917, they started returning to Finland.[26]

The decisive battle in the White push to reconquer southern Finland occurred at Tampere on April 4–6, 1918. For three days, White artillery pounded this Red bastion. When Red forces surrendered, much of the city had been destroyed, about 1,800 Red soldiers had died, and 11,000 were taken prisoner. As the Reds retreated southward, they did not know that the Svinhufvud Government had negotiated help from Germany, with the result that a German force of 9,500 men landed at the city of Hanko on the southwestern coast on April 3. On April 7, a smaller force of 2,500 Germans landed at Loviisa, east of Helsinki. The two forces advanced toward the capital, taking it by April 14. The Germans fanned out northward toward Hämeenlinna and Lahti, meeting White forces there. On May 5, the last Red units surrendered near Loviisa. The Civil War was over.

Finland's Civil War was short but bloody. According to recent figures, 3,458 Whites and 5,717 Reds were killed in battle. Beyond the battlefields, both sides perpetrated terror campaigns; more than 1,400 people died at the hands of the Red terror. The White terror campaign claimed over 7,300 lives. After the war, more than 13,000 of 75,000 Red prisoners died in prison camps, mostly as a result of malnutrition and epidemics such as the Spanish flu that ravaged Europe after World War I. In total, more than 27,000 died on the Red side.[27]

For years after 1918, the country remained divided over what to call the conflict. For White Finland, it was a war of independence, but this designation fails to address many aspects of the war. The White soldiers primarily fought their own countrymen, not Russian troops. The Red Government, while pursuing close relations with the Bolsheviks, had no intention of reincorporating Finland into Russia. In fact, one of its objectives was the incorporation of Russian or Eastern Karelia into Finland. The White Government, for its part, seriously hindered Finland's independence by signing very restrictive commercial treaties with Germany in exchange for military help. Red Finland considered the conflict a revolution of the workers against their capitalist masters. Indeed, the Red Guards consisted mostly of landless peasants and industrial workers. There is considerable doubt about the Reds' revolutionary fervor. The Reds had no interest in creating a dictatorship, as the Bolsheviks were doing in Russia. In fact, the Reds looked to the Swiss model of local, direct democracy for inspiration. As the divisions in the Social Democratic Party before the war indicated, the Marxist Left in Finland, even the radical Marxist Left, had a very pragmatic streak. The Left, as a whole, lacked an appetite for power. After World War II, the conflict became increasingly referred to as the Civil War. This term more accurately describes the struggle for authority among the people of Finland. Civil wars often have foreign participants, as this one did.[28]

From the 1890s until the end of World War I, Finland's people fought against various types of national and social oppression. The period produced some impressive accomplishments. Advances in art and culture helped construct a national identity that people of both language groups could embrace. The new Parliament gave all Finns a voice in the political process. The country achieved national independence but the Finns' journey as an independent people began with many burdens. The Civil War divided Finns into Red and White camps for decades to come. The victorious Whites struggled over whether Finland should become a republic or a constitutional monarchy, and the country was still divided over language. Relations with Russia still remained tense. Independent Finland was part of a new, turbulent Europe. The war transformed Europe, formerly a continent consisting largely of a handful of multinational empires, into a continent of tens of nation-states. These new, independent states, such as Finland, struggled to find their place in this new Europe.

NOTES

1. Toivo Nygård and Veikko Kallio, "Rajamaa," in *Suomen historian pikkujättiläinen,* ed. Seppo Zetterberg (Porvoo: WSOY, 1987), 546; Tuomo Polvinen, *Valtakunta ja rajamaa: N. I. Bobrikov Suomen kenraalikuvernöörinä 1898–1904* (Helsinki: WSOY, 1984), 35; Päiviö Tommila, *Suuri adressi* (Helsinki: WSOY, 1999), 20–29.

2. Nygård and Kallio, "Rajamaa," 545; Osmo Jussila, *Maakunnasta valtioksi: Suomen valtion synty* (Helsinki: WSOY, 1987), 123; Polvinen, *Valtakunta,* 36–37, 340–41; Edward C. Thaden, "Administrative Russification in Finland 1881–1914," in *Russification in the Baltic Provinces and Finland 1885–1914,* ed. Edward C. Thaden (Princeton, NJ: Princeton University Press, 1981), 76–88; Tommila, *Suuri adressi,* 22–23, 29–30.

3. Osmo Jussila "Suomi suuriruhtinaskuntana," in Osmo Jussila, Seppo Hentilä, and Jukka Nevakivi, *Suomen poliittinen historia* (Helsinki: WSOY, 2000), 66–67, 148–159.

4. Osmo Jussila, "Die russische Reichsgesetzgeburng in Finnland in den Jahren 1809–1898," *Jahrbücher für Geschichte Osteuropas* 33 (1985): 345–365.

5. Osmo Jussila, "Förfinskning och förryskning: Språkmanifestet år 1900 och dess bakgrund," *Historisk tidskrift för Finland* 65, no. 1 (1980): 1–17.

6. Jussila, "Suomi suuriruhtinaskuntana," 68–79; Polvinen, *Valtakunta,* 193; Markku Tyynilä, *Senaatti: Tutkimus hallituskonselji-senaatista 1809–1918* (Helsinki: VAPK, 1992), 310–311.

7. These various understandings of Finnish–Russian relations are outlined in Jussila, *Maakunnasta valtioksi.*

8. The address is covered thoroughly in Tommila, *Suuri adressi.*

9. Olavi Borg, *Suomen puolueet ja puolueohjelmat 1880–1964* (Porvoo: WSOY, 1965), 27–35; Nygård and Kallio, "Rajamaa," 556–563; Seppo Zetterberg, *Viisi laukausta senaatissa: Eugen Schaumanin elämä ja teko* (Helsinki: WSOY, 1988), 226–236.

10. Pirkko K. Koskinen, "Äänioikeuden lainsäädätöhistoria," in *Yksi kamari kaksi sukupuolta: Suomen eduskunnan ensimmäiset naiset,* ed. Eeva Ahtisaari (Helsinki: Gummerus, 1997), 27; Nygård and Kallio, "Rajamaa," 564–572; Heikki Waris, *Muuttuva suomalainen yhteiskunta* (Helsinki: WSOY, 1974), 34.

11. Jussila, "Suomi suuriruhtinaskuntana," 87–90; Nygård and Kallio, "Rajamaa," 573–579.

12. Osmo Jussila, *Suomen suuriruhtinaskunta 1809–1917* (Juva: WSOY, 2005) 711–739.

13. Ateneumin taidemuseo, *Ateneum opas* (Helsinki: Otava, 1997), 63–128; Riitta Konttinen et al., "Kuvataide suomalaisuuden ja muukalaisuuden puristuksessa," in *Suomen kulttuurihistoria*, vol. 3, ed. Anja Kervanto Nevanlinna and Laura Kolbe (Helsinki: Tammi, 2003), 395–417.

14. Antero Sinisalo, "Arkkitehtuuri," in *Suomen kulttuurihistoria*, vol. 2, ed. Päiviö Tommila, Aimo Reitala, and Veikko Kallio (Porvoo: WSOY, 1983), 431–444.

15. Aimo Reitala, "Kuvataide ja taideteollisuus," *Suomen kulttuurihistoria*, vol. 2, ed. Päiviö Tommila, Aimo Reitala, and Veikko Kallio (Porvoo: WSOY, 1983), 408–409.

16. Pirjo Lyytikäinen, "Kirjallisuus tienhaarassa," in *Suomen kulttuurihistoria*, in *Suomen kulttuurihistoria*, vol. 3, ed. Anja Kervanto Nevanlinna and Laura Kolbe (Helsinki: Tammi, 2003), 294–305.

17. Hannu-Iilari Lampila, "Musiikki kansakunnan käyntikorttina," in *Suomen kulttuurihistoria*, vol. 3 (2002), 426–427; Nygard and Kallio, "Rajamaa," 599–601. A wealth of information on Sibelius is available at http://www.sibelius.fi, a web site supported by the Finnish Club of Helsinki (accessed 3 January 2006).

18. Riitta Hjerppe, *Kasvun vuosisata*, (Helsinki: VAPK, 1990), 21–22; Eino Jutikkala, "Torpparikysymys," in *Suomen talous-ja sosiaalihistorian kehityslinjoja*, ed. Eino Jutikkala (Porvoo: WSOY, 1968), 189–205; Nygård and Kallio," Rajamaa," 587–591; Matti Peltonen, *Talolliset ja torpparit: Vuosisadan vaihteen maatalouskysymys Suomessa*, Historiallisia tutkimuksia 164 (Helsinki: Suomen Historiallinen Seura, 1992), 399–425; Kari Pitkänen, "Vaestonkehitys ja sosiaaliset ongelmat," in *Suomen taloushistoria*, vol. 2, ed. Jorma Ahvenainen et al. (Helsinki: Tammi, 1982), 138–140; Pentti Virrankoski, *Suomen taloushistoria kaskikaudesta atomiaikaan* (Helsinki: Otava, 1975), 181–186.

19. Hannu Soikkanen, *Kohti kansanvaltaa: Suomen sosiaalidemokraattinen puolue 75 vuotta*, vol.1 (Vaasa: Oy Kirjapaino Ab, 1975), 222.

20. Jussila "Suomi suuriruhtinaskuntana," 91–96.

21. Seppo Hentilä, "Itsenäistymisestä jatkosodan päättymiseen," in Osmo Jussila, Seppo Hentilä, and Jukka Nevakivi, *Suomen poliittinen historia* (Helsinki: WSOY, 2000), 98–103.

22. Hentilä, "Itsenäistymisestä," 99–103.

23. Hentilä, "Itsenäistymisestä," 98–99.

24. Hentilä, "Itsenäistymisestä," 104–106.

25. Hentti Virrankoski, *Suomen historia*, vol. 2 (Helsinki: Suomalaisen Kirjallisuuden Seura, 2001), 732.

26. Anthony A. Upton, *Vallankumous Suomessa*, vol. 1 (Helsinki: Kirjayhtymä, 1981), 44–45.

27. Aapo Roselius, *Amatöörien sota—Rintamataisteluiden henkilötappiot Suomen sisällissodassa 1918*, Valtioneuvoston kansalian julkaisuja 1/2006 (Helsinki: Edita, 2006), 19; *Sotaoloissa vuosina 1914–1922 surmansa saaneet*, ed. Lars Westerlund, Valtioneuvoston kansalian julkaisuja 10/2004 (Helsinki: Edita, 2004), 54–59.

28. Soikkanen, *Kohti Kansanvaltaa*, 275–289; Upton, *Vallankumous*, vol. 1, 60.

6

Finland between the World Wars (1918–1939)

In 1917, Finland became one of several newly independent countries arising from the collapse of the Russian and Austro-Hungarian empires at the end of World War I. These new states all struggled with problems of political authority, national identity, economic stability, and security in the new Europe. Compared to the countries in its peer group, Finland fared well in mastering these challenges.

CRISIS OF POLITICAL AUTHORITY: MONARCHY OR REPUBLIC?

The crisis of political authority that started with the demise of the Russian monarchy in March, 1917, continued even after the end of the Civil War. The White victory in the Civil War engendered yet another struggle for authority: Should Finland become a constitutional monarchy or a republic? In other words, should Finland be ruled by an unelected king or governed by an elected president?

The Old Finn Party, the Swedish People's Party, as well as scattered supporters in other non-Socialist parties backed a monarchy for four reasons. The first was tradition. Monarchs had ruled Finland throughout its history. Second, a monarch (who would come from abroad) would serve as an impartial outside force that could mediate the conflicts between the country's various political parties. Third, a king could serve as a barrier to the spread of violent radicalism that had ignited the Civil War. Many monarchists believed the expansion of democracy before independence had led to the chaos of 1918. Fourth, there was a foreign policy imperative. Choosing a German prince as king of Finland would cement ties with Germany, the country that aided the Whites in the Civil War. Many Finns considered Germany's help essential for the survival of national independence.

The supporters of a republic advanced three main arguments. First, strong democratic institutions would better facilitate needed reforms by giving all segments of the population a voice in the process. Second, since the parliamentary reform of 1906 Finland had been on the road to a republic and away from authoritarian, unelected, and unaccountable forms of governance. Third, a republican form of government was less divisive and more inclusive. A republic could be crafted in a way that would address some of the monarchists' concerns.

In the months after the Civil War, the absence of the Social Democratic Party from Parliament gave the monarchists a majority. In May 1918, Parliament approved a new monarchist-dominated Senate (now referred to with increasing frequency as the Government) under J. K. Paasikivi. The leader of the old Senate, P. E. Svinhufvud, was made temporary head of state, or regent, until the selection of a monarch. On October 9, 1918, Parliament elected a German, Prince Friedrich Karl of Hesse, to be king of Finland. The monarchists had wanted Prince Oskar, a son of Emperor William II of Germany. When William refused to place his son into the turbulent situation in Finland, the monarchists then settled for Friedrich Karl, William II's brother-in-law. A crown was made; it was widely believed that the new king would assume the throne under the Finnish name Väinö I. Then, on November 11, 1918, Germany, on the brink of collapse, sued for an armistice with its enemies. World War I was now over.[1]

Germany's capitulation meant the end of Finland's monarchy. Friedrich Karl abdicated the Finnish throne before he could assume it. The Paasikivi Senate resigned in favor of a Government that was both republican in orientation and friendly to the victors in World War I (above all, Great Britain, France, and the United States). Similarly, Svinhufvud resigned the regency in favor of General Mannerheim, who had better ties with the victorious Allies. The demise of the monarchist cause foreshadowed the thin line between foreign policy and domestic politics that would guide Finland's future as an independent country.

Meanwhile, the republican cause was organizing. After the Civil War, more moderate elements took over the Social Democratic Party and placed it on the side of the republic. On the non-Socialist side, the republicans in the Old and Young Finnish parties created a new party, the Progressive Party. In parliamentary elections in March 1919, the main republican parties, the Agrarian League, the Social Democrats, and the Progressives, won 148 seats in the 200-seat Parliament. This coalition not only implemented Finland's republican constitution but also supported the election of the constitution's main architect, K. J. Ståhlberg, to Finland's presidency.[2]

The constitution that was ratified in July 1919, most elements of which are still in force today, instituted a republic, but with some concessions to the monarchists. Finland's supreme law addressed both the republicans' desire for a strong legislature and the monarchists' call for a strong executive. In a wider sense, this compromise fused together the two systems of democratic governance: presidential and parliamentary. In a presidential system, the president is the sole chief executive. He or she is elected separately from the legislature. The ministers in the Cabinet serve solely at the pleasure of the president as extensions of presidential power. In a parliamentary system, the legislature formally elects the executive branch (usually a prime minister and the Government). The Government, or Cabinet, collectively acts as chief executive. Parliamentary democracies usually have a monarch or a president but, unlike in presidential systems, he or she is largely a figurehead.[3]

The Finnish constitution gave the president powers associated with a presidential democracy, the most important of which was the sole right to determine foreign policy. The president appointed and could remove the Government's ministers. He or she could dissolve Parliament and call new elections. In peacetime, the president served as commander in chief of the armed forces. In wartime, he or she could transfer this power to someone else. The granting of these wide powers placated many monarchists. Another concession to the monarchists was the election process. Instead of direct popular election, voters would select electors who would, in turn, choose the chief executive. This process ensured the elites' influence in choosing the president. When elected, a president could serve as long as any king: a term of six years without limits on reelection.

Presidents of the Republic

		Party	Term
Kaarlo Juho Ståhlberg	(1865–1952)	Progressive	1919–1925
Lauri Kristian Relander	(1883–1942)	Agrarian League	1925–1931
Pehr Evind Svinhufvud	(1861–1944)	National Coalition	1931–1937
Kyösti Kallio	(1873–1940)	Agrarian League	1937–1940
Risto Ryti	(1889–1956)	Progressive	1940–1944
Carl Gustaf Emil Mannerheim	(1867–1951)	Nonpartisan	1944–1946
Juho Kusti Paasikivi	(1870–1956)	National Coalition	1946–1956
Urho Kekkonen	(1900–1986)	Agrarian League/ Center	1956–1981
Mauno Koivisto	(1923–)	Social Democratic	1982–1994

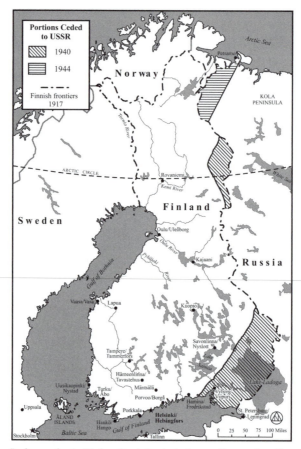

Independent Finland. Adapted from Osmo Jussila, Seppo Hentilä, and Jukka Nevakivi, *From Grand Duchy to Modern State: A Political History of Finland since 1809.* (London: Hurst, 1999), 100. Adapted with permission.

Martti Ahtisaari	(1937–)	Social Democratic	1994–2000
Tarja Halonen	(1943–)	Social Democratic	2000–

Source: Osmo Jussila, Seppo Hentilä, and Jukka Nevakivi, *Suomen poliittinen historia* (Helsinki: WSOY, 2000), 354.

Several factors, both within and outside of the constitution, kept Finland from having a full presidential system. The Finnish president could not expressly veto legislation passed by Parliament. He or she could refuse to sign a bill into law, but it automatically became law if a majority in Parliament again backed the bill. Furthermore, the president's powers have been limited by decades of practical politics that have given significant executive responsibility to the head of the Government, the prime minister, especially in

domestic politics. The Government's independence from the president in domestic policy also has stemmed from the fact that, in Finland's multiparty system, Governments with a parliamentary majority have consisted mostly of
ministers from outside of the president's own party. The spirit of the constitution called for the president to stay outside of daily domestic political battles.

Finland's constitution included aspects associated with a parliamentary system. The constitution expressly made Parliament the highest organ of state.
Article II states, "The sovereign power in Finland rests with the people, represented by the delegates assembled in Parliament." The constitution enshrined
a basic aspect of parliamentary democracy in that the Cabinet's mandate to
govern rested on Parliament's explicit confidence. In a parliamentary system,
Cabinets are called majority or minority depending on whether they consist
of parties that combined hold a majority or minority of seats in Parliament.
Majority Cabinets generally are able to govern more effectively, whereas minority Cabinets must seek backing from the opposition in order to succeed.[4]

Like most modern constitutions, Finland's constitution enumerated the
basic rights of the citizen. Among these rights included the explicit abolition
of any requirement for religious affiliation as a basis for citizenship. The constitution upheld the established status of the Lutheran Church, and the
Orthodox Church gained similar assurances of its continued status as a state-
supported church in the form of a Government decree in November, 1918.
The growing persecution of the Orthodox Church in Soviet Russia and a desire
to reduce Russian influence moved the members of Finland's Orthodox
Church to separate themselves from the control of the patriarch of Moscow.
In 1923, Finland's Orthodox Church became a church with wide-ranging au-
tonomy under the patriarch of Constantinople.[5]

POLITICAL PARTIES

In addition to a republican majority, the election of March, 1919, produced
a new spectrum of political parties that, for the most part, has survived to the
present day. This spectrum ranges from the Marxist Socialist parties of the
Left to the non-Socialist parties of the political Center and Right. On the Socialist Left, the pre-independence Social Democratic Party broke in two. Radical Socialists who had led the Red effort in the Civil War fled to Soviet Russia
and founded the Finnish Communist Party (SKP). This party was dedicated
to overthrowing Finland's elected leaders, with violence if necessary. It op-
erated in Finland through surrogate parties during the 1920s. These parties
suffered from official harassment, such as the arrest of 27 Communist members of Parliament in 1923. With the radicals gone, the Social Democratic Party
pursued the reformist course prevalent in Western European Social Democracy. The Social Democratic Party retained its pre-independence status as the
country's largest party. In spite of its size, Parliament's non-Socialist majority

largely kept the Social Democratic Party in opposition for most of the interwar period. During the 1920s, the Social Democratic Party entered the Government only once, when the party formed on its own a minority Cabinet during 1926–1927. This Cabinet is notable for including Finland's first female minister, Minna Sillanpää, who served as minister for social affairs.

Among the non-Socialist parties, there were continuities and discontinuities from the pre-independence period. The Agrarian League remained the largest non-Socialist party. Another holdover from the pre-independence period was the Swedish People's Party (SFP). The question of monarchy versus republic led to the dissolution of the Old Finn and Young Finn parties. Monarchist Old Finns and Young Finns formed the National Coalition Party. This party would become republican Finland's Conservative party. It represented the interests of big business, large landowning farmers, and a segment of the urban elite. It saw itself as a defender of the "inherited values" of "home, religion, and the fatherland." The republicans in the two Finnish parties formed the Liberal Progressive Party. In the mold of liberal parties in other European countries, the Progressive Party championed individual freedom by defending civil rights, rule of law, and the free enterprise system. The party drew its support primarily from the urban middle classes. The smallest of the four major non-Socialist parties, the Progressives played a role in politics disproportionate to its size for three reasons. First, the party had leaders who enjoyed popularity across party lines, such as President K. J. Ståhlberg. Second, the party's position in the political middle made it an attractive partner for larger parties wishing to build a governing coalition. Third, the party had a strong public voice through its ties to some major newspapers, above all Helsinki's daily, *Helsingin sanomat.*[6]

Parliamentary Seats Won in Elections 1919–1945

	Swedish People's Party (SFP)	National Coalition	Progressives	Agrarian League	Soc. Dem. (SDP)	Communist	Patriotic People's League (IKL)	Others*
1919	22	28	26	42	80	—	—	2
1922	25	35	15	45	53	27	—	0
1924	23	38	17	44	60	18	—	0
1927	24	34	10	52	60	20	—	0
1929	23	28	7	60	59	23	—	0
1930	21	25	11	59	66	—	—	1
1933	21	18	11	53	78	—	14	5
1936	21	20	6	53	83	—	14	2
1939**	18	25	6	56	85	—	8	2

* The Christian Workers' Party won the two seats in 1919. The seats won in 1930–1939 were won by various peasant parties.
** Due to World War II, the Parliament elected in 1939 remained in office until 1945.
Source: Osmo Jussila, Seppo Hentilä, and Jukka Nevakivi, *Suomen poliittinen historia* (Helsinki: WSOY, 2000), 357.

These four non-Socialist parties were deeply divided over ideology, language, and rural versus urban interests. For most of the interwar period, they were united only in their unwillingness to compromise with the Left. This was evident beyond the political arena as well. For example, the influential volunteer paramilitary organization, the Civil Guards, refused membership to Socialists of any kind. This refusal to integrate the Left into Finnish society was one of the long-term outcomes of the Civil War. In fact, some in the non-Socialist camp believed that the continued presence of large Socialist parties proved that the Whites had not yet won the Civil War.

THREATS TO DEMOCRACY

The introduction of the republican constitution did not completely resolve the crisis of political authority. As a result of the parties' unwillingness to overcome their many divisions, Finland suffered through the 1920s and most of the 1930s with short-term Governments. Between 1919 and 1939, Finland had 22 Cabinets, only 9 of which had majority backing in Parliament. In other words, a Government had an average life span of less than one year.

This inability to create strong, sustainable ruling coalitions prevailed in many of Europe's new democracies. This instability weakened support for democracy and encouraged the rise of various types of authoritarianism, the best-known type of which was Fascism. Fascism is a political ideology that consists of an emphasis on state power over the rights of the individual, a militarization of society, fanatical nationalism, and obedience to a charismatic leader that leaves no room for dissent. As an alternative to the uncertainties of democracy and industrial capitalism on one hand, and the threat of Communism on the other, Fascists offered to take people back to a more secure, predictable time—one that never existed. The best-known Fascist dictatorships of the time were those under Benito Mussolini in Italy, Adolf Hitler in Germany, and Francisco Franco in Spain.

At end of 1920s, the wave of authoritarianism reached Finland in the form of the Lapua Movement. The spark for this mobilization occurred on November 23–24, 1929 when Finland's Communist Youth League held a meeting in the village of Lapua. The selection of this location for the meeting was a deliberate provocation. Lapua lies in Ostrobothnia, Finland's most politically conservative region. Predictably, outraged local citizens broke up the meeting. Out of this action the Lapua Movement arose to eliminate Marxism "to the last vestige," to quote its leader, Vihtori Kosola. The movement pursued its goal by taking direct action against its enemies. The most frequent and best-known form of action was kidnapping. Over the course of 1930–1932, 254 victims consisting of Social Democrats, Communists, and other perceived enemies were kidnapped. Often the action ended in the victim left standing somewhere on the Soviet side of Finland's eastern border, where the kidnappers believed he should stay. On July 7, 1930, some 12,000 supporters of the movement marched on Helsinki. Obviously imitating the Italian Fascists' march on Rome in 1922 that brought Mussolini to power, the demonstrators demanded legislation against the Left, or they would take matters into their own hands.[7]

Many of Finland's leaders reacted the Lapua Movement's rise with appeasement, if not tacit approval. The movement's success in attracting supporters from the National Coalition Party and the Agrarian League held out the possibility of creating a large non-Socialist party that could rival the Social Democrats. The movement exploited a widespread view in White Finland that the danger to society came from the Left. Sympathizers did not want to see that the Lapua Movement was both anti-Marxist and anti-democratic.

In this atmosphere, the Lapua Movement pushed its agenda forward. In June 1930, the minority Government under Prime Minister Kyösti Kallio gave way to another minority Cabinet under the National Coalition Party's P. E. Svinhufvud, the movement's preferred candidate for prime minister. In order to realize the movement's minimum demand of a total criminalization of Communist activity, President Lauri Kristian Relander called new parliamentary elections for October 1930. The two-thirds majority won by the non-Socialist parties stemmed from both greater cooperation and administrative measures to prevent the election of Communists. The new Parliament then passed a series of laws formally outlawing Communist activity.

This zenith of the Lapua Movement's influence quickly turned into a steep decline. On October 14, 1930, military officers close to the movement organized the kidnapping of former president K. J. Ståhlberg and his wife, Ester. This action placed the movement beyond the pale of acceptability for many sympathizers. In the presidential election in February 1931, P. E. Svinhufvud was elected president. Although a popular figure in the Lapua Movement, he won the presidency in large part because President Relander had lost the support of his own party, the Agrarian League, for his reelection bid. Among the reasons for the party's decision was Relander's open sympathy for the Lapua Movement.

At the end of February, 1932, the Lapua Movement, in a final act of desperation, sought to employ illegal means to remove the very leaders they helped install. The leaders of this coup, headquartered in the southern village of Mäntsälä, called on the members of the Civil Guards to join them in overthrowing the government. The overwhelming majority stayed home. On March 2, President Svinhufvud, a man well-known for his strict adherence to law and order, condemned the action in a radio speech. Realizing that they had overplayed their hand, the rebels quickly gave up their attempt to end Finland's democracy. After the Lapua Movement was banned by the same laws passed to suppress Communist activity, a new and more openly anti-democratic party developed, the Patriotic People's League (IKL). This party was allowed to function because it pledged to operate within the constitution. It participated in elections, becoming one of the smaller parties in Parliament. The Patriotic People's League's openly Fascist program attracted only a fraction of those who had supported the Lapua Movement in its heyday. While support for Fascism was growing in other parts of Europe, it was on the decline in Finland.[8]

Even before the Mäntsälä rebellion, the tide had turned in favor of legality. Any successful defense of legality required a deeper and more inclusive cooperation among the country's democratic parties. The first Cabinet formed after the Mäntsälä rebellion, a minority Government under the Progressive T. M. Kivimäki, lasted a record four years. The major parties in Parliament, the Social Democratic Party (SDP) and Agrarian League in particular, supported this Government as a way of reestablishing order and stability. By 1937, the Social Democrats and the Agrarians had developed an alliance that could serve as the basis of a strong, broad-based coalition. The barrier to this coalition taking power was President Svinhufvud, who refused to allow the Social Democrats into the Government. In the presidential elections of 1937, the SDP used its position as the largest party to ensure the election of the Agrarian League's candidate, Kyösti Kallio, to the presidency. Kallio, in turn, named a Cabinet under the Progressive A. K. Cajander that consisted of a coalition of the Agrarian League, the Social Democratic Party, as well as the Progressives and the Swedish People's Party. This coalition, with the SDP and the Agrarians at its heart, would become known as the red earth coalition. This alliance would serve as the basis of every majority Government until 1987.

Finland's struggle for political authority ended in a victory for democratic rule. Of the newly independent countries in Eastern Europe after World War I, only Finland and Czechoslovakia had retained their democracies by 1935. The strengthening of democracy allowed the red earth coalition to pursue an ambitious agenda consisting of three points. First, it sought to improve the population's social safety net. Second, the Cabinet worked to improve cooperation with Finland's Scandinavian neighbors. Third, it aimed to achieve greater national unity at a time of growing tensions in Europe. The very creation of this coalition helped heal the Red–White split from the Civil War. It would have to act legislatively to alleviate the conflict between the country's linguistic camps.[9]

TOWARD A BILINGUAL NATIONALISM

The language conflict that had started in the mid-nineteenth century was suspended in the late 1890s by the crisis in relations with Russia. After the achievement of independence, the dispute resumed with many people continuing to adhere to the nineteenth-century ideal that a nation could only have one language. The prevalence of this belief in a bilingual country obviously hindered the development of a common sense of nationhood. Just as in the nineteenth century, the country's educational institutions served as the main battlefields in this renewed conflict.

Finland's republican constitution made both Finnish and Swedish official languages. A seeming act of inclusion in the short term did little to bridge differences between Finland's two main linguistic groups. Many in the Swedish-speaking population (about 10 percent during the interwar period) used their constitutional rights to the exclusion of Finnish. This was a problem for many Finnish speakers because Swedish speakers disproportionately held important places in society, such as in the country's one university in Helsinki. Some professors would teach in Swedish despite a majority of Finnish-speaking students in their classes. In many fields, such as law and medicine, a Finnish speaker would have few courses in his or her first language.

A movement known as the Ultra-Finns started in the 1920s to demand the introduction of Finnish as the sole language of Helsinki University and other public institutions. Ultra-Finns believed that public institutions should represent the reality that almost 90 percent of the population spoke Finnish as its first language and most of the rest spoke it well or fluently as a second language. Nowhere should a Finnish speaker have to master Swedish in order to advance in society.

At the same time, however, an alternative vision of bilingual nationhood was developing. In the Civil War, most Swedish speakers had sided with the Whites, leading some Finnish-speaking Whites to see a greater affinity with them than with the mostly Finnish-speaking Left. For its part, the Left saw the language question as a secondary issue for the working class. The leading Social Democrat of the time, Väinö Tanner, once condemned the entire language conflict as a "sixth-rate question." In the early years of independence, Swedish speakers rejected proposals to divide Finland into Swiss-style cantons based on language. They favored language rights for both groups throughout the country. Over the course of the 1920s and 1930s, Finnish gained ground as a language of the elites, education, and culture, weakening the Ultra-Finns' assertions of oppression by a small minority. Politicians who voiced sympathy for the Ultra-Finn cause were much more moderate in their actions. In short, despite all of the Ultra-Finn loud demands for "one language, one mind," many had already accepted some form of a bilingual nation.

The catalyst that crystallized these disparate sentiments into a comprehensive sense of nationhood lay outside of Finland's borders. Over the course of the turbulent 1930s, Finland's leaders saw cooperation with its Scandinavian neighbors as the best solution for its national security. The Scandinavian countries, Sweden in particular, considered the threats against the rights of Swedish speakers as a barrier to further cooperation. Any resolution of the language dispute would have to have Helsinki University as its focus. Already in the early 1920s, activists in both language camps hedged their bets over the future of the university by founding universities in Turku: the Swedish Åbo akademi and the Finnish Turun yliopisto (Turku University). In 1935, the Government proposed to a special session of Parliament a new law that would make Helsinki University primarily Finnish-speaking in terms of its teaching mission but would reserve 21 professorial chairs for Swedish-language instruction. This law failed to move forward because of opposition by Ultra-Finn parliamentarians (mostly in the Agrarian League) who felt that the proposal did not go far enough, and by the Swedish People's Party, which protested that the proposal went too far. In 1937, the new red earth coalition countered with a modified version of the law that reduced the number of Swedish-language professorships to 15. Citing the tense international situation, both Ultra-Finns and the Swedish People's Party accepted the measure.[10]

By the end of the 1930s, Finns had decided to build a national identity on the premise of "one nation, two languages." A Finn was both Swedish- and Finnish-speaking. Both languages would articulate Finnish nationhood.

CREATIVE COMMUNITIES BETWEEN THE WORLD WARS

Another factor that contributed to the growth of bilingual nationalism was the work of the country's creative communities: artists, musicians, writers, scientists, and athletes. Just as in the decades before independence, the entire population, regardless of language, embraced the achievements of these communities. Many stars of Finland's prewar cultural Golden Age, such as Jean Sibelius, remained productive into the first two decades of independence. Finland's creative communities were divided between those who looked to the rest of Europe and those who looked inside Finland for inspiration. They were joined in the broader national consensus that Finland was "the outpost of Western civilization." The writer Uuno Kailas expresses this sentiment in a poem: "The border opens like a chasm/Before me Asia, the East/Behind me Europe, the West/[which] I, the sentry, guard."[11] The consensus held that Finland was a Western country, to the east of which lay lands (the USSR) where Asiatic barbarity reigned.

National and European impulses infused many aspects of high culture. In literature, Frans Eemil Sillanpää (1888–1964) depicted the country's agrarian realities. In his book *Meek Heritage*, Sillanpää describes the plight of the landless peasantry before the Civil War. In the fall of 1939, when Finland was threatened with attack from the Soviet Union, Sillanpää was awarded the Nobel Prize for literature. The European movement of modernism heavily influenced Finland's literature. In poetry, this movement rejected established forms of rhyme and rhythm; in prose, modernism emphasized criticism and departures from traditional narrative. Moreover, modernism emphasized the

individual and the cosmopolitan. In Finnish-language literature, the important names in modernism are Aaro Hellaakoski (1893–1952) and Algot Untola
(1868–1918). Untola was so unconventional that he published many of his
works under the female pseudonym Maiju Lassila. Another modernist was
the best-known writer of the time, Mika Waltari (1908–1979). Waltari's body
of work encompasses virtually the entire range of literary genres, from detective stories to poetry. His short stories take place in urban, cosmopolitan settings and his historical novels embrace times and civilizations far away from
twentieth-century Finland. Of these, the best-known is *The Egyptian*, a story
about an abandoned baby who grows up to become the pharaoh's physician.
The novel was adapted into a Hollywood movie in 1954 of the same name.
In the country's Swedish-language literary community, important modernists
were Elmer Diktonius (1896–1961), Edith Södergran (1892–1924), and Hagar
Olsson (1893–1978).[12]

In the visual arts, the creative dynamic lay in sculpture and architecture.
An independent nation needed its own national monuments. The leading
figure in monumental sculpture was Väinö Aaltonen (1894–1966). Aaltonen
dedicated two statues to the great Olympic long-distance runner Paavo Nurmi
in Turku and Helsinki, both unveiled in 1924. He created the large statue of
the nineteenth-century writer Aleksis Kivi that stands to the north of Helsinki's central railroad station. In 1938, Aaltonen memorialized Finland's
achievements abroad by sculpting a monument in Chester, Pennsylvania com-
memorating 300 years of Finnish settlement in the United States.[13]

Finnish architecture became closely associated with functionalism. Functionalism is an architectural school of thought that holds that practical considerations such as use, material, and structure should determine the form of
a building. In other words, functionalism called for design in which "form
follows function" rather than function following form. Alvar Aalto (1898–
1976) rose to become one of the world's leading functionalist architects.
Among his earliest and best-known creations is the tuberculosis hospital in
the town of Paimio (completed in 1933). He achieved international notoriety
by designing the Finnish pavilions at the World's Fairs of 1937 and 1939. After
World War II, Aalto drew the plans for buildings, including Finlandia Hall in
Helsinki, the opera house in Essen, Germany, and the library of a Benedictine
monastery in the American state of Oregon.[14]

Finland's scientific community also established an international reputation.
The best-known of the scientists from this era is Artturi Ilmari Virtanen (1895–
1973). This Finnish biochemist's first significant innovation came in the 1920s,
when he was director of the laboratory of Valio, Finland's dairy cooperative.
Virtanen increased the shelf life of butter by raising the pH level from 6.0 to
6.5. This innovation, the secrecy of which Valio managed to preserve for
14 years, gave the cooperative an advantage in export markets. Virtanen's
research then focused on the preservation of fodder for livestock, dairy cows

in particular. His method, which he revealed in a monograph in 1943, improved the storage of green fodder by adding diluted hydrochloric or sulfuric acid to newly stored grain. For the creation of this new AIV-fodder, Virtanen was awarded the Nobel Prize in chemistry in 1945, the only Finn to win the prize. Like most of Finland's leading scholars in the interwar period, Virtanen received training in Germany, a leading country in the sciences before World War II.[15]

Growth in popular or mass culture matched the growth of high culture. The 1930s represented a golden age in Finnish film. There was a growth in the number of dance halls and, correspondingly, an increased cultivation of the imported tango as a Finnish form of dance. The most important development in popular culture, however, was in sports. During this time Finland was a sports superpower. On the international stage, Finland's athletic prowess was first established at the 1912 summer Olympic games in Stockholm. Among the 20 (mostly larger) countries that participated, Finland finished in a tie for fifth with Germany, with 26 medals. Finland's success surpassed the Russian team, which only won five. The long-distance runner Hannes Kolehmainen, who established a standard for future Finnish runners, won three of Finland's nine gold medals. After the First World War, Finland continued its success at the Olympics. In long-distance running events, Paavo Nurmi won in three Olympiads (1920, 1924, 1928) a combined total of nine gold and three silver medals. The high point of Finnish success came in the 1936 games in Berlin, where the Finns swept the 10,000-meter run. During the era 1908–1936, Finland won the fourth most medals in the summer games. In 1938, Helsinki was named host of the 1940 Olympic summer games. World War II and its aftermath would prevent Helsinki from hosting the Olympics until 1952.[16]

In part, the Finnish success at the Olympics stemmed from the fact that before World War II most of the world's countries did not participate in the games. Nonetheless, Finland enjoyed advantages that allowed it to exploit the situation. The country's sporting community was well-organized into resourceful if feuding sports federations. The culture supported competitive sports. Finnish athletes were the first in the world to train in a systematic, structured manner.[17]

It has been said that during this time Finland "ran itself onto the world's map." Indeed, success in sports did enhance Finland's global visibility, but the success had a greater impact on how Finns saw themselves. To this day, many Finns feel that their country's place in the world is that much more secure when they see the Finnish flag raised at a medal ceremony in an international competition. The use of sports in strengthening national consciousness was evident in the development of Finland's national sport, *pesäpallo*. This sport resembles baseball in that runners advance over bases by hitting a ball. The Civil Guards promoted it as a way of improving the basic military skills of both boys and girls. For example, throwing the ball was meant to develop the hand-eye coordination needed for throwing a hand grenade. In fact, the ball has the exact weight of an army hand grenade from the interwar period! A similar interest in developing military skills lay behind the cultivation of cross-country skiing.[18]

ECONOMIC PROSPERITY AND SOCIAL REFORM

Like most countries in Europe, Finland struggled after World War I to regain prewar economic prosperity. Between 1920 and 1940, Finland's population grew from about 3.15 million to 3.7 million. Some 70 percent of Finns lived on the land. Well over half of Finland's economic output came from agriculture. This source of wealth also engendered the country's biggest social problem: landless peasants. After the Civil War, tenant farmers were given the opportunity to buy their farms. In 1923, Parliament passed a law giving 20 hectares (49.4 acres) of state-owned land to peasants who completed a training course in agriculture. With various other economic incentives, the state encouraged all farmers to cultivate more land. Between the world wars, the number of hectares under cultivation grew by about 30 percent. The number of new independent farmers more than matched this growth in agricultural land. As a result, unlike in most other European countries at the time, the size of an average Finnish farm decreased. Nonetheless, these measures resolved the problem of landlessness as well as served national security interests. Finland became more self-sufficient in foodstuffs in case of war. A more even spread of population strengthened Finland's regional defense structure.

During the interwar period, Finland's industrial output increased on average by about eight percent annually, a leader in Europe. The industrial base was small to begin with, so that by 1940 less than 20 percent of the country's gross domestic product came from industry. Nonetheless, the growth in industrial output was important for two reasons. First, the increase in industrial jobs provided opportunities for some of the disadvantaged people on the land. Second, much of the industrial growth occurred in the production of export goods: wood products, paper, cellulose, and cut timber. Because Finland has a small domestic market, its prosperity has rested on its ability to export. With the closing of the Russian market after World War I, Finland had to find new customers for its exports. Great Britain became Finland's largest export market, followed by Germany, the United States, and Sweden.

During the 1920s and 1930s, Finland's economy grew at an average annual rate of 3.8 percent, estimated as the highest in Europe. By the end of the 1930s, Finland had a standard of living that, while behind that of Great Britain, Germany, and Sweden, was well above the European average. Finns lived better than people in many larger and more industrialized countries, such as Austria, Italy, and Czechoslovakia. The overall rise in standards of living overcame the worldwide depression of the late 1920s and early 1930s, as well as the fluctuations inherent in an agrarian economy.[19]

Some of the increase in national wealth was funneled into wider social reforms. In 1921, Finland introduced compulsory education for children aged 7 through 12. Over the course of the 1920s, legislation was passed that benefited workers. For example, in 1922 workers employed for a year in the same business were entitled to one week of paid vacation. The scale of unemployment compensation increased steadily. In 1937, the new red earth coalition instituted a pension insurance scheme. In the same year, Parliament approved an innovation in social policy not seen anywhere else in the world, the maternity package. This cardboard box includes some of the basic needs for the care of an infant: diapers, blankets, clothing, even a toy. The box itself was designed to serve as a bed for the newborn. At first, the benefit was granted to those below a certain income threshold, but in 1941 the package was made a universal benefit for all expectant mothers. The introduction of the maternity package is significant for three reasons. First, it gave national support to the efforts of Finland's communities in prenatal and early childhood care. These endeavors significantly lowered what had been one of Europe's highest infant mortality rates. Second, the maternity package foreshadowed the social benefits Finns would receive after World War II, regardless of income. Third, it reflected the importance placed on population growth in formulating social policy. By the end of the interwar period, Finland had a basic social safety net. The universal cradle-to-grave benefits associated with the Scandinavian welfare state would come after World War II.[20]

Although these reforms produced the desired outcome of a more prosperous and unified society, one did not: prohibition. The temperance movement had support in all of the political parties, especially in the Social Democratic Party and the Agrarian League. In 1907, the Finnish Parliament prohibited the production, sale, and possession of alcoholic beverages. Even though Emperor Nicholas II refused to sign the bill into law, most municipalities already had introduced some form of prohibition. In May 1917, the Russian provisional government approved the law, which came into force in 1919. The costs of enforcing the law proved greater than the costs of alcohol abuse. Finns who wanted to drink could obtain alcohol from moonshine stills in the forests. In restaurants and dance halls, one could order alcohol-fortified "strong tea." The law allowed medical doctors to prescribe alcohol "for medicinal purposes." Physicians used this right liberally. Thousands of bottles of Estonian spirits reached Finland's shores. In Finnish, one would say "spirits to Estonia" as one says in English "coals to Newcastle." With the rule of law threatened, by the beginning of the 1930s the political parties decided to change the law. In December, 1931, the Government proposed in a referendum an abolition of prohibition. In its place, a state monopoly would sell alcohol, with the profits going to the state. Seventy-one percent of voters approved this proposal. The state alcohol enterprise, Oy Alko Ab, still has a virtual monopoly over the sale of alcohol.[21]

FINLAND'S STRUGGLE FOR NATIONAL SECURITY

As a newly independent country in the eastern half of Europe, Finland lay in what the founder of Czechoslovakia, Thomas Masaryk, called Europe's "danger zone." Countries in this zone, such as Czechoslovakia and Finland, had to find security on a continent where larger powers looked upon their existence with disdain or indifference. Because they had once been parts of larger empires, these new countries feared losing their independence to larger neighbors, Germany and Soviet Russia in particular. Like the others in this danger zone, Finland failed to find an effective formula for national security before the outbreak of World War II.

Finland emerged from Civil War closely tied to imperial Germany. After its surrender to the Allies in November, 1918, Germany was no longer in a position to provide security to Finland. As neighboring Soviet Russia had descended into its own civil war, Finland quickly managed to improve relations with the victorious Allies. This new relationship did not measurably improve Finland's security, however. The Allies sought to use Finland as a staging area for an operation to capture St. Petersburg as a part of a larger effort to remove the Bolsheviks from power. Finland's leaders had little affection for the Bolsheviks, but they felt that the Allied offer of support to Finland was too little for such an operation. In addition, many anti-Bolsheviks wanted to reconstitute the old Russian Empire—Finland included. For these reasons, Finland refused to participate in the removal of the Bolsheviks.[22]

By the beginning of 1920, it looked increasingly clear that the Bolsheviks would keep their grip on power. The Finnish Government decided to normalize relations with its eastern neighbor by means of a formal peace treaty. Delegations from the two sides met in the Estonian city of Tartu in June, 1920. For the next five months, the two sides would argue over the border. The Soviet Russians wanted Finland's islands in the Gulf of Finland in order to enhance the defense of Petrograd (renamed Leningrad in 1924). The Finnish side opened the negotiations by demanding both Russian Karelia (also known as Eastern Karelia) and the Kola Peninsula. This claim reflected the desire of many in the political establishment to create a so-called Greater Finland that would include all speakers of Finnish and closely related languages. Units of Finnish volunteer soldiers were already occupying territories in Eastern Karelia. Regular Finnish army troops were occupying two locales on the Russian side of the border. These territories had never belonged to Finland in any political or administrative sense. The Finnish demands exemplified a destabilizing factor in interstate relations in Europe after World War I. On one hand, the war advanced the principle of national self-determination that allowed for nations such as Finland to become independent. On the other hand, the reorganization of Europe along national lines created new territorial conflicts. Many nations were not satisfied with independence within well-recognized boundaries. Rather, they pursued irredentism, the policy of seeking neighboring territories with ethnically related populations that historically had belonged to other countries.

On October 14, 1920, both sides compromised in signing a peace treaty. The Russians withdrew their demands for islands. The Finns gave up their dreams of a Greater Finland in exchange for the Arctic Sea corridor of Petsamo. Otherwise, the pre-independence border between the two countries was reconfirmed. The treaty brought formal peace to the Finnish–Soviet Russian relationship but did not erase mistrust or the dreams of territorial gain. The two chief Finnish negotiators in Tartu, Senator J. K. Paasikivi and Social Democratic leader Väinö Tanner, would encounter similar Soviet demands almost 20 years later, in the fall of 1939.[23]

Meanwhile, Finland had to confront an irredentist challenge from its western neighbor, Sweden. The point of conflict was the Åland Islands, Finland's Swedish-speaking archipelago. The upheavals of 1918 sparked a movement in the Åland Islands for union with Sweden. In February, 1918, King Gustav V of Sweden received the signatures of 7,000 Åland Islanders—more than a fourth of the total population—petitioning for incorporation into his kingdom. Sweden's leaders were extremely sympathetic to the islanders' wishes. The League of Nations eventually decided the future of the islands. This international body was created after World War I as a mechanism for resolving international disputes. In the spring of 1921, a committee deputed by the league concluded that the islands belonged historically, geographically, and economically to Finland. Both Sweden and Finland accepted the decision. This would be the one and only case in which the League of Nations would adjudicate an international dispute successfully.

Before the league's ruling, Finland had taken measures to weaken the separatist movement of the Åland Islanders. The new constitution of 1919 made both Finnish and Swedish official state languages. In the following year, Parliament passed a law giving the Åland Islands autonomy. The archipelago received its own legislature that could pass local laws. This autonomy has been expanded over the decades to include, among other things, a separate postal service. Swedish is the sole official language of the province. Taxpayer-funded schools provide instruction only in Swedish. Migration from the mainland is impeded by a law of domicile that prevents a new resident from voting in local elections, owning real estate, or owning a business unless that Finnish citizen has lived in Åland for at least five years and demonstrates a fair command of Swedish.[24]

With relations with its neighbors on a formal if not friendly basis, the country then pursued its major foreign policy objective—the neutralization of the

Soviet Russian threat. Two sources fed the Finnish fear of Soviet Russia (as of 1922, known formally as the Soviet Union or the USSR—the Union of Soviet Socialist Republics). The first was the worldwide fear of Soviet Communism. The second source stemmed from Finland's experiences with Russia during the so-called period of oppression. Finland's foreign policy leaders continued the pre-independence constitutionalist line toward the eastern neighbor. This approach to Russia, with its assumptions about perpetual Russian hostility toward Finland, guided the search for security. With the exception of the Communists, all parties (to varying degrees) supported this constitutionalist approach. It echoed a widespread feeling among the populace expressed in the saying, "A Russian is a Russian even if baked in butter." The threat from the East was both great and eternal. Considering the Soviets' overwhelming advantage in resources, Finns believed that they could not face the threat alone.

For the next two decades, the country searched for allies. The first attempt was the so-called border state policy. The countries that bordered Soviet Russia—Finland, Estonia, Latvia, Lithuania, and Poland—all saw the USSR as a threat to their security. In 1922, these countries signed a treaty of cooperation. The agreement was chiefly political in nature but it did have a clause for military cooperation in the event of an attack on one signatory. Even though the Finnish Government removed the military article before submitting the treaty to Parliament for ratification, the legislature rejected the treaty. The dissenting majority feared that the treaty threatened to draw Finland into conflicts in Central Europe.[25]

Finland then sought security from the League of Nations. Like its successor, the United Nations, the league aimed to promote international peace and security. The league's charter required member states to aid any other member state subject to aggression. Small countries, such as Finland, placed their hopes on the league's promise of security for all members. The league was divided over how to best provide peace and security. One faction, led by Great Britain, sought to achieve these goals through disarmament. The other faction, led by France, wanted to take the league more in the direction of a military alliance. Finland backed the French position. This division was never resolved and, by the mid-1930s, Finland's foreign policy makers concluded that the league could not protect the security of small states. The events of the late 1930s would validate this conclusion.

In 1935, Finland officially embarked on a policy of closer security cooperation with other Scandinavian states. The launch of the so-called Scandinavian orientation came at a time of growing tensions throughout Europe. In Germany, Adolf Hitler became dictator in 1933. His rearmament of Germany and territorial demands heightened the desire of the Soviet dictator, Josef Stalin, to enhance the USSR's security. The Scandinavian orientation would encounter three roadblocks. First, there was widespread opposition in Sweden to any improvement of security ties with Finland until the language question was resolved. Second, even with the resolution of the language question in 1937, the four Scandinavian states could not agree on a common enemy. For Norway and Denmark, the major threat was Germany; for Finland, it was the Soviet Union. Sweden could not decide between the Soviet Union or Germany. Third, Finland's Scandinavian neighbors had small defense establishments that might not be able to provide the help needed in the face of a Soviet attack. In the final analysis, the attractiveness of Scandinavian cooperation for Finland lay not in military power but in the Scandinavian countries' reputations as reliable neutrals in a war among the great powers.[26]

The lack of suitable allies frustrated Finland's search for security. The country wounded itself with respect to security policy as well. Many of the country's foreign policy leaders were inexperienced or, in some cases, uninterested in foreign policy. Of Finland's four interwar presidents, only P. E. Svinhufvud had significant foreign policy experience before winning the office. Despite all of the fear of a Soviet invasion, Finland's political parties were reluctant to spend money on the armed forces until the 1930s. Finland's leaders never seriously considered that an improvement of relations with Moscow might enhance national security. The only real milestone in Finnish–Soviet relations after the Peace of Tartu was a mutual nonaggression pact signed in 1932. This treaty fulfilled the constitutionalist ideal of making Finnish–Soviet relations as legalistic as possible. The Finnish side never saw it as a possible confidence-building measure toward better relations. In all fairness, the Soviets did little to ease tensions between the two countries. In the spring of 1938, the Soviets opened up a dialogue with an offer they believed the Finns could not refuse.

NOTES

1. This whole episode is covered in detail in Anders Huldén, *Kuningasseik-kailu Suomessa 1918* (Helsinki: Kirjayhtymä, 1988); see also George C. School-field, *Helsinki of the Czars* (Columbia, SC: Camden House, 1995), 263–264.

2. Raimo Salokangas, "Itsenäinen tasavalta," in *Suomen historian pikkujätti-läinen*, ed. Seppo Zetterberg (Porvoo: WSOY, 1987), 617–619.

3. Wikipedia contributors, "Parliamentary system," in *Wikipedia: The Free Encyclopedia*, http://en.wikipedia.org/w/index.php?title = Parliamentary_system&oldid; = 29258758 (accessed 30 November 2005).

4. *Constitution Act and Parliament Act of Finland* (Helsinki: Ministry for Foreign Affairs, 1967).

5. Tapani Kärkkäinen, *Kirkon historia: Ortodoksin käsikirja* (Jyväskylä: Gummerus, 1999), 194–195.

6. Salokangas, "Itsenäinen tasavalta," 620–627.

7. This topic is covered in excruciating detail in Juha Siltala, *Lapuan liike ja kyyditykset 1930* (Helsinki: Otava, 1985).

8. Seppo Hentilä, "Itsenäistymisestä jatkosodan päättymiseen," in Osmo Jussila, Seppo Hentilä and Jukka Nevakivi, *Suomen poliittinen historia* (Helsinki: WSOY, 2000), 148–159.

9. Salonkangas, "Itsenäinen tasavalta," 650–654, 660–662.

10. Göran von Bonsdorff, *Självstyrelsetanken i finlandssvensk politik åren 1917–1923*, Bidrag till kännedom av Finlands natur och folk 94 (Helsingfors: Centraltryckeriet, 1950). Pekka-Kalevi Hämäläinen, *In Time of Storm: Revolution, Civil War, and the Ethnolinguistic Issue in Finland* (Albany, NY: University of New York Press, 1978); Henrik Meinander, *Finlands Historia*, vol. 4 (Esbo: Schildts, 1999), 165–168.

11. Eino Jutikkala and Kauko Pirinen, *Suomen historia* (Helsinki: Weilin & Göös, 1981), 342.

12. Pirjo Lyytikäinen, "Kirjallisuus tienhaarassa," in *Suomen kulttuurihistoria*, vol. 3, ed. Anja Kervanto Nevanlinna and Laura Kolbe (Helsinki: Tammi, 2003), 294–305; Salokangas, "Itsenäinen tasavalta," 695–699; George C. Schoolfield, "The Age of Modernism 1916–1960," in *A History of Finland's Literature*, ed. George C. Schoolfield (Lincoln, NE: University of Nebraska Press, 1998), 453–589.

13. Aimo Reitala, "Kuvataide," in *Suomen kulttuurihistoria*, vol. 3, ed. Päiviö Tommila, Aimo Reitala, and Veikko Kallio (Porvoo: WSOY, 1984), 435–447.

14. Göran Schildt, *Alvar Aalto: A Life's Work—Architecture, Design, and Art* (Keuruu: WSOY, 1994), 310–313.

15. Pekka Pyykkö, "Biokemian nousu," in Päiviö Tommila et al, *Suomen tieteen historia*, vol. 3 (Helsinki: WSOY, 2000), 173–174.

16. Finnish Olympic Committee web site, http://www.noc.fi/olympiahistoria/suomalaisten_historia (accessed 30 November 2005); Leena Laine, "Suomi huippu-urheilu suurvaltana," in Antero Heikkinen et al., *Suomi uskoi urheiluun: Suomen urheilun ja liikkunnan historia* (Helsinki: VAPK, 1992), 216.

17. Heikki Ylikangas and Kalervo Immonen, "Miksi Suomi on urheilun suurvalta?" in *Citius, Altius, Fortius: Suomen olympiayhdistys ry 1907–1982*, ed. Helge Nygrén (Helsinki: Suomen olympiayhdistys, 1982), 32–45.

18. Tuoko Perko, "Urheilu- ja liikuntakulttuuri," *Suomen kulttuurihistoria*, vol. 3, ed. Päiviö Tommila, Aimo Reitala, and Veikko Kallio (Helsinki: WSOY, 1982), 577–586; Salokangas, "Itsenäinen tasavalta," 701–702.

19. Salokangas, "Itsenäinen tasavalta," 684–686; several articles in *Suomen taloushistoria*, vol. 2, ed. Jorma Ahvenainen et al. (Helsinki: Tammi, 1982), 175–316.

20. Jorma Ahvenainen and Henri Vartiainen, "Itsenäisen Suomen talouspolitiikka," Jorma Ahvenainen, "Taloudellinen kasvu ja elintaso," in *Suomen taloushistoria*, vol. 2, ed. Jorma Ahvenainen et al. (Helsinki: Tammi, 1982), 175–191, 308–315.

21. Henrik Ekberg, "Förbudslagen," in Henrik Meinander, *Finlands Historia*, vol. 4 (Esbo: Schildts, 1999), 111; Jorma Kallenautio, *Kieltolaki ja sen kumoaminen puoluepoliittisena ongelmana*, Alkoholitutkimussäätiön julkaisuja 31 (Jyväskylä: Gummerus, 1979), 11–13; Matti Peltonen, *Viinapäästä kolerakauhuun: kirjoituksia sosiaalihistoriasta* (Helsinki: Hanki ja jää, 1988), 17; Pentti Virrankoski, *Suomen historia*, vol. 2 (Helsinki: Suomalaisen Kirjallisuuden Seura, 2001), 559.

22. Jorma Kallenautio, *Suomi katsoi eteensä: Itsenäisen Suomen ulkopolitiikka 1917–1955* (Helsinki: Tammi, 1955), 59–60.

23. Hentilä, "Itsenäistymisestä jatkosodan päättymiseen,"134–136.

24. Hentilä, "Itsenäistymisestä jatkosodan päättymiseen," 133–134; Salonkangas, "Itsenäinen tasavalta," 633–634; "Åland in Brief" at Åland Islands' government web site, http://www.aland.fi/alandinbrief (accessed 3 January 2006).

25. Kallenautio, *Suomi*, 86–91; Hentilä, "Itsenäistymisestä jatkosodan päättymiseen," 136–138.

26. Kallenautio, *Suomi*, 158–171.

7

Finland at War (1939–1945)

During the years 1939–1945, Finland's place between East and West was never more visible—or more dangerous. On one hand, Finland lay in the middle of a German–Soviet struggle for hegemony in Eastern Europe. On the other, Finland stood between fellow Western democracies and their wartime ally, the Soviet Union. Despite long odds, Finland endured years of conflict that resulted in many other small countries losing their independence. Finland's wartime experience is not just a story of survival, but also of transformation. The country emerged from the conflict both unconquered and healed of most of its deep prewar divisions. The war years formed Finland's national identity for decades to come.

SECRETARY JARTSEV'S OPENING

Finland's road to war is widely understood to have begun on April 14, 1938. On this day, an official at the Soviet embassy in Helsinki, Boris Jartsev, met with Finland's Foreign Minister Rudolf Holsti. Jartsev related his country's concern about German expansion in Eastern Europe. In the previous month, Hitler's Germany had annexed Austria. Now Czechoslovakia was next in the German dictator's sights. The Soviets did not intend to wait passively until German expansion reached their borders. More specifically, the Soviet representative proposed formal military ties between Finland and the USSR in the event of a German attack.

For the next several months, Jartsev conducted talks with Holsti, Prime Minister A. K. Cajander, and Finance Minister Väinö Tanner. These discussions stagnated for two reasons. First, Finnish officials did not take Jartsev seriously because of his relatively low status at the Soviet embassy. They did not know that Jartsev had received his instructions directly from the Soviet leader, Josef Stalin, bypassing the bureaucracy of the Soviet Foreign Ministry. Second, Finnish foreign policy had long defined security as protection from, rather than cooperation with, the eastern neighbor. Holsti's successor as foreign minister, Eljas Erkko, ended the talks in November 1938.[1]

The end of Jartsev's initiative occurred against a backdrop of further German expansion. With the blessing of Great Britain, France, and Italy, Germany annexed the Sudetenland of Czechoslovakia in September 1938. In March of the next year, Germany took the rest of Czechoslovakia. The complicity of Britain and France in the German actions, coupled with the reluctance of any power to join the Soviets in an anti-German alliance, drew the Soviets to make their own deal with the Germans. On August 23, 1939, Nazi Germany and Communist Russia shocked the world by signing a nonaggression pact. The agreement's real impact would not lie in its public clauses but, rather, in a secret rider that divided Eastern Europe into German and Soviet spheres of influence. Finland, the Baltic republics of Estonia, Latvia, and Lithuania, and the eastern parts of Poland were placed in the Soviet sphere. The Soviets gained both a stay of an expected German invasion and an opportunity to extend their power westward. The treaty allowed Germany to invade Poland without having to fear a two-front war between the USSR on one hand and the Western Allies, Britain and France, on the other. Finland and other countries in Eastern Europe were the losers in the deal. They had based their security assumptions on a balance of power maintained by tensions between Germany and the USSR.

With Germany's invasion of Poland on September 1, 1939, the Second World War began. Redeeming its agreement with Germany, the Soviets demanded military bases from the Baltic states in September 1939. Lacking the internal resources and foreign allies to oppose the Soviets, these three states quickly acquiesced. Next, the Soviets turned to Finland. On October 5, the Soviet foreign minister Vyacheslav Molotov called for discussions on "concrete political questions." The Finnish Government responded militarily by mobilizing the regular army and reservists. Diplomatically, the Finns responded by sending to Moscow J. K. Paasikivi, Finland's chief negotiator for the Tartu peace treaty of 1920 between the Soviet Union and Finland.[2]

FINNISH–SOVIET NEGOTIATIONS

On October 12, Paasikivi met Stalin and Molotov in Moscow. Two days later, they presented to the Finnish diplomat demands packaged in terms of the

Soviets' desire to enhance the security of Leningrad (St. Petersburg). As in Bobrikov's time, the Finnish-Soviet border lay about 20 miles (32 kilometers) from Leningrad. The Soviets wanted enough Finnish territory on the Karelian Isthmus to place the greater Leningrad area outside of the range of Finnish artillery. They also demanded several large islands in the Gulf of Finland and a 30-year lease for the port of Hanko (west of Helsinki). With Hanko and naval bases in Estonia, the Soviets aimed to have the capability of closing off the Gulf of Finland in the event of a German invasion. In a demand farther afield, the Soviets wanted the Finnish part of the Fisherman's Peninsula (also known as the Rybachii Peninsula), which lay at the approaches to Finland's Arctic Sea port of Liinahamari. The Soviets claimed that they needed this land for the defense of the ice-free port of Murmansk. In exchange for Finnish cessions, the Soviets promised to cede to Finland an area twice as large along the central part of the Finnish-Soviet border. The Soviets wanted to amend the nonaggression pact between the two countries so that neither state could enter into an alliance targeted against the other party. The Finnish Government had anticipated these demands. With the possible partial exception of some islands in the Gulf of Finland, Paasikivi was instructed to reject all Soviet demands. The negotiations did not go beyond the opening gambits. On October 15, Paasikivi left Moscow.

On October 21, Paasikivi departed again for Moscow. This time he took with him Finance Minister Väinö Tanner. Tanner had helped Paasikivi negotiate the Peace of Tartu. He also was the dominant figure in the country's largest party, the Social Democratic Party. His presence in Moscow would signal to the Soviet leadership that the party of Finland's working class stood behind the Government. As a Cabinet minister, he could be helpful in convincing his fellow ministers to make concessions in order to achieve an agreement. The Government's instructions for Paasikivi and Tanner revealed little new flexibility. The Government was prepared to discuss a small cession of land on the Karelian Isthmus in addition to some islands in the Gulf of Finland. Any discussions beyond these parameters were not permitted.[3]

In Moscow, negotiations again went nowhere. The Soviets considered their demands to be at a minimum already and they were not prepared to bargain. The Finnish delegation returned to Helsinki empty-handed on October 26. On October 31, Paasikivi and Tanner led another delegation to Moscow.[4] The Finnish side was now prepared to cede to the Soviets the Rybachii Peninsula as well as an island off the Karelian Isthmus. Under no circumstances was Paasikivi's delegation to discuss a Soviet base on Finnish territory. When negotiations started on November 3, the Soviets focused on their demand for a naval base. The Finnish delegation, realizing that the Soviets were not going to accept a resolution without a base, left Moscow on November 13 without any resolution. The silence from the Soviet side in the days after talks in Moscow ended led many Finns to assume that indeed the Soviets had been bluffing and that the worst was over. Mobilized reservists received extended leave; evacuees from urban areas were permitted to return home; and schools that had been closed were reopened.[5]

Over the course of the negotiations, Paasikivi and the head of the National Defense Council, Marshal Carl Gustaf Emil Mannerheim, counseled the Government to acquiesce to some of the Soviet demands. They believed that the Soviets were not bluffing. Finland's defenses could not withstand a Soviet attack. However, the elected political leadership largely opposed their calls for concessions. Why, in the face of such overwhelming force, did the Finnish Government remain unwilling to compromise? First, the country's conduct of relations with the USSR rested on the Young Finn or constitutionalist ideology, which posited that legality, not power politics, should govern Finnish–Soviet relations. Since independence, Finns had voted in overwhelming majorities for political parties that followed to various degrees the Young Finn line. The country's leadership felt it had a mandate from the voters for its intransigent stance. Even if it had wanted to accept some of the Soviet demands, the constitution required approval by a five-sixths majority in Parliament for changes in the country's boundaries. An alternative route to approval consisted of receiving three-quarters of the vote in one Parliament, then calling elections for a new Parliament that would have to approve the proposal by the same margin. The breadth of the Young Finn consensus would have made it virtually impossible to achieve such majorities.[6]

Second, by the fall of 1939 the appeasement of large, expansive powers during the 1930s had proved disastrous for large powers and suicidal for small powers. Finland's leadership in late 1939 had seen how the appeasement of Nazi Germany and Soviet Russia had resulted in several small countries losing their independence. The Baltic States' agreements with the USSR resulted in the military occupation of those three countries. In June 1940, the three countries were formally annexed into the Soviet Union. The eventual Soviet invasion of Finland only confirmed the argument that appeasement would not have worked.

Third, many Finns believed that their country would receive foreign help in the event of a Soviet attack. This expectation of foreign help was based on the country's self-defined position as "the outpost of Western civilization" against Soviet Bolshevism. In particular, Finns looked to Sweden for help. For some two decades, Finland's military establishment had maintained informal but wide-ranging cooperation with the Swedish armed forces. These contacts gave Finland's leaders, Foreign Minister Eljas Erkko in particular, the impression that Sweden would come to Finland's aid in event of a war. This belief in Swedish help was maintained despite messages from the Swedish Government in the fall of 1939 that it would not come to Finland's defense in the event of war.[7]

The expectation that Finland would receive help from the West underpinned a fourth reason for its intransigence. Many of Finland's leaders, including Foreign Minister Erkko, believed that the Soviet threats of force only constituted a bluff. They assumed that Soviets would not risk a loss of standing in the world by invading Finland. As the Finnish delegation was about to enter the train on October 31 for the last round of talks, Foreign Minister Erkko placed into Paasikivi's hand a brief note that read "Forget that Russia [sic] is a great power. . . . We have justice on our side and Russia is bound by agreements with us and in the eyes of the whole world."[8]

About 10 days after the end of negotiations, Finnish assumptions about Soviet bluffing began to be proved false. On November 26, the Soviets claimed that Finnish artillery had fired on Soviet troops near the village of Mainila on the Karelian Isthmus, resulting in the deaths of four Soviet soldiers. Finnish artillery was not within range of the Soviet soldiers. A Finnish investigation concluded that shots were fired from the Soviet side of the border. Two days later, the Soviets declared the nonaggression pact between the two countries null and void and on November 30 at 6:50 A.M., Soviet troops crossed the border on the Karelian Isthmus. At 9:20 A.M., Soviet airplanes began dropping bombs on Helsinki. The Winter War had begun.[9]

FINNISH AND SOVIET WAR AIMS

The outbreak of the war changed the objectives of both sides. In invading Finland, the Soviets were no longer satisfied with taking some of the Karelian Isthmus and a naval base. On December 1, 1939, the Soviets announced the establishment of a Government for the new so-called Democratic Republic of Finland in Terijoki, the first town on the Karelian Isthmus taken by the Soviet Red Army. The prime minister of this Government was Otto Ville Kuusinen, the head of the Finnish Communist Party (SKP), then in exile in Moscow. Other ministers in this Cabinet were, like Kuusinen, Finnish Communist exiles. The Soviet Government signed a treaty with this puppet regime, opening diplomatic relations and changing the border in accordance with the Soviets' prewar proposal. The Soviets promised to give the Kuusinen Government all possible assistance to establish its authority over Finland. The formation of the Terijoki Government gave the strongest possible signal of Moscow's intention to occupy Finland entirely. For the Soviets and their Finnish puppets, victory was just a matter of days.[10]

The Soviet invasion changed goals and personnel in Helsinki as well. Finland's war aims were to avoid surrender, seek outside help, and to reopen negotiations with the USSR. To meet these goals, a new wartime Cabinet was created. The Cabinet included representatives from all political parties with the exception of the anti-democratic, far-Right Patriotic People's League (IKL). A member of the Progressive Party, Risto Ryti, replaced the ineffectual Prime Minister Cajander. Ryti had been the director of the Bank of Finland, the country's central bank. His connections to Western Europe, Great Britain in particular, were seen as a possible means of gaining foreign support for the war effort. Väinö Tanner replaced Foreign Minister Erkko, the man most closely associated with the prewar policy. His assumption of the foreign minister's portfolio was supposed to signal Finland's desire to negotiate.

"ONE FINN EQUALS TEN RUSSIANS"

In pursuing the goal of no surrender, Finland faced a Soviet army larger than Finland's total population. Moreover, Finland's armed forces were woefully underequipped for the task at hand. There were not enough guns for all of the soldiers. The official uniform for many soldiers consisted of only a belt and a cockade. In spite of this lack of resources and manpower, the Finnish armed forces thwarted the Soviet invasion for 105 days. The so-called miracle of the Winter War is very often explained, especially to foreigners, in mystical terms: the Finns had *sisu* and the Soviets did not. *Sisu* loosely translates as "guts." According to Finland's national mythology, *sisu* is an intestinal fortitude that only Finns possess. These types of explanations insult both the audience to which they are directed and those who themselves did the fighting. Explanations relying on *sisu*, of course, need to be distinguished from the exceptional willingness of Finns to pay any price for the defense of their country. In the final analysis, the reasons for the miracle of the Winter War lay in Soviet blundering as well as Finnish ingenuity and sacrifice.

The Soviets' incompetence and arrogance matched their military power. The Soviets invaded Finland with 450,000 men. While clearly the larger force, it was not enough. Military planning usually calls for an invading force to have three times as many soldiers as those on the defensive. If one concedes that not all of Finland's 300,000 soldiers had weapons, the Soviet advantage in manpower might have been two to one, at best. Assuming a quick Finnish surrender, the Soviets did not see the need for a larger force. Another factor that weakened the Red Army was Stalin's war on his own people. Stalin's purges in the 1930s had decimated the experienced officer corps. The lack of planning and leadership was evident in how the Soviet army tried to advance into Finland: either by marching in broad waves in open land or in narrow columns on roads through dense forests. Both approaches made them vulnerable to Finnish counterattack. To add to their self-inflicted handicaps, the Soviets launched an invasion during the coldest winter in decades. The persistently bad weather nullified their overwhelming air superiority.[11]

The Finns did many things right. What they lacked in manpower and materiel they compensated for in strategic preparedness and tactical ingenuity. The mobilization of the army in October placed the country on a wartime footing before the outbreak of hostilities. Military planners correctly surmised before the war that a Soviet invasion would take place primarily through the Karelian Isthmus. The rest of the border largely consisted of dense forests and few roads. As a result, the Finns focused their border defenses on the isthmus.

A defensive line known as the Mannerheim Line stretched some 70 kilometers (43.75 miles) across the land bridge. It was largely a system of trenches, tank barriers, and minefields integrated with natural barriers, such as rivers and swamps. Lacking the concrete and steel of the French Maginot Line, it nonetheless proved an effective impediment to the Soviet invasion.[12]

The Finns developed tactics and technologies that maximized their strengths and exploited Soviet weaknesses. The Finns compensated for their lack of heavy firepower with speed and mobility. While the Soviets marched through snow, the Finns skied. Skiing was key to the Finns' most effective tactical maneuver against the Soviets: the *motti*. This Finnish word literally means a bundle of firewood. The *motti* tactic consisted of attacking in quick, hit-and run, encircling pincer movements that would chop up enemy troops in segments, or *mottis*. The Soviets allowed the Finns opportunities for using the *motti* tactic with their tendencies to advance on roads in long columns or to congregate into tighter formations when faced with attack. In both instances, Finnish troops could ski out of the woods and cut the larger Soviet force into *mottis*. If a Soviet *motti* was large enough, it could withstand Finnish attacks and receive supplies from the air. Finland had no air power to destroy the larger *mottis* or anti-aircraft weapons to stop these supply operations. The *motti* tactic was employed in the Finns' greatest military victory of the war, at the village of Suomussalmi in northern Finland. The Soviet incursion near Suomussalmi was meant to dissect Finland at its "waist," or geographically narrowest point, and prevent the Finnish army from retreating northward to fight a guerilla-style war. Between December 11, 1939 and January 2, 1940, a Finnish brigade under Colonel Hjalmar Siilasvuo smashed the Soviet force consisting of two divisions, keeping Finland intact.[13]

Another Finnish innovation came in the form of antitank warfare. The Finnish army entered the conflict with virtually no antitank guns. In the years before the outbreak of the war, the Finnish army worked on developing a type of firebomb that was used against motorized vehicles in the Spanish Civil War. The bomb consisted of a bottle and combustible fluid that was lit by a rag and thrown at the vehicle. The Finns improved the weapon by making a longer-burning wick and adding tar to make the fire stick to the target. The Finns cynically christened their weapon the Molotov cocktail in honor of the Soviet foreign minister. Finnish soldiers would stop a tank with a barrier or by placing a block of wood in its tracks, and then they would throw the lit bottle toward the tank's engine, causing a fire inside. The Soviets often made the Finns' job easier by deploying tanks without any infantry or air support.[14]

FOREIGN RESPONSES TO THE WINTER WAR

Finland's heroic struggle captured the world's imagination. In an age in which democracy and national self-determination were suffering loss after loss, the bleeding stopped for a moment. Outpourings of private sympathy and support ran contrary to the reluctance of foreign governments to help Finland. The Winter War had an impact on Finland's ties with four important countries: Germany, Britain, the United States, and Sweden.

Germany reacted to the war by scrupulously adhering to the Nazi-Soviet Pact, which assigned Finland to the Soviet sphere. As the war ground on, Germany became increasingly concerned about British and French plans to intervene in the conflict, a move that would have deployed Allied troops in Germany's backyard. The Germans sought to keep the Allies out of Scandinavia in two ways. First, they planned an invasion of Denmark and Norway. Second, in February 1940, German leaders unofficially encouraged their Finnish counterparts to accept Soviet terms for peace. Some German communications held out the possibility of Finland regaining lost territories at a later time. These messages seemed to have comforted Finnish leaders as they confronted Soviet terms for peace.[15]

For the British Government, there was only one question concerning the Winter War: How did it affect the war effort against Germany? Seeing the Nazi–Soviet friendship as a short-term expedient, the British were at first wary of aiding Finland and thus antagonizing the USSR. As British leaders realized that Finland was not going to collapse, their attitude changed. Britain supplied Finland with about 100 combat aircraft and both Britain and France gave the Finns artillery and ammunition. With shortages in the arsenals for their own war efforts, the Allies refrained from giving the Finns much-needed antitank weapons. On February 5, the British and French agreed on a plan to send 150,000 troops to conquer the Norwegian port of Narvik, the ice-free port used by the Germans to transport Swedish iron ore to Germany in the winter. After taking the port, the Allies would march into northern Sweden and take the iron mines themselves. Then the Allies would march on to Finland to fight the Soviets. The goal was to "kill two birds with one stone," as Prime Minister Neville Chamberlain stated.[16]

The Finnish Government balked at accepting the offer of help for three reasons. First, the Allies refused to move without a formal and public Finnish request for help. This placed Finland in the difficult position of asking Britain and France to invade their Scandinavian neighbors, since Norway and Sweden refused to allow Allied forces to enter their countries. Second, the Allies changed plans and troop numbers many times, creating doubt about the effectiveness of an Allied intervention. Third, if an Allied force reached Finland, the Finns risked losing control of their own war. Finland would become a great-power battlefield between the Allies, the Soviet Union, and possibly Germany.

In the United States, fundraisers were conducted all over the country. Those who wanted the United States to intervene in the world war on the side of the Allies backed Finland's cause. At the time of the Winter War, American intervention in the world war was still almost two years away. President

Franklin Delano Roosevelt's desire to help Finland was reined in by isolationist sentiment and neutrality legislation, on one hand, and a reluctance to inflame relations with the USSR on the other. Like the British, the Americans anticipated that the Soviet Union might become an ally against Nazi Germany. The president managed to arrange for a $10 million loan from the U.S. Treasury for Finland in early December. The loan was granted with strings attached—the money could not be spent on arms. The Finns wanted a loan for purchasing arms. Finland's resourceful minister in Washington, D.C., Hjalmar Procopé, resolved the problem by buying food with the loan, selling the food to Great Britain, and using the profits for arms. At the end of February, Congress approved an additional loan of $20 million, also for nonmilitary items. Finland's success in gaining any American help at all was as much a tribute to the county's struggle against as to its status as the only debtor after World War I not to default on American loans.[17]

Although the Winter War edged the United States away from neutrality, an opposite development occurred in Sweden. The outbreak of the war divided Sweden's Social Democratic government. A majority of the ministers, including Prime Minister Per Albin Hansson, opposed intervention in the war. They feared that intervention might leave Sweden exposed to German military action. They calculated that Sweden had more to lose in a war with the USSR than in a Soviet conquest of Finland. An interventionist minority, led by Foreign Minister Rickhard Sandler, saw a Soviet conquest of Finland as a grave threat to Sweden's security. These divisions resulted in the demise of the Hansson Cabinet. It was replaced on December 13 by a new national unity government that represented all parties in the Swedish Parliament except for the Communists. Sandler and other interventionists were excluded. This government swore to keep the country out of war. Although it refused to intervene formally, the Swedish Government aided Finland in two important respects. First, it gave wide latitude to private initiatives to help Finland. About 8,000 Swedish volunteers joined Finland's army. Private organizations following the battle call of "Finland's cause is ours" helped make Sweden Finland's largest supplier of arms and nonmilitary supplies. Second, the Swedish Government acted as the key intermediary once talks between Finland and the USSR reopened at the end of January.[18]

THE PEACE OF MOSCOW

Although Finland did not receive all of the foreign help it wanted, the possibility of larger powers coming to Finland's aid, along with the military stalemate, helped the Finns reach their third war aim: the achievement of a negotiated settlement with Moscow. For the first two months of the war, the Soviets insisted that they would only negotiate with the Terijoki Government. By the end of January, after two months of military embarrassment and the looming threat of foreign intervention, the Soviets signaled their willingness to negotiate with the Ryti Cabinet.[19]

Finland's success in breaking the Soviets' diplomatic resistance came just in time. As the war entered its third month, Finnish military resistance was weakening. From the first days of the war, the Soviets had focused their invasion on the town of Summa located in the middle of the Karelian Isthmus. The area around Summa had the fewest natural obstacles and Summa also lay at one of the points along the Mannerheim Line closest to Viipuri (Vyborg). On February 11, the Soviets launched an offensive on the isthmus and on February 15, Finnish troops withdrew from the Summa area. The Soviets then pushed Finnish troops to the outskirts of Viipuri by the end of February. The Finns' fighting spirit and ingenuity were now losing ground to superior Soviet resources.[20]

On February 23, the Finns received the Soviets' conditions for peace. The Soviets wanted all of the Karelian Isthmus, as well as islands in the Gulf of Finland, a base at Hanko, and all of the Fisherman's Peninsula. Nonetheless, the Soviets were no longer seeking to end Finland's national independence. The Finnish Government reluctantly started negotiations with the Soviets at the beginning of March. Time for achieving an acceptable peace was running out; Finland's brave army was on the brink of exhaustion. After the Finnish delegation arrived in Moscow on March 7, 1940, the Soviets added to their demands Finland's Salla region along the central border. Salla was where the Finnish border was both the highest and nearest to Murmansk railway, the Soviets' lifeline to the Atlantic. In addition, Finland had to build a railroad line from the Swedish to the Soviet border that would connect with a branch of the Murmansk railroad. Officially, the Soviets wanted the rail line to better facilitate Soviet–Swedish trade, but the Finns saw it as a possible conduit for a future Soviet invasion. Historians remain puzzled over what the Soviet demand meant. In any case, the railroad was never built. A very divided Finnish Government accepted this and other Soviet conditions for peace on March 12. On the next day, the Peace of Moscow was signed.[21]

OUTCOMES OF THE WINTER WAR

Finland won the Winter War, if victory is defined by meeting war aims. Finland did not surrender to Soviet occupation; it achieved a negotiated settlement. Even in seeking foreign help, Finland partially succeeded. Finland became a more visible member of the international community at a time when many small countries were disappearing from the map.

The war advanced the healing of longstanding divisions in Finnish society. It furthered the growing prewar harmony between Finnish and Swedish speakers, and between Finns who had fought against each other in the Civil War fought together against the USSR. In January, 1940, Finland's employers officially recognized the workers' right to organize themselves. The Civil Guards, defenders of White Finland, opened their membership to the Left.

The war transformed national identity in three ways. First, the Winter War served as the glorious war of national independence that the Civil War was not. Such struggles often play an important role in the formation of national identity. Second, the war gave Finns a collective frame of reference for the future. The war provided justifications for policies ranging from high agrarian subsidies to restrictive immigration policies for decades after the war. Third, the war triggered a change in how Finns saw themselves in Europe. The lack of help from the West undermined Finland's claim as "the outpost of Western civilization." Marshal Mannerheim proclaimed at the end of the war, "We have paid our debt to the West to the final penny." Only after another three years of war would a wide segment of Finns embrace Mannerheim's conclusion.

These outcomes demanded a very high price. Some 27,000 Finnish soldiers died in the defense of their country. The Soviet losses were five times as great (about 126,000 soldiers) but the population of the USSR was at least 40 times larger than Finland's. The loss of territories totaled about 10 percent of Finland's prewar land area. Economically and culturally, the loss was greater. In the Karelian Isthmus lay some of Finland's best agricultural lands and its second-largest city, Viipuri. The loss of territories saddled the country with the challenge of resettling the refugees from those ceded areas, more than 400,000 people, about 11 percent of the country's population. The peace agreement gave the populations of the ceded areas 10 days to evacuate. Virtually nobody stayed to welcome the Red Army; many left with only what they could carry.[22]

Although the war left Finland free and formally at peace with its eastern neighbor, it did not remove the basic mistrust between the two countries. The Soviets still saw Finland as a potential corridor for invasion by a larger power. Finnish foreign policy was still guided by the goal of neutralizing the Soviet threat. Added to this was a strong feeling of revenge. The Finnish desire for recouping the losses of the war was reflected in the common reference to the Peace of Moscow as an interim peace.

THE INTERIM PEACE AND COLLUSION WITH GERMANY

Finland continued its search for security by reviving its prewar Scandinavian orientation. In August 1940, Sweden's Foreign Minister Christian Günther proposed a union with Finland for the conduct of common foreign and defense policies. This union would aim to keep the two countries out of the world war. In April 1940, Germany conquered Denmark and Norway and in June 1940, the USSR formally annexed the Baltic republics of Estonia,

Latvia, and Lithuania. Both Sweden and Finland were now caught between two totalitarian dictators. Soviet and German opposition made the proposal for a union a dead letter by the end of 1940.[23]

Finland had better success in cultivating Germany as a counterweight to the USSR. In June 1940, the two countries signed a trade agreement whereby the Germans achieved one of their goals with respect to Finland: access to Finland's nickel deposits, most of which were located in the Arctic Petsamo region. In September 1940, the Finnish Government agreed to allow Germany to transfer troops in and out of Norway through Finland to Germany. In return, Finland started receiving major infusions of war materiel. In December 1940, German dictator Adolf Hitler approved an invasion plan of the USSR known as Operation Barbarossa. This plan assumed that Finland would join Germany in the attack. At the beginning of 1941, Finnish military officials began to involve themselves in the planning of the invasion.[24]

The development of Finnish–German relations was aided by a corresponding deterioration in Finnish–Soviet ties. After signing the Peace of Moscow, the Soviets sought to involve themselves in Finland's domestic affairs. One example of this occurred in connection with the election of a new president in December 1940. President Kyösti Kallio, disabled by a stroke in August 1940, resigned in December. The same electoral college that elected Kallio in 1937 met to elect Prime Minister Ryti to the presidency. The Soviets openly campaigned for the election of J. K. Paasikivi, now Finland's ambassador to Moscow and not a presidential candidate. The Soviets then began to demand control of Finland's nickel mines in Petsamo. Finland was ready to grant the Soviets preferential purchasing rights but not monopoly control. Finland's response to this and other Soviet demands hardened as its cooperation with Germany deepened.

In May 1941, the Finnish Government formally decided to join the German invasion of the USSR. By this time, the Finns had painted themselves into a corner. For almost a year Finland had been privy to some of Germany's most important military secrets. A break with Germany might have meant war. At the same time, however, Finland's cooperation with Germany had raised Soviet ire. In June, Finland tied itself closer to the German invasion plans by allowing the German army to station itself in northern Finland and the German navy to mine the waters of the Gulf of Finland. At its height, the German army in Finland consisted of 220,000 men. The Finnish Government gave the Germans its conditions for participating in the invasion of the USSR; the most important of these was that Finnish military operations would begin only after the Soviets started hostilities. This condition kept Finland out of war for three days after the Germans launched their invasion on June 22. The Finns launched their own invasion on June 25, after German incursions on Soviet airspace from Finland provoked the Soviets to bomb several cities in Finland.[25]

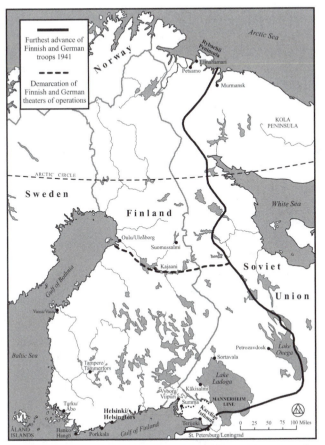

Finland during World War II. Adapted from Osmo Jussila, Seppo Hentilä, and Jukka Nevakivi, *From Grand Duchy to Modern State: A Political History of Finland since 1809.* (London: Hurst, 1999), 200. Adapted with permission.

THE CONTINUATION WAR

Finland's so-called Continuation War started off well. In September 1941, Finland captured the last of the territories ceded at the end of the Winter War. The Finnish army then continued to move eastward into Soviet Karelia. By the end of the year, with most of Soviet Karelia in hand, the Finnish army had stopped its advance and dug into a defensive posture.

The Finns were much better prepared to face the Soviets in 1941 than they were in 1939. With the infusions of German arms, Finland's armed forces had none of the shortages in weaponry that prevailed during the Winter War. The number of fighting men was increased by employing women in the civilian workplace and noncombat military jobs. German troops manned Finland's eastern border north of the Oulu River, allowing the Finnish army to concentrate on retaking the lost territories. The allocation of scarce consumer items, such as food, was regulated through a system of rationing.[26]

In comparing this conflict to the Winter War, what Finland had in resources it lacked in clarity of mission and moral authority. This ambivalence appeared on several levels. Finland considered itself a cobelligerent rather than an ally of Germany. In other words, Finland and Germany shared a common enemy but not common war aims. The Finns asserted that they were continuing a defensive struggle started during the Winter War; hence the name Continuation War for the war that started in June, 1941. Indeed, the Finns made some decisions to separate themselves from the Germans' war of conquest. For example, the Finns refused to participate in the German siege of Leningrad in late 1941, which allowed the Soviets to hold Leningrad during a three-year-long German siege. Finland also balked at cutting the Murmansk railway. In struggling to assert the distinctiveness of their war, the Finns hoped to keep open the possibility of a separate peace with the Soviet Union. Interestingly, the Soviets held open the possibility of a separate peace with Finland as a means of focusing resources on defeating Germany.

Finland also distanced itself from Germany by upholding its democratic form of government. Moreover, the Finns rejected Nazi Germany's program of genocidal anti-Semitism. Finland refused German requests to cleanse its army of Jews and to surrender its Jewish citizens to German death camps. Finland's record, however, was not completely without blemish. In November 1942, five Jewish refugees were deported to Germany. Three family members accompanied these five back to Germany. Of the eight, seven perished in the Holocaust. This Finnish decision did not stem from any German pressure; the deportations occurred at a time when Finnish authorities were seeking to expel all refugees who had acted in a delinquent fashion. Nonetheless, the deportation of these Jewish refugees was inexplicably insensitive. Of the nearly 3,000 Soviet prisoners of war whom Finland deported to Germany, it is estimated that as many as 74 were Jews. These prisoners were deported not because of their ethnicity but, rather, because of their military rank. None of these deportees is known to have survived the war.[27]

In spite of distancing itself from Germany, Finland bore the dubious distinction as the only democracy on the side of Germany during World War II. As such, it lost the moral authority that it had during the Winter War. The world's democracies did not fully accept Finland's claim that it was fighting its own separate war. On Finland's independence day, December 6, 1941, Great Britain, now an ally of the USSR, declared war on Finland because of its conquest of territory beyond the 1939 borders. Most other Allied powers followed suit, with the notable exception of United States. Even at the beginning of the twenty-first century, Finns still were debating the separateness of Finland's war. The arguments on all sides ignore the fact that Finland's war was and still is primarily understood by outsiders in the context of the larger war between Germany and its enemies.[28]

Finland did not fight with clear war aims, as it had in the Winter War. A national consensus backed the reconquest of the lost territories. Finns and their leaders were less united over additional conquests. The quick success convinced most of the country's leaders to take additional territory. Some wanted to take land as a bargaining chip in a final peace settlement; others wanted to realize the dream of a Greater Finland that would encompass the Finnish-speaking population of Soviet Karelia. The Government took measures in the direction of a Greater Finland by ethnically cleansing the newly conquered lands. The flight of almost 70 percent of Soviet Karelia's population into the USSR left only about 85,000 inhabitants, half of whom were deemed nationals, that is, ethnic Finns and others who spoke Finnic languages such as Karelian and Veps. The non-national half of the population, mostly Russian, was subjected to various resettlement schemes. Some were resettled in abandoned villages away from the population of nationals. At varying times, 15,000 to 20,000 were placed in internment camps for deportation to Russia after the war. In return, it was hoped that Finnish and ethnically related populations elsewhere in Russia would replace the deportees.[29]

Finland's conduct of the war was rife with paradoxes. It fought to defend its democracy by allying with a dictatorship that had expansionist and genocidal aims. In a purported defensive war, it conquered foreign territory. It rejected the Holocaust but conducted a less-murderous form of ethnic cleansing. It hedged its bets in case of a German or Soviet victory. The soldiers at the front reflected this ambivalence. The best-known literary account of the war, Väinö Linna's *The Unknown Soldier*, portrays ordinary soldiers who were willing to fight and die for their country but not for their leaders' delusions of grandeur.

WITHDRAWAL FROM THE WAR

In June 1941, Finland's leaders assumed there would be a swift German victory. After Germany's surrender at the battle of Stalingrad in February, 1943, Finland sought an exit from the war. In August 1943, 33 members of Parliament signed a letter to President Ryti requesting that the Government seek an end the war. These advocates of peace did not know that their Government was already looking for a way out. In February 1943, President Ryti wrote to his American counterpart, Franklin Delano Roosevelt, asking for mediation with the Soviets. Finland was ready to sue for peace if it could return to the 1939 borders, although changes to the border on the Karelian Isthmus could be discussed. The Soviets responded with conditions of their own: the 1940 borders and war reparations. The American mediation effort failed for two reasons. First, the two sides were too far apart to make an agreement.

Second, Germany, upon finding out about the initiative, succeeded in pressuring the Finns to stop.[30]

In January 1944, the Soviets broke the Germans' three-year siege of Leningrad. Facing a resurgent Soviet army on the Karelian Isthmus, the Finns sought to reopen talks. With the military momentum in its favor, the Soviets raised the price for peace. In addition to the 1940 borders and reparations, the Soviets wanted removal of the German troops from Finnish soil, as well as a base at either Petsamo or Hanko. Meanwhile, Germany had learned of Finland's renewed drive for a separate peace. As a means of keeping Finland fighting on its side, Germany suspended grain and arms shipments. Meanwhile, Finland's defenses were crumbling under the weight of the Soviet advance. In the hope of restarting German shipments, on June 26, 1944, President Ryti gave German Foreign Minister Joachim von Ribbentrop a written personal promise that, as long as he was president, Finland would make no separate peace. Recent scholarship has shown that Ryti probably did not have to make the agreement. Neither Hitler nor the German military shared the foreign minister's interest in such a Finnish pledge. The Soviet advances precipitated the resumption of German some aid even before Ryti made his pledge, and that pledge further weakened Finland's claim to fighting a separate war. In protest, the United States broke off diplomatic relations.[31]

Instead of painting Finland deeper into a corner, Ryti's move actually opened the door wider to a separate peace. With new infusions of German supplies, the situation stabilized temporarily on the Karelian Isthmus. This, in turn, bought the Finns time for negotiations before the Soviets overran the country. Progress in these talks reached a point where Ryti decided to use the escape hatch of his agreement with Ribbentrop. The promise of no separate peace bound Ryti, but no future Finnish president. On August 4, 1944, Ryti resigned from the presidency. On the same day, Parliament by emergency law elected Marshal Mannerheim president for a full six-year term. Only he had the credibility and prestige to maintain national unity during a difficult transition to peace. The new president named a new Cabinet under Antti Hackzell, formerly Finland's ambassador to Berlin. The real strongman of the Government was Mannerheim's confidant, Foreign Minister Carl Enckell. This new executive was deputed with the express mission of extracting the country from of the war. Although the situation was difficult, the Finns had two factors in their favor: the Finnish army was still fighting, and the Soviets were more concerned about reaching Berlin than Helsinki.

Negotiating through the Soviet embassy in Stockholm, the Finns received the terms for peace. In addition to previous demands, the Soviets now wanted Finland to break off diplomatic relations with Germany and remove German troops from Finland. On September 2, 1944, Parliament accepted the conditions, and on September 4, Finnish troops ceased military operations. On September 7, a Finnish delegation arrived in Moscow. The armistice agreement, signed on September 19, 1944, was in a legal sense an agreement between Finland and the Allies that had declared war on it. In reality, it was a treaty between Finland and the USSR. The Allies already were dividing Europe into spheres of influence and, as in 1939, Finland fell into the Soviet sphere of influence—a fact recognized, albeit reluctantly, by Moscow's democratic allies. According to the treaty, the Finns agreed to retreat to the 1940 borders. They accepted war reparations of $300 million based on the currency's 1938 value, payable over six years. Per capita, this indemnity exceeded Germany's reparations bill after World War I. In addition to these longstanding demands, the Finns had to consent to a list of new Soviet conditions. The Soviets satisfied their desire for Finnish nickel by taking the Petsamo region. Instead of Hanko, the Finns had to lease the Soviets the Porkkala Peninsula, about 30 kilometers (20 miles) west of Helsinki. The exchange of Hanko for Porkkala reflected not only the longstanding Soviet goal of lordship over the Gulf of Finland, but also a larger desire for increased influence in Finland. The armistice called for the legalization of the Finnish Communist Party (SKP), in exile since 1918. Finland agreed to ban "Fascist" and "Hitlerite" organizations, and war criminals would be prosecuted. A Soviet-dominated Allied Control Commission based in Helsinki would monitor the implementation of the armistice until a final peace treaty was signed.

THE LAPLAND WAR

The armistice ended the Continuation War, but Finland was not yet at peace. Finland still had to remove the German troops on its soil. The Finnish military high command secretly agreed with the Germans on a staged withdrawal. It was staged in two respects. First, the Germans, who were now retreating all over Europe, would leave northern Finland according to a mutually agreed timetable. Second, Finland would pretend to push the Germans out. The Germans would pretend to defend themselves by destroying certain bridges and roads as they withdrew into Norway. Soviet impatience with the slowness of the German withdrawal forced the Finns to open formal hostilities with Germany. On October 1, 1944, a Finnish force made a surprise attack on the Germans by landing at Tornio at the head of the Gulf of Bothnia. The Germans methodically withdrew northward over the next seven months, leaving scorched earth in their wake. The evacuation of the civilian population, primarily to neighboring Sweden, saved the civilian population. On April 27, 1945, the last German troops left Finland.[32]

THE COSTS AND OUTCOMES OF THE WAR YEARS

During the Continuation War, Finland lost about 60,000 soldiers. The Lapland war took nearly 1,000. In all three conflicts, approximately 90,000 died from combat. Many of the inhabitants of the areas ceded in 1940 returned to their homes in the summer and fall of 1941. They now had to be again resettled elsewhere in Finland. In addition, the smaller populations of Petsamo and Porkkala also faced resettlement. The departing Germans burned about one-third of the country to the ground. The country now faced years of paying war reparations.[33]

While Finland's losses were great, many European countries would have traded their war experiences for those of Finland. The country never suffered occupation. Among European combatants in World War II, only three were able to protect their capitals from occupation: London, Moscow, and Helsinki. The country's institutions were intact; and the populace stood ready to support its leaders in peace as it had in war.

In spite of these many achievements, Finland failed in war to achieve what it had tried to achieve in the two decades before 1939: the neutralization of the Soviet threat. Finland could not realistically consider any country as an ally against the Soviet Union, now the dominant power in Eastern Europe. Germany was heading toward defeat and the world's major democracies were aligned with the USSR. Finland's Scandinavian neighbors would enter the postwar period even more divided over foreign and defense policy. Finland would have to choose a new course in relations with Moscow, one based on the realities of the time and the lessons of the past.

NOTES

1. Raimo Salonkangas, "Itsenäinen tasavalta," in *Suomen historian pikkujättiläinen*, ed. Seppo Zetterberg (Porvoo: WSOY, 1987), 677–681.

2. Antti Laine, "Suomi sodassa," in *Suomen historian pikkujättiläinen*, ed. Seppo Zetterberg (Porvoo: WSOY, 1987), 705.

3. Seppo Hentilä, "Itsenäistymisestä jatkosodan päättymiseen," in Osmo Jussila, Seppo Hentilä, and Jukka Nevakivi, *Suomen poliittinen historia* (Helsinki: WSOY, 2000), 173–174; Laine, "Suomi sodassa," 705; Max Jakobson, *The Diplomacy of the Winter War* (Cambridge, MA: Harvard University Press, 1961), 113–114; Tuomo Polvinen, *J. K. Paasikivi: Valtiomiehen elämäntyö 3: 1939–1944* (Helsinki: WSOY, 1995), 38–39;

4. Polvinen, *Paasikivi*, 48.

5. Jakobson, *Winter War*, 139–140.

6. Jakobson, *Winter War*, 63–65, 99, 113–114; Polvinen, *Paasikivi*, 38–39.

7. Martti Turtola, *Tornionjoelta rajajoelle: Suomen ja Ruotsin salainen yhteistoiminta Neuvostoliiton hyökkäyksen varalle vuosina 1923–1940* (Helsinki: WSOY, 1984).

8. Polvinen, *Paasikivi*, 48.

9. Jakobson, *Winter War*, 147–154.

10. Osmo Jussila, *Terijoen hallitus 1939–1940*, (Helsinki: WSOY, 1985).

11. Hentilä, "Itsenäistymisestä," 176.

12. Anthony F. Upton, *Finland 1939–1940* (Newark, NJ: University of Delaware Press, 1979), 54–55.

13. Upton, *Finland*, 83–90.

14. Keijo Heinonen, "Kuka keksi 'Molotov cocktailin'?" *Sotahistoriallinen Aikakauskirja* 24 (2005): 131–153; Esko O. Toivonen, "Molotovin cocktail eli polttopullo," *Ase-lehti*, no. 4 (1996): 24–27; William R. Trotter, *A Frozen Hell: The Russo-Finnish War of 1939–1940* (Chapel Hill, NC: Algonquin Books, 1991), 73.

15. Jakobson, *Winter War*, 184–190; Mauno Jokipii, "Mitä Göring tarkoitti helmikuussa 1940," *Kanava*, 28, no. 6 (2000): 373–377; Upton, *Finland*, 125–126, 157–159; Heikki Ylikangas, *Tulkintani talvisodasta* (Juva: WSOY, 2001).

16. Jukka Nevakivi, *Apu jota ei pyydetty: Liittoutuneet ja Suomen talvisota 1939–1940* (Helsinki: Tammi, 1972); Upton, *Finland*, 80–81.

17. Jakobson, *Winter War*, 190–195; Robert Sobel, *Origins of Interventionism: The United States and the Russo-Finnish War* (New York: Bookman, 1960), 89–107, 109–111.

18. Upton, *Finland*, 77–78, 94.

19. Upton, *Finland*, 94.

20. Upton, *Finland*, 109–111.

21. Hentilä, "Itsenäistymisestä," 181; Lasse Laaksonen, "Olisi taisteluja pystytty jatkamaan? Suomalaisten tilanne kannaksella talvisodan lopussa 1940," *Sotahistoriallinen Aikakauskirja* 19 (2000): 128–174; Upton, *Finland*, 134–148;

22. Hentilä, "Itsenäistymisestä," 186; *Soviet Casualties and Combat Losses in the Twentieth Century*, ed. G. F. Krivosheev (London: Greenhill Books, 1993), 79; Riita Lentilä and Antti Juutilainen, "Talvisodan uhrit," in *Talvisodan pikkujättiläinen*, ed. Jari Leskinen and Antti Juutilainen (Porvoo: WSOY, 1999), 825.

23. Hentilä, "Itsenäistymisestä," 190.

24. Hentilä, "Itsenäistymisestä," 190–191; Hans Peter Krosby, *Finland, Germany, and the Soviet Union 1940–1941: The Petsamo Dispute* (Madison, WI: University of Wisconsin Press, 1968), 27.

25. Hentilä, "Itsenäistymisestä," 190–192.

26. Hentilä, "Itsenäistymisestä," 196.

27. Max Jakobson, "Suomesta luovutetut," *Helsingin sanomat*, 13 March 2003; Jukka Lindstedt, "Juutalaisten sotavankien luovutukset," *Historiallinen Aikakauskirja* 102, no. 2 (2004): 144–165; Hannu Rautkallio, *Finland and the Holocaust: The Rescue of Finland's Jews* (New York: Holocaust Library, 1987), 229–238; Elina Sana, *Luovutetut: Suomen ihmisluovutukset Gestapolle* (Helsinki: WSOY, 2003), Heikki Ylikangas, *Heikki Ylikankaan selvitys valtioneuvoston kanslialle*, Valtioneuvoston kanslian julkaisusarja 5/2004 (Helsinki: Edita, 2004).

28. Tuomo Polvinen, *Between East and West: Finland in International Politics 1944–1947* (Helsinki: WSOY, 1986), 9.

29. Antti Laine, "Suomi sodassa," in *Suomen historian pikkujättiläinen*, 725–726; Antti Laine, *Suur-Suomen Kahden Kasvot: Itä-Karjalan Siviiliväestön asema suomalaisessa miehityshallinnossa 1941–1944*, Joensuun yliopiston julkaisuja ser. A, vol. 24 (Helsinki: Otava 1982), 102–121, 488–490.

30. Hentilä, "Itsenäistymisestä," 198–199; Juhani Suomi, *Myrrysmies: Urho Kekkonen 1936–1944* (Helsinki: Otava, 1986), 368–387.

31. Markku Jokisipilä, *Aseveljiä vai liittolaisia? Suomi, Saksan liittosopimusvaatimukset ja Rytin-Ribbentropin sopimus* (Helsinki: Suomalaisen Kirjallisuuden Seura, 2004).

32. Hentilä, "Itsenäistymisestä," 197–206; Jukka Nevakivi, "Jatkosodasta nykypäivään 1944–1999," in Osmo Jussila, Seppo Hentilä, and Jukka Nevakivi, *Suomen poliittinen historia* (Helsinki: WSOY, 2000), 208–215.

33. Ari Raunio et al., eds., *Jatkosodan historia*, vol. 6 (Porvoo: WSOY, 1994), 489, 492.

8

Finland during the Cold War (1944–1991)

After World War II, Europe became center stage of a bipolar world dominated by the American–Soviet Cold War. The line between East and West had been redrawn again, with Finland falling in the Soviets' political and military sphere of influence. At the same time, Finland retained its Western market economy and democratic institutions. Finland was widely viewed as having an unenviable and ultimately untenable position as a small democracy in the shadow of Soviet power. Out of this dilemma, Finland created for itself a secure and prosperous niche in the Cold War divide.

CHANGES IN FOREIGN POLICY: THE PAASIKIVI LINE

Finland's surrender to the Soviet Union meant the end of the constitutionalist Young Finn approach toward its eastern neighbor. In November 1944, a new Cabinet was formed under J. K. Paasikivi, Finland's chief ambassador to the USSR since the fall of 1939. With the failing health of the elderly President Mannerheim, Paasikivi was expected, unlike previous prime ministers, to set domestic and foreign policy. Paasikivi's foreign policy (or line) consisted of four premises based on Old Finn appeasement of Russian power. First, Finns had to recognize that they could no longer seek allies to neutralize Soviet power. The Western democracies were fighting on the side of the USSR. With

Germany's demise in May 1945, the Soviet Union became the only major military power in the Baltic. The only possibility for maintaining national independence lay in accommodating Soviet power. Second, the USSR had legitimate defensive interests in Finland. The Soviet Union justifiably sought to ensure that Finland no longer posed an invasion corridor for a third power. If Finland recognized this Soviet interest, the USSR would most likely leave Finland alone. Paasikivi saw Finnish–Russian relations in the nineteenth century (at least before Bobrikov) as a precedent. Third, Paasikivi preferred a flexible rather than a legalistic conduct of relations with the Soviet Union. Paasikivi once upbraided supporters of the constitutionalist approach to the USSR by saying, "the Kremlin is not a court of law." Fourth, foreign policy held priority over domestic policy.

Paasikivi's Cabinet reflected the widespread support for his new foreign policy. This Government consisted of the prewar coalition partners, the Social Democratic Party and the Agrarian League. Paasikivi, a former leader of the National Coalition Party, included the newly legalized Finnish Communist Party (SKP). The inclusion of the SKP constituted both a conciliatory gesture to the USSR and a shrewd move to saddle a revolutionary party with the heavy responsibility of postwar reconstruction. In parliamentary elections in March 1945, the voters gave Paasikivi a mandate. In the election campaign, Paasikivi called on voters to elect "new faces," in other words, people not burdened by the war. In the first parliamentary elections since 1939, 92 of the 200 members of Parliament were new. The Social Democrats remained the largest party, with 50 seats. The Agrarian League won 49 seats. The biggest winner was a new political movement—the Finnish People's Democratic League (SKDL)—also with 49 seats. The Finnish Communist Party created this movement as a vehicle for unifying the Marxist Left, as well as so-called enlightened non-Socialists. The SKDL never succeeded in achieving this goal, but it did attract Marxists who considered the SDP too conservative. The big three parties reconstituted their coalition after the election with Paasikivi as prime minister.[1]

MEETING THE TERMS OF THE PEACE

The first step in building new ties with the USSR lay in meeting the terms of the armistice agreement. In October 1944, the Allied Control Commission established operations in Hotel Torni in Helsinki. The hotel, with its tall tower, gave the commission an imposing physical presence in the heart of Finland's capital. This commission monitored the treaty's implementation. Although the commission included British representatives, it was essentially a Soviet body. This foreshadowed the larger division of Europe into spheres of influence.

Before the commission arrived in Helsinki, Finland already had met some of the most difficult treaty obligations. It was expelling German troops from Lapland. Finnish officials were banning organizations that the Soviets deemed as Fascist or Hitlerite. The best-known of these organizations were the Civil Guards, the Lotta Svärd women's auxiliary, and the Patriotic People's League (IKL). The largest of the banned organizations, the Finnish Association of Brothers-in-Arms (*Aseveljien liitto*), cared for war veterans and their families. Most of these associations were not Fascist, but Moscow saw them as anti-Soviet.[2]

The territories along the eastern border were ceded, and the leased area of Porkkala had been evacuated. Finland's leaders now had to decide on a way of permanently resettling about 10 percent of the population. These refugees, mostly farmers, were resettled on land taken from the state and large, private landowners. Private landowners were compensated through bonds redeemable in 15 years. The postwar inflation ultimately rendered these obligations worthless. In terms of long-term economics, the resettlement program made no sense. Most new farms were too small for viability. In the short term, the resettlement made social and political sense: people had work while the country industrialized. Internal peace prevailed at a time of external danger.[3]

Since the end of the war, Finland officially has renounced all claims to the ceded territories. Nonetheless, regaining the lands has remained a dream among much of the public and political leadership. Since 1963, Finland has leased the Saimaa canal from its eastern neighbor. Running across the postwar border, this waterway links eastern Finland to the Baltic. In 1968, President Urho Kekkonen proposed to Soviet leader Leonid Brezhnev an exchange of eastern Finnish Lapland as well as Finnish diplomatic recognition of the Communist German Democratic Republic (East Germany) for the return of the city of Viipuri (Vyborg) and its environs. In public opinion polls as recent as 2004 and 2005, as many as nearly 40 percent of Finns backed to varying degrees the return of the ceded territories.[4]

On December 17, 1944, the Soviets and Finns signed a formal reparations agreement for $300 million based on the dollar's 1938 value. In the fall of 1945, the Soviets extended the period of payment from six to eight years; in 1948, they reduced the total sum to $226.5 million. In comparative terms, Finland paid more war reparations per capita than Germany was scheduled to pay after World War I. The reparations, paid on time, created the conditions for increased Finnish–Soviet trade.[5]

In signing the armistice agreement, Finland agreed to prosecute war criminals. The Finnish side considered war criminals as soldiers who violated the Geneva Conventions. In the summer of 1945, the Soviets and their Allies expanded this definition to include political leaders responsible for starting aggressive war. The Finns argued that indicting the country's wartime leadership would mean the imposition of an ex post facto law (a law that

criminalizes conduct after the fact). Such laws violated the Finnish constitution as well as Western jurisprudence. The Soviets insisted that the Finns prosecute their wartime leadership or they would do it for them. Paasikivi's
Government decided to keep the matter in Finnish hands as a means of having
control over the verdicts. Between November 1945 and February 1946, a court
consisting of members of Parliament presided over the prosecution of wartime
leaders. At the top of the Soviets' list of indicted persons, wartime president
Risto Ryti received a sentence of 10 years in prison; wartime Prime Minister
Jukka Rangell received 6 years; and Foreign Minister Väinö Tanner and Prime
Minister Edvin Linkomies received 5½ years each. Finland's wartime ambassador to Berlin, T. M. Kivimäki, was sentenced to 5 years, Foreign Minister
Henrik Ramsay received 2½ years, and ministers Antti Kukkonen and Tyko
Reininka 2 years each. None of the convicted served his full sentence. In the
larger context of postwar war crimes prosecutions, Finland was the only defeated country allowed to conduct its own trials. It was the only country to
not condemn the guilty to death. The Soviets primarily sought to punish the
wartime political leadership. Marshal Mannerheim and other military leaders
were spared prosecution. With the trials over, Mannerheim, who had feared
prosecution, left the protection of the presidency. On March 4, 1946, he resigned. Parliament by emergency law made Paasikivi president for the rest of
Mannerheim's term. In 1950 the voters reelected President Paasikivi to a six-
year term.

The last step in fulfilling the terms of the armistice was the negotiation of
a final peace treaty. On February 10, 1947, Finland signed the Peace of Paris
with the Soviet Union, the United Kingdom, and other countries that had
declared war against Finland. The peace treaty reaffirmed the armistice agreement. It added limitations on Finland's military potential, such as a ban on
submarines. After ratification of the peace treaty, the Allied Control Commission left Helsinki.[6]

THE YYA TREATY AND THE CZECHOSLOVAK ROAD

The Peace of Paris sealed the Soviets' war aims with respect to Finland
during World War II. The treaty did not address the rise of a Europe divided
between the Soviet empire and the American-led West. The year 1948 represented a turning point in this polarization. In February, Communists took
power in Czechoslovakia. In June, the Soviet Union started a nearly year-long
blockade of the Western occupation zones of Berlin. On February 22, 1948,
Soviet leader Josef Stalin, in a personal letter to President Paasikivi, proposed
a military alliance. This idea was not new to the Finnish–Soviet postwar
dialogue—President Mannerheim had offered the Soviets a limited joint

defense pact in 1945. In this tense environment, however, Stalin's letter caused great alarm. Was the Soviet proposal just a step toward the Sovietization of Finland? The Soviet proposal came just days before the Czech coup on February 25. As of early 1948, both Finland and Czechoslovakia had many things in common. In both countries, Communists were in Government. A Communist minister of the interior had control of the police. Although Finland was not occupied like Czechoslovakia, all of Helsinki lay within reach of Soviet artillery at Porkkala. According to urban legends of the time, Hertta Kuusinen, daughter of the Terijoki Government's prime minister and head of the Finnish People's Democratic League's parliamentary faction, had called on her countrymen to follow the "Czechoslovak road."

President Paasikivi responded to the Soviet request by stating that neither he nor Parliament could accept a general military alliance. The Finnish president proposed negotiations on a narrower and less-binding arrangement. Negotiations in Moscow started on March 25, 1948. The two sides signed the agreement known as the Treaty of Friendship, Cooperation, and Mutual Assistance (frequently known by its Finnish initials, the YYA Treaty) on April 6, 1948. The treaty basically followed the original Finnish proposal. Finland pledged to defend itself against any attack on Finland or on the USSR through Finland "by Germany or any State allied with the latter." Only in the event of an attack would both sides discuss specific military cooperation. The treaty recognized "Finland's desire to remain outside the conflicting interests of the Great Powers."

Why did the Soviets yield from their original demands and accept the Finnish proposal? The Soviets had more important concerns to attend to in central Europe, specifically in Germany. The agreement addressed the Soviets' primary concern about Finland as a possible corridor for a third-party attack on the USSR. Moreover, recent archival discoveries suggest that the Soviets interpreted the treaty as a military alliance, qualifications notwithstanding. For the Finns, the treaty was proof to the world of the distance between Finland and its eastern neighbor. Finland never belonged to the any of the Soviet alliance systems, such as the Warsaw Pact. Finland and the USSR recognized the treaty as the cornerstone of their bilateral relationship.[7]

The treaty weakened rather than strengthened Communist power. In May 1948, Parliament gave Communist Minister of the Interior Yrjö Leino a vote of nonconfidence for his overtly political leadership of the police. In turn, President Paasikivi fired Leino. In July, the SKDL suffered a devastating defeat in parliamentary elections, losing 12 seats; it would remain in opposition until 1966.

In the final analysis, Finland did not travel the Czechoslovak road for a variety of reasons. First, the Communists did not have a sufficient appetite for power. The rumors and threats of a takeover never reached the level of specific plans and actions. The YYA Treaty, a possible mechanism for the

Soviets to achieve a Communist takeover, seems to have further weakened the Communists' sense of urgency. Second, the Communists themselves admitted that they lacked the qualified and politically reliable personnel needed for a successful coup. Third, the Soviets were reluctant to help Finland's Communists seize power, especially after the signing of the YYA Treaty. The Soviets had found non-Communist politicians who recognized their vital defensive interests in Finland. Moreover, the Soviets lacked confidence in the ability of Finland's Communists to execute a successful coup. Fourth, non-Communist Finland stood united against a Communist takeover. The Social Democrats were key in this struggle. They had stopped the Communists from taking over the trade union movement in the immediate postwar era. The SDP's work helped convince Finns that their future as a society lay in Social Democratic Scandinavia, not people's democratic Eastern Europe.[8]

In the years after 1948, Finland's place in Europe steadily improved. In 1952, Finland paid the last of its war reparations. In the same year, Helsinki hosted the Olympic summer games. In 1955, the Soviets returned Porkkala. In the same year, the Soviets dropped their opposition to Finland's membership in the Nordic Council, a cooperative body for the Scandinavian countries. At the same time, the United States and the USSR ended their long-running disagreement over new members of the United Nations. As a result, Finland was able to join the UN in 1956. These achievements validated Paasikivi's belief that an improvement in relations with the USSR would result in greater freedom with the West. Good Finnish–Soviet relations made it possible for the West to deal with Finland without antagonizing the USSR.

On Finland's Independence Day in 1944, Paasikivi had told his people that Finland had fallen into an abyss "as deep as a ravine." Paasikivi left office in 1956 having led his country out of the ravine to a plain of security and prosperity. Paasikivi, a president who enjoyed trust and respect across party lines, handed the presidency over to one of the most controversial figures of the era, Urho Kekkonen.[9]

KEKKONEN AND FINLANDIZATION

Before winning the presidency in 1956, Urho Kekkonen had already been involved in national politics for some 30 years. He started his political career in the 1920s as a student activist in the Ultra-Finn movement. A competitive athlete in his younger years, Kekkonen led the Finnish Athletics Federation (SUL) 1929–1947. In 1936, he won a seat in Parliament representing the Agrarian League. He served in the Government as minister of justice (1936–1937) and minister of the interior (1937–1939). Already considered a divisive political figure, he was kept on the political sidelines during the war years. Starting in 1942, under the pseudonym Pekka Peitsi, he began to advocate a new policy toward the USSR After the war, he became one of President Paasikivi's trusted ministers, serving as minister of justice 1944–1946 and then as prime minister of five Cabinets during 1950–1956. Despite his impressive credentials, Kekkonen barely won the presidency. A charismatic and gifted politician, his persona attracted as many voters as it repulsed. He was known for his heavy drinking and extramarital affairs. In the third round of voting in the electoral college, Kekkonen, largely with the support of his party and the SKDL, defeated Social Democrat Karl-August Fagerholm by 151 votes to 149.

Kekkonen held the presidency for the next quarter-century. In a democracy, an elected head of state or Government rarely remains in office for so long. Kekkonen benefited from no constitutional limit on terms in office. More important to Kekkonen's longevity was his successful manipulation of relations with Moscow for domestic gain. Kekkonen's presidency has been synonymous with the term Finlandization. During the Cold War, scholars and politicians outside of Finland defined Finlandization as a small power's servile policy toward its larger neighbor. Finland served for many in the West as a warning example to other democracies facing Soviet power. This unfavorable perception of Finnish–Soviet relations made the term taboo in Finland. Finland's public diplomacy during the Cold War consisted of trying to convince the outside world that the USSR did not have extraordinary influence in Finland. Finns frequently complained that the ideological blinders of anti-Communism prevented foreigners from understanding their foreign policy. Since the end of the Cold War, Finns have embraced the term Finlandization to mean, as defined by the historian Jukka Tarkka, "the conduct of domestic policy through foreign policy." Finnish history is replete with examples of politicians seeking to strengthen their position in domestic politics by currying Russian favor. During Kekkonen's presidency, this practice was carried to unprecedented heights.[10]

At three important junctures the political consensus moved from containing to welcoming Soviet power into the domestic sphere. The first of these turning points, the so-called Night Frost Crisis, occurred in the fall of 1958. After parliamentary elections, a new Cabinet was formed under the Social Democrat Karl-August Fagerholm. The new Government raised Soviet ire for two reasons. First, it left in opposition the Finnish People's Democratic League (SKDL), the winner of the elections and largest party in Parliament. Second, the Social Democratic Party recently had returned to its chairmanship Väinö Tanner, a convicted war criminal. The Soviet leadership feared that the new Cabinet would entrench Finland more deeply into the Western camp. The Soviets responded by freezing all forms of diplomatic interchange and subjecting the Fagerholm Government to blistering media attacks. Kekkonen did little to defend the Cabinet that he had appointed. By the end of the year, the Government collapsed. Never before had a Finnish Cabinet resigned under such overt Soviet pressure. After the crisis, Soviet leader Nikita Khrushchev called the crisis in Finnish–Soviet relations a brief "night frost." Kekkonen would work to ensure that such a chill never would occur again during his presidency.

The second and even more controversial affair, the Note Crisis, erupted in October 1961, when the Finnish Government received a Soviet note requesting consultations based on the YYA Treaty. The note reached Kekkonen while he was vacationing in Hawaii at the end of a three-week state visit to Canada and the United States. The note shook the Finns: Accepting the Soviet request could end Finland's claims to neutrality in the Cold War. Refusing the Soviet request could end Finland's independence. Kekkonen completed his North American visit and then traveled to Siberia in November 1961, to discuss the note with Soviet leader Khrushchev. The Soviets ultimately decided to suspend their request for formal consultations. Scholars have long debated the reasons for the Soviet action: Were the Soviets motivated by growing tensions in Europe, or by fears of Kekkonen's possible defeat in the presidential election scheduled for January 1962? The note served several Soviet goals with respect to Finland and Europe. The note signaled concerns about West German rearmament, as well as Danish and Norwegian military cooperation within the Western alliance. The note had its greatest effectiveness on the outcome of the 1962 presidential election. The crisis broke the unity of Kekkonen's opponents, the Social Democrats and the Conservative National Coalition Party in particular, who supported a common candidate, Olavi Honka, for the presidency. During the crisis Honka withdrew his candidacy in the name of national unity, ensuring Kekkonen's reelection by a wide margin. Although Kekkonen received some warning about a possible note, no evidence suggests that he orchestrated the action.[11]

A third turning point came during the late 1960s and early 1970s. At this time, relations between the United States and the Soviet Union entered the era of *détente*, or a relaxation of tensions. The Soviets feared that reduced international tensions could encourage their satellites to drift into the Western sphere or become neutral in the Cold War. This fear fueled the Soviet decision to invade Czechoslovakia in 1968. At the same time, the USSR put Finland on a shorter leash by no longer recognizing Finland as a neutral country. The Soviets thought that they could take advantage of the student radicalism of the time and the Left's growing influence to effect a gradual transition to Communism in Finland. Although the Soviets failed to achieve such a transition, many Finns saw the end of the Prague Spring as a possible foreshadowing of a Soviet occupation of Finland.[12]

Each of these three crises resulted in the conclusion by political parties that supporting Kekkonen was the only way to gain power. The Soviets went to great lengths to keep Kekkonen in power; the president, in turn, played the Moscow card to stay in power. In 1968, when Kekkonen ran for a third term in office, the Social Democrats joined the Agrarian League (now known as the Center Party) and the Finnish People's Democratic League in reelecting Kekkonen to a third term. In 1970, the Conservative National Coalition Party was the last of the country's four major parties to officially support Kekkonen. Conservative support was key in extending Kekkonen's term of office, scheduled to end in 1974. In order to overcome the president's reluctance to campaign for a fourth term, in 1973 Parliament, by a five-sixths majority, extended Kekkonen's term by emergency law until 1978. Supporters of the law argued that the president needed more time to complete important diplomatic initiatives, such as a free trade agreement with the European Community (EC) and a European security conference. Some in the political establishment feared Soviet occupation if Kekkonen left office. Obviously, keeping Kekkonen in power was in the interest of those parties that had tied their political futures to the president.

Parliament passed the emergency law under the assumption that Kekkonen would retire in 1978 at age 78. Instead, he decided to run again for another six-year term. He won 82 percent of the popular vote and 260 out of 301 electoral votes. The political elites demonstrated their determination to keep Kekkonen in office by concealing the president's worsening physical condition from the public. News of the president's resignation in October 1981, shocked, confused, and, in some cases, even frightened Finns. The public largely had been kept in the dark about the serious health problems that had prompted him to relinquish power.

To this day, Finns still debate the Kekkonen era. The balance sheet of Kekkonen's presidency is indeed complicated. One needs to separate the benefits of better relations with the USSR from the domestic political culture. Kekkonen's foreign policy scored three important achievements. First, even though Kekkonen played the Moscow card, he used his influence with Moscow to rebuff many Soviet attempts to draw Finland even closer militarily and politically. The best-known example of this is Kekkonen's rejection of a Soviet proposal for joint Finnish-Soviet military maneuvers in 1978.

Second, Kekkonen's foreign policy made Finland wealthier. Finnish-Soviet trade grew during his presidency. Kekkonen used the diplomatic room to maneuver granted by Moscow to secure Western markets. In 1961, Finland joined the European Free Trade Association (EFTA) as an associate member. EFTA consisted of Finland's Scandinavian neighbors, the United Kingdom, Austria, and Switzerland, that is, many of Finland's trading partners, as an alternative trading bloc to the EC. As an associate member, Finland obtained trade benefits but, in deference to Moscow, refrained from many aspects of EFTA's decision making. In joining EFTA, Finland also promised to keep the Soviets' most-favored-nation status in trade. After Kekkonen received an extension of his term in 1973, Moscow let Finland sign a free trade agreement with the EC. Finland's ability to stay connected to an increasingly integrated Western European economy significantly contributed to its postwar prosperity. The West (not the USSR) bought Finland's most valuable exports—wood and paper products. If Finland had not managed to make these agreements, it might have remained outside of the trade barriers created by Western European integration. The securing of these Western markets, in turn, enhanced Finland's economic independence from the USSR.

Third, Kekkonen's foreign policy made Finland a reliable partner in the easing of East–West tensions. Helsinki became a frequent meeting place for meetings between American and Soviet leaders. In the late 1960s, President Kekkonen proposed a European security conference. In 1975, he hosted the Conference on Security and Cooperation in Europe. At this meeting, leaders of Europe and North America signed the Helsinki Accords that eased Cold War tensions and gave hope to dissidents in Communist Eastern Europe. The conference, Kekkonen's most lasting achievement, became a permanent organization, the Organization for Security and Cooperation in Europe.

One must consider these accomplishments when examining the abuses of the era. The weakening of democratic values did not stem primarily from overwhelming Soviet pressure or even Kekkonen's thirst for power but, rather, from the collaboration of the elites in Finnish society. Particularly in Kekkonen's last decade in office, political leaders sought mandates not so much through elections as through participation in the president's "court" and sauna evenings at the Soviet embassy. Any criticism of the president was, by definition, considered detrimental to national unity and the trust between Finland and the USSR. In addition to the major political parties, other organizations and citizens measured themselves through their loyalty to Moscow. The media became notorious for self-censoring news critical of the Soviet Union. In the 1960s, foreign literature critical of the Soviet Union still appeared in translation in Finland, but in the 1970s Finnish publishers refused to publish such works as Alexander Solzhenitsyn's *The Gulag Archipelago*. In 1983, Finland's Journalists Union called on its members to report on events in keeping with the official foreign policy. Participation in international nongovernmental organizations, such as Greenpeace and Amnesty International, was discouraged; for many, membership in the Finnish-Soviet Friendship Society was a requirement for professional advancement. Moscow demanded or expected little of what Finns did internally in the name of Finnish–Soviet relations. The Moscow card was played for domestic reasons. As the Finnish scholar and journalist Kaarle Nordenstreng, a self-admitted player of the Moscow card, has concluded, "[E]ach sought to raise their Soviet stock and use it as political capital to the best of one's ability." Some commentators today call the period of Finlandization a time of national self-deception. The level of conscious participation in this political culture suggests a time of national opportunism.[13]

MAUNO KOIVISTO AND THE END OF THE PAASIKIVI-KEKKONEN LINE

In the fall of 1981, Finns, some of whom had begun to refer to their country snidely as "Kekkoslovakia," now had to choose a new president. The voters made a clear decision for change by electing Social Democrat Mauno Koivisto to the presidency. Koivisto had enhanced his image with voters as prime minister (1979–1982). During his tenure as prime minister, he dared to defy the president on domestic policy. In the first round of voting, Koivisto won 144 electoral votes, narrowly missing outright election. When the electoral college convened, the candidate of the SKDL, Kalevi Kivistö, asked his electors to support Koivisto. In the first round of voting, Koivisto won with 167 votes. Koivisto's election was historic in many respects. He was Finland's first president from the Left. He was Finland's first president born in an urban area, Turku. He was also Finland's first president of the working class. After serving in World War II, Koivisto had worked as a stevedore in Turku harbor. While working there, he pursued university studies, earning in a doctorate in social sciences in 1956. He then made a career in politics, serving as finance minister (1966–1967, 1972), and prime minister (1968–1970, 1979–1982). When not in Government, he served as director-general of the Bank of Finland from 1968 to 1982.

Despite being a new kind of president, Koivisto pledged to continue the Paasikivi-Kekkonen Line. In Koivisto's first term, the first signs of the end of the Cold War appeared. In 1985, Mikhail Gorbachev became the leader of the Soviet Union. His agenda of reform unleashed movements for democracy and national self-determination throughout the Soviet empire. By the time Koivisto won reelection to a second term in 1988, the future relevance of the Paasikivi-Kekkonen Line stood in serious doubt. Tensions between East and West were decreasing and the Soviet empire had shown the first signs of disintegration. The agitation in the Baltic states for national independence brought the USSR's problems to Finland's doorstep. Leaders of independence movements in the Baltic states were calling on Finland to help them, and many private Finnish organizations did help; official Finland kept its distance until the USSR collapsed. Western Europe was taking steps toward greater political and economic integration. The divide between East and West, within which Finland had created a comfortable and isolated niche, was disappearing. Many Finns greeted these developments with paranoia. With respect to Western Europe, many Finns had nightmares of their country in a European confederation in which the Germans had bought up all of Finland's summer cottages. Looking eastward, some worried that if Gorbachev failed to reform the USSR, Finland would find itself on an even shorter Soviet leash. Others feared the possibility of success. What if Gorbachev opened the Soviet Union's borders? More people lived in the greater Leningrad area than in all of Finland. Would millions of Russians stream into Finland?

On August 19, 1991, Finns woke up to see some of their worst fears realized. Soviet leader Gorbachev had been overthrown in a coup. The farcical putsch lasted only four days, and the Soviet Union dissolved at the end of 1991. In the face of this instability, President Koivisto decided to lead his country toward deeper integration with Western Europe. Much of the country was ready for some kind of change in foreign policy. Finland had reached the end of the Paasikivi-Kekkonen Line.[14]

PARLIAMENTARY POLITICS AND PRESIDENTIAL POWER

After the 1948 parliamentary elections, the cooperation of the big three parties came to an end. For the next 18 years, short-term Governments ruled Finland. The Agrarian League (after 1965 the Center Party) and the Social Democrats continued their prewar red earth cooperation enough to form 7 of the era's 18 Cabinets. In many of the other 11 Cabinets, one party formed a minority Cabinet with the support or toleration of the other. Many factors contributed to a fractious political environment. After years of sacrificing for a nation in danger, the political parties wanted a share of the growing prosperity for their constituents. After the experience with big three cooperation, both the Social Democrats and the Agrarian League/Center Party were reluctant to cooperate with the Finnish People's Democratic League (SKDL). Starting in 1957, the SDP suffered divisions that would last for the next decade. Old grudges and foreign policy concerns kept the Center Party from seeking lasting cooperation with the National Coalition Party as the basis of an alternative, non-Socialist coalition.

In the mid-1960s, the Social Democrats began to heal their divisions, moved to the Left, and looked again to cooperation with the SKDL. In 1966, the Socialist parties won a majority in Parliament. The Center Party joined the Left in a coalition Government led by Social Democrat Rafael Paasio. The big three (now more frequently called popular front coalition) would govern Finland for most of the period between 1966 and 1982. Although the Center Party, the SDP, and SKDL together controlled a large majority in Parliament, their coalition frequently collapsed. The weak link in this coalition was the Finnish People's Democratic League or, more specifically, its primary component, the Finnish Communist Party (SKP). Since the mid-1960s, the Communists split into an orthodox, hard-line, Stalinist minority and a moderate wing. The staying power of this coalition had less to do with voter approval than with the rise of presidential power. During the Cold War, the importance of foreign policy over domestic policy gave Presidents Paasikivi and Kekkonen greater influence in domestic affairs. President Kekkonen used this influence to keep this coalition together despite eroding support for the Center Party and the SKDL, as well as the Conservatives' success at the polls. When the popular front would suffer one of its temporary breakups, Kekkonen often responded by naming a nonpartisan Cabinet of civil servants until the popular front was reconstituted. Consisting mostly of Kekkonen parties, Parliament did not assert itself in the formation of Governments. The constitutional balance of presidential appointment of and parliamentary confidence in Cabinets thus tipped in favor of the president. The strength of presidential power is seen in the case of Prime Minister Mauno Koivisto's refusal to resign in the fall of 1981 at Kekkonen's behest while he had the support of Parliament. Although legally correct, Koivisto's decision to defy the president was seen as a great act of political courage.[15]

Drawing on his experiences as prime minister, Mauno Koivisto assumed the presidency in 1982 with the intention of reducing the president's activity in domestic affairs. He welcomed constitutional reform toward this end. In the meantime, he voluntarily retreated from domestic affairs. Election results and parliamentary politics, rather than presidential preferences, would increasingly determine the basis of governing coalitions. Koivisto let the popular front era end in the fall of 1982, when the SKDL left the Government over proposed increases in defense spending. The SKDL's departure signaled the further decline of the far Left as a political force. The movement that after the war had won a fourth of the electorate declined to about 10 percent by end of the 1980s. The transformation of the Finnish People's Democratic League into the Left-Wing Alliance in 1990 did not stop the slide of the far Left.

After the 1983 parliamentary elections, a red earth coalition was formed. It was augmented by the inclusion of a winner in the election, the Finnish Farmer's Party, a small populist party that had opposed President Kekkonen. This Cabinet, headed by Social Democrat Prime Minister Kalevi Sorsa, was the first to last the entire four-year period between parliamentary elections. The growing durability of this and successive Cabinets weakened the president's ability to interfere in daily politics.

In the 1987 elections, the Conservative National Coalition Party was the big winner with a nine-seat pickup. Now controlling a majority in Parliament, the leaders of the Center Party, the National Coalition Party, and the Swedish People's party sought to implement a pre-election agreement to form a non-Socialist Cabinet. President Koivisto, offended by this challenge to his right to name the Cabinet, instead appointed a new type of coalition: a so-called blue-red coalition with the Conservatives and the Social Democrats as the main partners. For the first time since the early 1960s, Conservatives were represented in Government. New Prime Minister Harri Holkeri became the first head of Government from the National Coalition Party since J. K. Paasikivi. Although in many countries a coalition of Social Democrats and Conservatives might seem incongruous or impossible, the two parties in Finland have many common interests. Both parties draw their support primarily from middle-class wage-earners in southern Finland. The Left–Right divide in Finnish politics is made more complicated by a north–south divide, in which the Center Party and SKDL/Left Wing Alliance have drawn support disproportionately from the north and Social Democrats and Conservatives from the south.

The Holkeri Government aimed to facilitate a "controlled structural change" from an industrial to a postindustrial economy. Instead of leading Finland to new prosperity, the blue-red coalition in its last year in office presided over the worst depression in the history of independent Finland. In 1991, the voters punished both the Conservatives and the Social Democrats and rewarded the Center Party. The election resulted in the creation of a Government coalition under Center Party Chairman Esko Aho, with the Conservatives and Center as the main partners. This non-Socialist Cabinet with majority backing in Parliament had not been seen in Finland since the 1930s.

Many factors facilitated the growth of parliamentary power: the reticence of President Koivisto to intervene in domestic affairs, the conclusion of the Cold War, the narrowing ideological differences between major parties, and a greater desire for consensus over conflict. These changes in political culture would be institutionalized in constitutional reform that would result in a new constitution in the year 2000.

CORPORATISM AND CONSENSUS

Presidents and parties of Cold War Finland accommodated the rise of corporatism. Corporatism consists of cooperation between major economic interest groups, such as labor unions and employer organizations that form public policy for the entire country. Corporatism grew in many Western European democracies during the Cold War era. The first steps toward corporatism in Finland developed during the war years. In January 1940, employers agreed to recognize workers' right to organize. Membership in the unions that belonged to the largest trade union confederation at the time, the Confederation of Finnish Trade Unions (SAK), rose from about 66,000 in 1941 to nearly 300,000 in 1945. Union membership grew in the Cold War period to well over 80 percent of the workforce. By the end of World War II, both labor and employers were dissatisfied with heavy state regulation of wages and prices. Both sides felt that they could get a better deal on wages and prices through collective bargaining. In the spring of 1945, employers' associations accepted the unions' call for collective bargaining agreements that would regulate wages and work conditions in specific industries. After the war, the growth of Communist power in the labor movement encouraged cooperation between employers and the Social Democrats of the labor movement. Since 1968, collective bargaining agreements have been supplemented by comprehensive income policy agreements between labor, employers, and the Government. The first income policy agreement included improvements in wages and work rules between labor and employers. The Government agreed to regulate rents and prices, as well as to index benefits to inflation without a threshold. These income policy agreements have included the employers' associations, labor unions, as well as the major agrarian interest group, Central Union of Agricultural Producers and Forest Owners (MTK).

Over the course of the 1970s and 1980s, the willingness of labor, employers, and the Government to make income policy agreements increased because all sides benefited from them. Employers experienced a decline in days lost to strikes and were able to implement needed structural changes though the income agreement process. Workers experienced an increase in wages, workplace protections, and social benefits. Governments could make policy knowing what the major economic actors planned to do. In broader social terms, income differences between rich and poor narrowed.[16]

SOCIETY AND ECONOMICS

In the Cold War era, Finland's population grew from 3.8 million in 1945 to more than 5 million in 1991. The population grew fastest in the decade after the war, during which Finland experienced, like most European countries, a baby boom. Population growth occurred despite many burdens. Until the 1980s, Finland lost hundreds of thousands of working-age adults who emigrated, mostly to Sweden, in the hope of better economic opportunities. This outward migration reached a height in 1969 and 1970, when almost 80,000 more people left Finland than moved into the country. Another drag on population growth, the decline in the birthrate, had many factors behind it. Women were increasingly entering the workforce, and contraception and abortion became more available. In 1945, Finnish women gave birth to an average of 3.1 children. By 1970, this declined to below 2.1 children, the rate needed to maintain a population. The rate decreased to 1.5 in 1973 but since then has risen to as high as 1.9. This decline in the birthrate, while significant, was actually less than that in many other European countries. Premature death rates did not decrease as steeply as in other European countries. Finns (men, in particular) led the world in deaths due to cardiovascular and respiratory diseases, as well as suicide. Finland's rate of violent crime remained well above the Western European average.[17]

By 1948, Finns had rebuilt their country so that economic productivity as well as most living standards had returned to prewar levels. This reconstruction occurred while paying war reparations to the USSR. Soviet opposition prevented Finland from taking American Marshall Plan aid, a basis for reconstruction elsewhere in Western Europe. Over the course of a generation after 1945, Finland transformed itself from an overwhelmingly agrarian to an industrial and urban society. According to the traditional explanation for Finland's rapid industrialization, the USSR's demand for war reparations in industrial goods rather than forest products forced the country to industrialize. More recent scholarship has questioned the impact of war reparations on industrialization. At the end of World War II, Finland possessed the necessary industrial know-how and infrastructure; only capacity and access to raw materials were lacking. Often overlooked is the wartime industrialization. Industrial products would have to be produced for reconstruction after the war. Nonetheless, the reparations payments built the foundation for significant trade between Finland and the Soviet Union. By the early 1980s, trade with the USSR accounted for more than a fifth of Finland's foreign trade, making the Soviet Union Finland's largest trading partner.[18]

Per Capita Gross Domestic Product Measured in 1990 Dollars (Geary-Khamis Method)

Year	1945	1950	1960	1970	1980	1990	2000
Finland	3,450	4,253	6,230	9,577	12,949	16,866	20,235
Sweden	5,568	6,739	8,688	12,716	14,937	17,695	20,321
(West) Germany	4,514	3,881	7,705	10,839	14,114	15,929	18,596
United Kingdom	7,056	6,939	8,645	10,767	12,931	16,430	19,817
United States	11,709	9,561	11,328	15,030	18,577	23,201	28,129
USSR/Russia	1,913	2,841	3,945	5,575	6,426	6,878	4,351

Source: Angus Maddison, *The World Economy: Historical Statistics* (Paris: Organization for Economic Cooperation and Development, 2003), 50–53, 101.

The industrialization of Finland, like in many other parts of the world, was spurred on by changes in the agrarian sector. As elsewhere in Europe, agriculture experienced improved efficiency in the postwar years. Fewer workers and acres were needed to feed the population. As a result of resettlement after the war, the size of farms actually deceased while they increased in size elsewhere. In 1941, Finland had 136,000 farms of 10 hectares (24.71 acres) or less. By 1959, this number had jumped to 203,000. By the 1960s, people were leaving the land for work in the industrial economy of Finland or neighboring Sweden. In 1945, slightly more than one-quarter of Finland's population lived in urban areas. In 1970, the growth of the urban population reached the 50-percent mark; 30 years later, 80 percent of Finns lived in urban areas. Finland's architects sought to create new urban neighborhoods that included nature and open space. The best-known achievement in this respect was the creation in the 1950s of the "garden city" of Tapiola within the city of Espoo.[19]

By the 1960s, Finland had become one of the world's wealthiest countries. One scholar has suggested that Finland's economic development was more important than its foreign policy in preserving national independence during the Cold War. The ability of a market economy to provide wealth and social security blunted the appeal of Soviet Communism. Nonetheless, Finland had to contend with structural problems, some of which continue to the present day. As already mentioned, unemployment has been a challenge, even in times of high economic growth. Another intractable problem has been uneven regional development. Finland's urbanization not only led to the growth of cities, but also to the shift of population and wealth from the north and east to the south and west. Various regional development schemes have failed to stem this tide.

Until the early 1980s, the postwar Finnish economy was sensitive to inflationary pressures. In the years immediately after the war, inflation was fueled, in part, by the indexing of incomes to the cost of living as a means of buying labor peace. During the years when Finland was paying war reparations, Governments could not afford long strikes. In 1956, the Government's decision to end indexing and price controls provoked a three-week general strike. In the 1970s, Finland (and many other countries) suffered from inflationary pressures due to spikes in oil prices. The most persistent inflationary pressure, however, stemmed from success in foreign trade. Extended periods of favorable trade led to increased prosperity, and Finns bought more imported goods, increasing the trade deficit. Wages went up, often leading to a competitive disadvantage for Finnish firms in the world market. In order to keep the national balance of payments in equilibrium and export industries competitive, the Bank of Finland devalued the mark 14 times in the years 1945–1991. Devaluation made Finnish goods cheaper abroad but imports became more expensive, thus fueling inflation. Jobs were saved at the cost of inflation.[20]

As elsewhere in Scandinavia, much of wealth created by the postwar prosperity was funneled into the creation of a universal welfare state. Such a welfare state provides benefits to its citizens regardless of income. In 1948, the first of the significant universal benefits was the child allowance that gave families a cash payment for every child. Over the next 30 years, benefits ranging from universal health care to free day care to income-indexed unemployment benefits were created. The welfare state was built on the basis of a broad national consensus. The growth of the Left's political power put social benefits at the top of the political agenda. Many on the Right saw the expansion of the welfare state as a way to maintain national unity by reducing social conflict. In creating a welfare state, Finns did not shirk their traditional fiscal discipline and aversion to public debt. Growing national wealth and increased taxation paid for this growth in public-sector spending. Throughout the Cold War, a national consensus maintained that the welfare state represented investments that would provide, as returns, more productive workers and fewer social problems. The sustained economic growth of the era prevented the premise of this consensus from being tested.[21]

The services provided by the welfare state contributed to the growth of gender equality. Women were more easily able to work outside the home as well as have a family. Income disparities between men and women were narrowed by Finland's labor unions in negotiating income policy agreements. In politics, women increased their visibility and influence. In the parliamentary elections of 1991, women won 39 percent of the seats Parliament, a record at the time.[22]

CULTURAL DEVELOPMENTS

The outcome of World War II changed Finns' basic assumptions about their place in the larger world. Before the war, Finns struggled to build a national identity in larger, especially European, contexts. After the war they believed that insulating themselves from the outside world best preserved national identity. The Paasikivi-Kekkonen Line encouraged Finns to think that they stood between East and West, really belonging to neither. Finns spoke of Europe as if their country lay on another continent. While Finland's Scandinavian neighbors were welcoming immigrants, Finland became more homogenous. In 1938, some 21,000 foreigners lived in Finland; by 1955, this number had decreased to just over 7,000. In the early 1980s, Finland ranked second in Europe to hermitically sealed Communist Albania with the fewest foreigners as a percentage of population. In fairness, Finland did not suffer from the labor shortages that made other Western European countries open their doors to immigrants. However, Finland, unlike its Western European neighbors, refused to accept significant numbers of refugees. In the name of good relations, Finland during the Cold War returned the vast majority of defectors from the USSR.[23]

In spite of this insularity, some Finns shared their creativity with a wider world. In industrial design, Tapio Wirkkala (1915–1985) became famous for his work with glass. His most ubiquitous creation is the bottle for Finlandia vodka. The entrepreneur Armi Ratia (1912–1979) made Marimekko an internationally known brand name of clothing by the early 1960s. In literature, Mika Waltari gained an audience outside of Finland. His work, *The Egyptian*, reached the top of the American bestseller list in 1950. His other historical novels, *The Adventurer* and *The Wanderer*, made the American bestseller list in the 1950s as well. Tove Jansson's (1914–2001), Moomin Valley series of children's books was translated into several languages. Väinö Linna, (1920–1992) is widely regarded as the most influential author of post-World War II Finland. His novel about Finnish soldiers during the Continuation War, *The Unknown Soldier* (1954), has gone through more than 40 printings and twice has been made into a motion picture. His other famous work, the trilogy *Here Under the Northern Star* (1959–1962), chronicles in epic sweep the transformation of a Finnish village between the 1880s and 1940s. Both books provoked debate about difficult episodes in Finland's past.[24]

In music, Finns made their presence felt in the world of opera. Einojuhani Rautavaara (1928–) led the movement to remove Finnish opera from its national framework and merge it into larger European trends. Rautavaara produced critically acclaimed works in the twenty-first century with productions such as *Rasputin* (2003). In the 1970s and 1980s, Joonas Kokkonen (1921–1996) and Aulis Sallinen (1935–) became leading opera composers with works such as Kokkonen's *The Last Temptations* (1975) and Sallinen's *The King Goes Forth to France* (1983). Martti Talvela (1935–1989) is regarded as the greatest vocal bass of his generation. During most of the 1970s, he led the Savonlinna Opera Festival as its artistic director, making the festival a significant event in the world of opera. During the 1980s, Karita Mattila (1960–) established herself as a leading soprano.[25]

In sports, Finns became less visible in track and field than they were before World War II, but they became more competitive in other sports. Finns established themselves as a force in nordic skiing, that is, cross-country skiing and ski jumping. Cross-country skier Veikko Hakulinen (1925–2003) won seven medals in three Olympiads (1952, 1956, and 1960). In the Olympic winter games in Sarajevo (1984) and Calgary (1988), Marjo Matikainen (1965–) and Marja-Liisa Kirvesniemi (1955–) distinguished themselves in women's cross-country skiing. Matti Nykänen (1963–) won gold medals in both the Sarajevo and Calgary games. In North America, top Finnish players started making an impact on the National Hockey League, beginning in the 1980s. Jari Kurri (1960–), who played alongside Wayne Gretzky, became in 2001 the first Finn inducted in the Hockey Hall of Fame. At the same time, Finns established themselves in Formula One auto racing. In 1981, Keijo "Keke" Rosberg (1948–) won the Formula One title. Mika Häkkinen (1968–) won the championship twice (1998, 1999). As Finland entered the twenty-first century, Kimi Räikkönen (1979–) was a top contender on the Formula One circuit.[26]

Finland's religious communities faced the challenges of secularization and alienation from organized religion prevalent throughout Europe during the second half of the twentieth century. In addition, Finland's two largest religious communities experienced unique problems of their own. The Orthodox Church survived the war in a precarious state. The territory in Karelia that Finland ceded to the Soviet Union contained most of Finland's prewar Orthodox population and infrastructure. Two-thirds of Finland's Orthodox population had to be settled from the ceded areas. Ninety percent of the Church's real estate remained behind the new border, and the lack of new infrastructure led to decline in church membership. The decline was furthered by a growth of interfaith marriages whose offspring were baptized Lutheran. Its prewar membership of over 80,000 declined to around 52,000 by 1990.[27]

In the Lutheran Church, as in many Christian churches, internal divisions developed over questions of sexuality and the family. The most protracted dispute came over the ordination of women into the clergy. In 1963, the Synod, the Lutheran Church's supreme decision-making body, rejected a proposal for ordination, although it did offer the possibility for women to serve as deacons. In 1976, the Synod by an overwhelming majority, 70 to 33, accepted the ordination of women. However, this majority fell short of the three-quarters needed to change Church policy. In 1984, ordination of women again failed to win the needed majority. In 1986, Finland's Lutheran Church became the last of the Scandinavian Lutheran churches to approve the ordination of women. The first women were ordained to the ministry in March 1988. As of 2003, about one-third of Lutheran pastors in Finland were women.[28] At the end of the Second World War, Finland faced daunting tasks. By the 1980s, Finns often told themselves that they had a "completed" country. The country's place in Europe was secure. Economic prosperity was widespread. Political consensus eliminated serious ideological conflict. It indeed seemed that, as many Finns at the time said, to be born in Finland was to win the lottery of life. The end of the Cold War would end this national smugness.

NOTES

1. Jukka Nevakivi, "Jatkosodasta nykypäivään," in Osmo Jussila, Seppo Hentilä, and Jukka Nevakivi, *Suomen poliittinen historia* (Helsinki: WSOY, 2000), 222–226.

2. Nevakivi, "Jatkosodasta nykypäivään," 216–221; Jouko Vahtola, *Suomen historia jääkaudesta Euroopan unioniin* (Helsinki: WSOY, 2003), 379–380.

3. Lauri Haataja, "Jälleenrakentava Suomi," in *Suomen historian pikkujättiläinen,* ed. Seppo Zetterberg (Porvoo: WSOY, 1987), 750–751; Nevakivi, "Jatkosodasta nykypäivään," 232–234.

4. Jason Lavery, "All of the President's Historians: The Debate over Urho Kekkonen," *Scandinavian Studies* 75, no. 3 (2003): 389; "Yhä harvempi suomalainen mielii Karjalaa takaisin," *Helsingin sanomat,* 21 August 2005.

5. Lauri Haataja, "Jälleenrakentava Suomi," 748; Hannu Heikkilä, *Liittoutuneet ja kysymys Suomen sotakorvauksista 1943–1947,* Suomalaisen Kirjallisuuden Seura: historiallisia tutkimuksia, vol. 121 (Helsinki: Suomalaisen Kirjallisuuden Seura , 1983), 213–217; Riitta Hjerppe, Hyödyttivätkö sotakorvaukset Suomea?" *Helsingin sanomat,* 27 February 1998; Bartell C. Jensen, *The Impact of Reparations on the Post-War Finnish Economy: An Input-Output Study* (Homewood, IL: R. D. Irwin, 1966), 109; Charles P. Kindleberger, "Suomen sotakorvaukset," *Kansantaloudellinen Aikakauskirja* 83, no. 2 (1987): 149–159.

6. Nevakivi, "Jatkosodasta nykypäivään," 218–219.

7. Finnish Ministry for Foreign Affairs, *Treaty of Friendship, Co-operation and Mutual Assistance between Finland and the USSR,* (Helsinki, Finnish Ministry for Foreign Affairs, 1983); Nevakivi, "Jatkosodasta nykypäivään, 235–241; Vahtola, *Suomen historia,* 388.

8. Mikko Majander, *Pohjoismaa vai kansandemokratia? Sosiaalidemokraatit,kommunistit ja Suomen kansainvälinen asema 1944–51* (Helsinki: Suomalaisen Kirjallisuuden Seura, 2005).

9. Haataja, "Jälleenrakentava Suomi," 836–840.

10. Lavery, "All of the President's Historians, 378–388; Timo Vihavainen, *Kansakunta rähmällään: Suomettumisen lyhyt historia* (Helsinki: Otava, 1991), 1–76.

11. Lavery, "All of the President's Historians," 381–383.

12. Kimmo Rentola, *Vallankumouksen aave: Vasemmisto, Beljakov ja Kekkonen 1970* (Keuruu: Otava, 2005); Raimo Väyrynen, "Paineet kasvavat: Suomi ja Neuvostoliitto 1968–1973," *Historiallinen Aikakauskirja* 102, no. 1 (2004): 5–22.

13. Kaarle Nordenstreng, "Me, media ja menneisyydenhallinta," in *Entäs kun tulee se yhdestoista? Suomettumisen uusin historia*, ed. Johan Bäckman (Helsinki: WSOY, 2001), 218–230; Vahtola, *Suomen historia*, 476, Pentti Virrankoski, *Suomen historia*, vol. 2 (Helsinki: Suomalaisen Kirjallisuuden Seura, 2001), 964–965.

14. Jason Lavery, "Finland at Eighty: A More Confident and Open Nation," *Scandinavian Review* 85, no. 2 (1997): 13–19; Timo Vihavainen, "Hyvinvointi-Suomi," in *Suomen historian pikkujättiläinen*, ed. Seppo Zetterberg (Porvoo: WSOY, 1987), 900–906.

15. Jukka Nevakivi, "Jatkosodasta nykypäivään," 253–282; Vihavainen, "Hyvinvointi-Suomi," 847–869.

16. Tapio Bergholm, "A Short History of SAK," http://www.sak.fi/englanti/whatissak.shtml/02?10048 (accessed 15 January 2006); Jukka Pekkarinen and Juhana Vartiainen, *Suomen talouspolitiikan pitkä linja* (Porvoo: WSOY, 1995), 275; Juhana Vartiainen, "Suomalainen korporatismi ja talouspolitiikan vastuu," *Kansantaloudellinen Aikakauskirja* 87, no. 4 (1991): 491.

17. "Kokonaishedelmällisyysluku 1900–2001," web site of Statistics Finland, http://www.tilastokeskus.fi/tk/he/tasaarvo_hedelmallisyys.xls (accessed 16 January 2006); Markku Lehti, *Henkirikoskatsaus* (Helsinki: Oikeusministeriö, 2005) web site, http://www.om.fi/optula/uploads/t9qsbsx3velm.pdf (accessed 16 January 2006); "Maahan ja maastamuuttaneet vuosina 1945–2004," web site of Finnish Institute of Migration, http://www.migrationinstitute.fi/db/stat/fin/art.php?artid = 4 (accessed 16 January 2006); *Statistical Yearbook for Finland 1971* (Helsinki: Tilastokeskus, 1972), 5; Vahtola, *Suomen historia*, 409–410, Tapani Valkonen, "The Mystery of the Premature Mortality of Finnish Men," in *Small States in Comparative Perspective: Essays for Erik Allardt*, ed. Risto Alapuro et al. (Oslo: Norwegian University Press, 1985), 229–241.

18. Haataja, "Jälleenrakentava Suomi," 748; Heikkilä, *Liitoutuneet*, 213–217; Hjerppe, "Hyödyttivätkö sotakorvaukset Suomea;" Jensen, *Reparations*, 109; Kindleberger, "Suomen sotakorvaukset," 149–159.

19. Kirsi Saarikangas, "Metsän reunalla: Suomen rakentaminen 1900-luvulla," in *Suomen kulttuurihistoria*, vol. 4, ed. Laura Kolbe et al. (Helsinki: Tammi, 2004), 22–61; *Statistical Yearbook for Finland 1960* (Helsinki: Tilastokeskus, 1961), 5; *Statistical Yearbook for Finland 1971* (Helsinki: Tilastokeskus, 1970), 5; *Statistical Yearbook for Finland 2004* (Helsinki: Tilastokeskus, 2005), 71; Vahtola, *Suomen historia*, 418.

20. Martti Häikiö, "Uusia lähteitä ja moralisointia Kekkosesta," *Historiallinen aikakauskirja* 98, no. 3 (2000): 282–284; Pekkarinen and Vartiainen, *Pitkä linja*, 43–45, 245; Eero Tuomainen, *Inflaatio: Syyt, vaikutukset, torjunta* (Helsinki: Taloudellinen suunnittelukeskus, 1975), 82–84; Virrankoski, *Suomen historia*, vol. 2, 982.

21. Eric S. Einhorn and John Logue, *Modern Welfare States: Scandinavian Politics and Policy in the Global Age*, 2nd ed. (Westport, CT: Praeger, 2003), 259–261; Pekka Haatainen, "Suomalaisen hyvinvointivaltion kehitys," in *Sosiaalipolitiikka 2017: Näkökulmia suomalaisen yhteiskunnan kehitykseen ja tulevaisuuteen*, ed. Olavi Riihinen (Juva: WSOY, 1993), 46–47, Pauli Kettunen, "The Nordic

Welfare State in Finland," *Scandinavian Journal of History* 26, no. 3 (2001): 225–247; Pekkarinen and Vartiainen, *Pitkä linja*, 44; Pertti Pesonen and Olavi Riihinen, *Dynamic Finland: The Political System and the Welfare State* (Helsinki: Suomalaisen Kirjallisuuden Seura, 2002), 214.

22. Maria Lähteenmäki, "Vastuu kasvattaa itsenäisyyttä: Naisliikke Suomea rakentamassa," in *Suomalainen nainen*, ed. Satu Apo et al. (Helsinki: Otava, 1999), 39–53; "Naiset Suomen eduskunnassa," http://www.eduskunta.fi/fakta/opas/tiedotus/naised.htm (accessed 10 January 2006).

23. Arto Astikainen, "Suomi jätti palauttamatta joka neljännen neuvostoloikkarin," *Helsingin sanomat*, 15 September 2005; Lavery, "Finland at Eighty," 13–19; *Statistical Yearbook for Finland 1955* (Helsinki: Tilastokeskus, 1956), 45.

24. Owen Witesman, "Life after Waltari: The Current State and Influence of Finnish-Language Literature in English Translation," paper presented at the annual conference of the Society for the Advancement of Scandinavian Study, Redondo Beach, CA, April, 2004.

25. Pekka Hako, "Finnish Opera," web site Virtual Finland, http://virtual.finland.fi/netcomm/news/showarticle.asp?intNWSAID = 26983 (accessed 16 January 2006); Pekka Hako, "Suomalainen oopperamusiikki," web site of Finnish Music Information Center, http://www.fimic.fi/fimic/fimic.nsf/mainframe?readform&18A3B01E4D18013542256C46003DA4A8 (accessed 15 January 2006).

26. "Formula One World Champions," web site of All Formula One Info http://www.allf1.info/champs.php (accessed 16 January 2006); web site of International Olympic Committee, http://www.olympic.org/uk/athletes/index_uk.asp (accessed 16 January 2006).

27. Tapani Kärkkäinen, *Kirkon historia: Ortodoksin käsikirja* (Jyväskylä: Gummerus, 1999), 202–206.

28. Simo Heininen and Markku Heikkilä, *Suomen kirkkohistoria* (Helsinki: Edita, 1996), 238, 244–245; Mikko Juva, "Suomen kirkko seksuaalisen muutoksen vuosina 1944–2002," in Martti Nissinen and Liisa Tuovinen, *Synti vai siunaus? Homoseksuaalit. kirkko ja yhteiskunta* (Helsinki: Kirjapaja, 2003), 23–32.

9

European Finland in a Globalizing World

With the end of the Cold War, Finland again had to redefine its place in Europe—and the world. The twin processes of European integration and globalization have had and will continue to have their greatest impacts on foreign policy, economics, and national identity.

FINLAND LOOKS WEST

The reduction in East–West tensions during the 1980s allowed Finland to remove some of the Soviet filter in its relations with the West. In 1986, it became a full member of the European Free Trade Association (EFTA). In 1989, Finland became the last European democracy at the time to join the Council of Europe. This organization, founded in 1949, has worked to advance the causes of human rights, rule of law, and democracy on the European continent.

At the same time, Finland had to confront new developments in the decades-long process of Western European economic integration. The members of the European Community (EC) moved toward greater economic cooperation in the face of the growing economic integration of North America, as well as competition from Japan. In 1987, the EC approved the Single European Act, which mandated by 1992 the creation of an internal market based on the so-called four freedoms: the free flow of labor, capital, goods, and services between member states. The community proposed the creation of a similar internal market or European Economic Area (EEA) with the countries of the European Free Trade Association (EFTA). In the fall of 1991, Finland joined other EFTA and EC member states in signing the EEA agreement. In doing so, Finland protected its access to vital foreign markets.

Meanwhile, Europe underwent revolutionary change. In the fall of 1989, the Berlin Wall fell. A year later, Germany was reunified. Germany's European partners, and the Germans themselves, saw an opportunity and need to further the process of European integration. In December 1991, the EC's member states signed the Maastricht Treaty, which changed the community's name to the European Union (EU), revised the Union's decision-making processes, and placed the Union on a path of cooperation beyond the purely economic. The treaty's most significant aspect was an outline for the implementation of a single currency for the EU. The end of the Cold War forced not only Finland but also other Western European neutrals to reconsider their place in Europe. In October 1990, the Swedish government announced that it would seek membership in the EC. Sweden's decision to integrate, along with the continuing disintegration of the USSR, threatened to marginalize Finland in the new Europe.

In January 1992, just days after the collapse of the USSR, President Mauno Koivisto proposed Finnish membership in the EU. After approval by the Cabinet and Parliament, Finland opened accession talks with the EU. After completion of the treaty in 1994, 56.9 percent of voters in a consultative referendum approved membership. Parliament then approved membership, 152 to 45. On January 1, 1995, Finland, along with Sweden and Austria, joined the EU. In 1999, Finland joined 10 other EU countries in adopting the single European currency, the euro.[1]

Many supporters of EU membership shared opponents' concerns about Finland's future in the EU. Many feared that Germans and other foreigners would buy up the country. Agriculture, heavily protected and subsidized, would face greater competition from other European countries. How much national sovereignty would be lost to the EU? Would Finns have to sacrifice their welfare state? Despite these fears, a majority of Finns embraced EU membership for three reasons. First, membership could open new markets for a depressed economy. Second, and more important, membership could enhance national security with respect to a chaotic Russia without joining a military alliance. Third, many Finns saw membership in the EU as a way of leaving Moscow's political sphere of influence once and for all.

As Finland observed its first decade of EU membership in 2005, opinion polls suggested a widespread belief that membership secured the country's place in Europe after the Cold War. Finns, like most other EU citizens, supported the union as an economic community but balked at deeper political integration. Economists concluded that EU membership made the country more prosperous. In 2004, Finns paid about 10 percent less for food in real terms than they had in 1994. Increased competition in general lowered consumer prices, which still remained some of Europe's highest. Moreover, none of the major fears about membership came to pass. Increased competition and more restrictive EU rules concerning subsidies did reduce the number of farms from 115,000 to 71,000 during the years 1995–2004. Although significant, the reduction was much less than predicted. Instead of stoking fears about Germans buying up the country, the mass media started wondering why Finland did not attract more foreign investors.[2]

After joining the EU, national discussion turned to possible membership in the North Atlantic Treaty Organization (NATO). Supporters for joining the military alliance pointed to a future possible Russian threat. The EU, in spite of many proposals, was not able to offer its members any firm collective security guarantees. As Finland entered the twenty-first century, the vast majority of Finns remained opposed to NATO membership. This opposition grew with the outbreak of the Iraq War in 2003. In the fall of 2004, the Government, in a formal statement before Parliament, maintained the post-Cold War policy of "military non-alignment" or, as some put it, "neutrality that follows the times." The Government expressed the hope that the EU could provide greater security guarantees for its members; it left open the possibility of NATO membership at a later time.[3]

Since the end of the Cold War, Finland's foreign policy leadership has placed relations with its eastern neighbor on a back burner. Russia's reduced importance on the world stage after the Cold War does not change its status as Finland's largest neighbor. To paraphrase President Paasikivi, Russia might not always be a great power in the world, but it is always one to Finland. For their part, Finnish businesses have seized the opportunities offered by an economically reviving Russia. By 2004, trade between the two countries rose to the level of the late 1980s. In 2004, Russia was Finland's third-largest export market, after Sweden and Germany.[4]

FROM CONSUMPTION PARTY TO DEPRESSION

During much of the twentieth century, Finland had experienced some of the highest levels of economic growth in Europe. As it entered the 1990s, Finland faced an economic depression not seen among industrialized nations since the depression of the 1930s. The depression of the 1990s had its roots in the previous decade, when Finland's leaders, following a worldwide trend, decided to deregulate the economy and allow for greater market forces. In Finland, the deregulation focused on the banking industry. One of Western Europe's most heavily regulated banking sectors was deregulated almost overnight. Banks reacted by loaning out money hand over fist; people took the loans in similar measure. The strong Finnish mark encouraged private individuals, businesses, as well as the state and municipalities to take advantage of the removal of restrictions on taking out cheaper loans in foreign currency. The new debt fueled a growth in consumer spending known as "the consumption party." Spending was further encouraged by a strong mark that kept imports inexpensive and made foreign travel outright profitable. Debt turned the wheel of the so-called casino economy, a speculative boom in stocks and real estate.

Economists have concluded that deregulation was necessary and intrinsically beneficial, but its sequence and timing were disastrous. The reforms should have been implemented during an economic downturn when the economy could have more easily absorbed the new stimulus. Instead, the reforms brought an already overheated economy to a meltdown. In the second half of 1989, the bubbles in real estate and stock prices burst. At the same time, Finland's overvalued currency and rising labor costs were rendering its exports less competitive in world markets. In 1991, Finland lost one of its largest trading partners with the collapse of the USSR

In this gloomy economic situation, people and businesses rushed to pay off their debts by selling their assets. This further depressed the value of real estate and stocks. Individuals could not get out from under their debts. Heavily indebted businesses began to eliminate jobs. Traditionally, Finns responded to such economic downturns by devaluing the mark as a means of making Finnish export goods more competitive abroad, thus spurring employment at home. Devaluation in this situation threatened to depress the economy even more, since so much debt was in foreign currency. A devalued mark would make paying off debts in foreign currency even more expensive. Furthermore, the political consensus since the early 1980s had backed the idea of a strong mark as a means of creating economic stability. With unemployment increasing to record levels, the Aho Government in November 1991, reversed course and approved a 12-percent devaluation. In September of the next year, the mark was allowed to float freely on world markets without intervention from the Bank of Finland, resulting in a de facto devaluation.

As predicted, devaluation precipitated more bankruptcies. The wave of business failures even engulfed the Finnish Communist Party, whose speculative investments in the 1980s were as risky as those of any capitalist. Unemployment rose to almost 20 percent by 1994 and Finland's gross domestic product dropped by 14 percent in the years 1990–93. Bread lines spread throughout the country. The increase in unemployment, in turn, saddled the state with even more social costs. The rising social costs pushed the Government to cut spending and raise taxes—measures that further depressed the economy. The most dangerous aspect of the depression was the so-called banking crisis. During the 1980s, banks had shoveled out loans to people who could not repay them. Two drastic measures prevented widespread bank failures. First, the government initiated a massive taxpayer-funded bailout of the banks, savingsbanks in particular, that cost Finns more per person than had war reparations after World War II. Second, banks merged with each other, resulting in fewer but stronger banks.

The depression altered Finns' images of themselves. The archetypal Finn who paid back his debts was replaced by one whose arrears were resolved through repossession. Schoolteachers no longer taught their pupils that to be born in Finland was to win the lottery of life. Instead, they had to confront the depression's impact on children. The depression challenged two important institutions: the welfare state and corporatism. Both were founded on the assumption of steady, continuous economic growth and high levels of employment. Both proved to be stronger than their founding assumptions. In terms of the welfare state, the level of many cash benefits did decline, but many services, such as the availability of free day care for children, actually improved during the depression. With respect to Finland's corporatist decision-making processes, the Aho Government sought to weaken the scope of national incomes policy agreements by devolving collective bargaining to local workplaces as a way of making the labor market more flexible, thus hopefully enhancing employment. Organized labor as well as some employers' organizations successfully opposed these moves. The Aho Government's more-targeted attacks on organized labor proved equally as ineffective. Finns' unwillingness to sacrifice these institutions in order to end the depression was expressed in the victory of the Social Democrats at the polls in the 1995 parliamentary election. For the following eight years, Social Democratic Chair Paavo Lipponen led a so-called rainbow coalition consisting of his party, the Left-Wing Alliance, the Swedish People's Party, and the National Coalition Party. This coalition, which included Conservatives and one-time Communists, reflected Finns' desire to continue the politics of consensus. This coalition followed a largely successful policy of pursuing economic growth within the contexts of the welfare state and corporatism.

By the end of 1993, the measures taken to aid the export industries began to have positive effects. The rise in unemployment ended in 1994, although domestic consumption remained sluggish into 1996. Scholars are still scrutinizing the lasting impact of the depression. The depression seems to have had the most lasting effects on the labor market. A decade after the depression's end, unemployment still remained around 10 percent, and most of these unemployed people will probably never again have regular jobs because of age and lack of skills. For many Finns, work after the depression became less lucrative and less secure. Employers became reluctant to grant long-term employment to workers. Lower-paying jobs from the service sector replaced many of the high-paying industrial jobs lost in the depression. Since the depression, a new, small group of workers has developed—the working poor. A large segment of the working poor consists of families with children, threatening to create a permanent underclass. A decade after the depression, the number of Finns below the poverty line continued to grow, even though this number is small by international standards. Much of this employment insecurity might have occurred without the depression, as a result of a more competitive world economy. Moreover, not all Finnish workers were worse off after the depression. Many benefited from the rise of a new information economy.[5]

RISE OF AN INFORMATION ECONOMY

In a report by the respected World Economic Forum in 2003, Finland was identified as the world leader in the use of information and communications technologies. Several long-term developments contributed to the quick rise of Finland's information economy. First and foremost is Finland's consistent national investment in education, as well as significant public and private investment in research and development. Instead of cutting money for research during the depression, the Aho Government increased spending with the goal of creating an information-based economy. Second, Finns traditionally have embraced new technologies, especially those that make labor more efficient. Third, the state has provided basic infrastructure for private enterprise to flourish. For example, Finland joined its Scandinavian neighbors in the creation of a common public platform for mobile telephones. Launched in the early 1980s, the so-called NMT platform provided a much larger market for pioneers in wireless technologies to develop and sell products. Fourth, state deregulation of the telecommunications industry in the 1980s enhanced the spirit of entrepreneurship that already existed among the country's privately owned community telephone companies.

All four factors explain not only the rise of Finland as an information economy, but also the rise of its most visible enterprise, Nokia. This industrial conglomerate had ventures in telecommunications as well as computers since the 1960s. However, as late as the early 1980s, Nokia was better known as a producer of rubber boots and toilet paper. Nokia first established itself as a mobile telephone producer with the creation of the NMT zone. In 1984, Nokia moved beyond Scandinavia by making an agreement with the American Tandy Corporation to sell its products in Tandy's Radio Shack stores. In the depression of the 1990s, Nokia's enterprises were either sold off or went into bankruptcy, with the exception of its small mobile telephone division. Nokia emerged from the depression as one of the world's leading mobile telephone producers. In the year 2000, it was ranked fifth among the world's 10 most valuable brand names—the only non-American company on the list.[6]

CONSTITUTIONAL AND POLITICAL CHANGES

In the year 2000, Finns completed almost two decades of constitutional reform that focused on the powers of the presidency or, more specifically, the growth of presidential power during the Kekkonen era. During the 1980s, many concluded that direct popular election would make the presidency less imperial and more accountable. The presidential election of 1988 included an element of direct election. Voters received two ballots: one for an elector and the other for a presidential candidate. If a candidate failed to receive at least 50 percent of the popular vote, then the electoral college would convene to select the president. In that election, President Koivisto won 47.9 percent of the popular vote, barely missing outright election. In the Electoral College, Koivisto won on the first ballot.

For the election of 1994, the Electoral College was abolished, leaving only a direct election. If no candidate won more than 50 percent of the vote in the first round, the top two finishers would face each other in a runoff. Furthermore, any new officeholder would be limited to serving two consecutive six-year terms. The voters selected two finalists for the 1994 runoff who were, in their own ways, atypical. The winner of the first round was the Social Democratic candidate Martti Ahtisaari. A career diplomat, he achieved national visibility as the United Nations' high commissioner for Namibia during that country's transition to independence from South Africa in the years 1989–1990. Many voters wanting change saw his potential weakness—a lack of experience in Finnish politics—as a plus. His opponent, Minister of Defense Elisabeth Rehn, was a minority in three respects. She was a woman, she came from a small party, and she was of Finland's Swedish-speaking minority. In the two weeks before the runoff election, Ahtisaari built on his first-round lead to defeat Rehn.

In many respects, the 2000 presidential election represented a break with the past. For the first time in decades, there was no clear favorite. President Ahtisaari refused to participate in the Social Democratic Party's new primary election process for selecting its candidate, thus leaving him unable to seek a second term. For the first time in Finland's history, the majority of the candidates, four of seven, were women. Three women ranked among the top four finishers in the first round; in the second round, the first-round winner, Foreign Minister Tarja Halonen of the Social Democratic Party, faced Center Party Chair and former Prime Minister Esko Aho.

In many ways, Tarja Halonen fit the traditional presidential mold. Her Social Democratic Party had produced the two previous presidents; she is a lawyer by training—a background shared by 5 of Finland's previous 10 presidents; and she gained significant foreign policy experience in her tenure as foreign minister in 1995–2000. In other respects, Ms. Halonen's candidacy openly challenged Finns' conception of the president as the representative of the country's official values. She is a professed atheist in an overwhelmingly Lutheran country, and she was a single mother (after winning the presidency, she did marry her longtime partner, Dr. Pentti Arajärvi). As a practicing lawyer, she challenged the limits of tolerance by working for greater legal protections for sexual minorities.

In the second round of voting, Esko Aho tried to convince voters that Tarja Halonen did not share their "family values." Ms. Halonen overcame voters' prejudices in three ways. First, she benefited from her position as foreign minister at a time when Finland held the presidency of the EU for the first time. Her skill in helping guide Finnish foreign policy at this critical juncture created for her a more positive image among voters. Second, she only started campaigning seriously in January, after the end of the Finnish EU presidency. Her late start gave her the benefit of being a fresh face at the end of a long election campaign. Third, she had the undivided support of the main organizations of the Finnish Left: the Social Democratic Party, the Left-Wing Alliance, and the Central Organization of Finnish Trade Unions (SAK). In the decisive second round, many women who never had voted for the Left identified with Ms. Halonen, who, like most Finnish women, was a working woman herself. When the votes were counted on February 6, 2000, Tarja Halonen won with 51.6 percent of the vote versus Esko Aho's 48.6 percent. Finland had elected its first woman president. [7]

On the same day that President Halonen took office, March 1, 2000, a new constitution came into force. It shifted power away from the president to the Cabinet and Parliament. The new constitution charged the president to conduct foreign policy "in cooperation with the Government." The Cabinet was specifically responsible for maintaining Finland's relations with the EU. The president is still expected by the constitution and the public to serve as Finland's leader in relations with powers outside of the EU—the United States and Russia, in particular. Parliament, not the president, would select the prime minister, whom the president would then appoint. The president could dissolve Parliament and call new elections only at the request of the prime minister. The new constitution also took away the president's right to name the high officials of the Evangelical Lutheran and Orthodox Churches. [8]

With the constitutional powers of the presidency reduced, President Halonen strove to maintain the role of the president as an advocate for national concerns and values that transcend daily political fights. With relations with the EU largely in the hands of the Cabinet, the president focused her activity in foreign policy on larger issues concerning globalization. For example, President Halonen organized a formal dialogue between developed and developing countries known as the Helsinki Process. Voters were satisfied enough with President Halonen that they elected her to a second term in 2006.

The first test of the new constitution came after the parliamentary election of March 2003. The Center Party, in opposition since 1995, became the largest party in Parliament. In accordance with Parliament's decision, President Halonen named Center Party Chair Anneli Jäätteenmäki prime minister. She formed a coalition Cabinet consisting of her Center Party, the Social

Democratic Party, and the Swedish People's Party. The return of the old red earth coalition was historic in that Jäätteenmäki became Finland's first female prime minister. Half of the Cabinet's ministers were women. However, scandal rendered the achievement short-lived. During the election campaign, Anneli Jäätteenmäki claimed that the incumbent Prime Minister Paavo Lipponen was planning to bring Finland into the American-led coalition that invaded Iraq in March 2003. She based her claim on a distorted reading of classified—and illegally obtained—documents. This scandal forced Jäätteenmäki to resign in June 2003, after less than two months in office. Parliament approved a new red earth Cabinet in which fellow Center Party member Matti Vanhanen replaced Jäätteenmäki as prime minister and party chair.

Parties in Finland's Parliament 2005

Party	Seats
Center Party	55
Social Democratic Party	53
National Coalition Party	41
Left-Wing Alliance	19
The Greens	14
Swedish People's Party	9
Christian Democrats (former Christian League)	6
True Finns Party	3

POPULATION TRENDS

By 2005, Finland had a population of about 5.2 million inhabitants. The main demographic trends of the Cold War era continued into the twenty-first century. The trend that has raised the most concern is the low birthrate. In the year 2000, about 56,000 children were born in Finland, the lowest number since the famine year of 1868, when Finland had only 1.7 million people. The reluctance to have children has provoked a broad national discussion. Some claim that the welfare state gives little incentive and support for having children, although support for families since the 1970s has steadily increased. Others point to the increasing demands and insecurities of the workplace that make it difficult for men and women to harmonize work and family. Commentators criticize the growth of a so-called singles culture in which young people put off having a family in order to pursue self-fulfillment. If current trends continue, Finland's population will begin to decline around the year 2020. For Finland and other industrialized countries, the decline in the birthrate is not just a statistical curiosity, but also an economic and social challenge. A decreasing number of working-age Finns must support a growing elderly population. As of the year 2000, a Finnish worker supported less than one Finn; in the year 2050, if current demographic trends hold, one worker will have to support two Finns.[9]

While the birthrate has remained sluggish, immigration has been allowed to grow. At the beginning of the twenty-first century, immigration accounted for almost 40 percent of Finland's population growth. Several factors have opened up a steady stream of immigrants. Finland's leaders have bowed to both domestic and foreign pressure to accept more refugees. The collapse of the Soviet Union in 1991 opened the eastern border. Many arrivals from the former USSR have skills desired by Finland's employers. The country's entrance into the EU in 1995 eased movement into Finland by citizens of other EU member states. The first significant loosening in Finland's traditionally restrictive immigration policy came in 1990, when President Mauno Koivisto allowed Finns from the Russian region of Ingria to move to Finland in a way that bypassed most immigration barriers. In part, the president wanted to make restitution to the Ingrian Finns who migrated to Finland during World War II, and then were returned to the Soviet Union after the war. Also, President Koivisto, like many Finns at the time, erroneously feared the imminent onset of a labor shortage.

Since 1990, the largest group of immigrants has come from the territory of the former Soviet Union, largely Russia and Estonia. In eastern Finland, many communities have experienced small-scale immigration from Russia because Finns are moving out of those communities for the south and west. Another visible immigrant group consists of refugees from Somalia, who fled that country's civil war in the early 1990s. Immigrants are most visible in Helsinki, where in some eastern sections of the city one-fifth of the residents are immigrants. In spite of the fourfold growth in the immigrant community in the 1990s, Finland in 2005 had one of the smallest immigrant communities in Europe (less than two percent of the population). Even though continued immigration will help maintain population levels, immigration does not immediately create a larger workforce of people to pay for those who need public support. Many immigrants themselves need state support for several years in the form of education and job training. The ability of immigrants to contribute will ultimately depend on the willingness of Finns to integrate them into society. The country's political leadership has so far proven reluctant to openly address both justifiable concerns and primitive xenophobia concerning the growth of immigration.[10]

CULTURE: FROM IDENTITY TO DIFFERENCE

Since the end of the Cold War, Finland has moved from a culture that maintained a narrow national identity toward one that has begun to tolerate greater diversity. A newer, broader definition of Finnishness was exemplified by the selection in 1996 of Lola Odusoga as Miss Finland. The winner of this beauty contest is expected to present a proper image of Finland abroad. Ms. Odusoga, a native-born Finn, is black. While Finland has been making room for new minority groups, historical minority groups have worked to redefine themselves. In the 1990s, Parliament granted the Sámi greater cultural autonomy; the Sámi still seek greater control over the land and natural resources in areas where they predominate. The Swedish-speaking minority has been involved in an internal debate over how to protect the future of the Swedish language in Finland. Some argue for the maintenance of the country's Swedish-language institutions, especially schools, only for those who consider themselves Swedish-speaking. Others advocate opening these institutions to the growing number of those who come from bilingual environments. Neither vision offers an easy solution to the problem of a steady overall decline in the population of Swedish speakers.[11]

The basic unit of Finnish society—the family—has developed more diverse culturally and legally accepted forms. Many of these forms, such as nonmarried couples, single parents, and blended families, had taken root starting in the 1970s. By the beginning of the twenty-first century, about a third of all children were born outside of marriage (half of all first-born children). The growing acceptance of non-nuclear families was seen in the election of Tarja Halonen to the presidency in the year 2000. In 2001, Parliament approved a law allowing same-sex couples to register their unions, giving them most of the same rights as heterosexual couples.[12]

New legislation supported religious diversity as well. In 2003, a new law on religious freedom bound the state to support freedom of worship. The state may give financial support to smaller religious communities, such as Roman Catholicism and Islam, which have grown due to immigration. Children of smaller religious communities have received greater opportunities for religious instruction at school. The new law also made it easier for people to leave the Evangelical Lutheran Church; as a result, the number of Finns belonging to the Church declined by almost 25,000 in the years 2000–2004. Still, as of 2005 more than 80 percent of Finns belonged to the Evangelical Lutheran Church. Since 1990, the Orthodox Church in Finland has experienced a small but steady increase in membership, largely as a result of immigration from Russia. It has been estimated that by the year 2030 the number of Orthodox will double to more than 100,000, largely as a result of immigration.[13]

FINLAND IN A GLOBALIZING WORLD

Like other nation-states, Finland entered the twenty-first century facing the challenge of globalization, the process of worldwide economic integration. In many respects, Finland is well-equipped to benefit from a globalizing world. Finland's economic prosperity has long rested on the ability of its domestic industries to compete in a world economy. Finland is already a leader in information technology, which drives much of the process of globalization. The education system provides Finns with knowledge and skills needed for a global economy, and Finland offers the world a stable, transparent, and efficient environment in which to conduct business of all kinds. In 2004, the organization Transparency International ranked Finland as the world's least-corrupt country. Although Finns pay very high rates of taxes, Finland's public sector has been ranked among the world's most efficient.[14]

In spite of these advantages, Finns have approached globalization with a great deal of concern. These concerns relate to globalization's impact on foreign policy, economics, and national identity. Globalization has unleashed a national discussion on the future scope of Finland's foreign policy. So-called realists argue that Finland's security is best ensured by keeping the country's traditional focus on relations with the world's major powers, especially the EU and the United States. Others argue that Finland needs to recognize that threats to security and prosperity no longer lie solely within a Euro-Atlantic context. These so-called globalists want Finland to play a stronger role in such issues as Third World poverty and human rights throughout the world. The debate between the realists and globalists ignores the fact that independent Finland's foreign policy always has had a global, or at least a multilateral, dimension. Since the 1950s, Finland has sent tens of thousands of troops to United Nations peacekeeping operations throughout the world. Finns traditionally have given strong support to international organizations ranging from the League of Nations to the Nordic Council.[15]

The second challenge of globalization lies in the economic realm. Even though Finland's economy has been ranked one of the most competitive in the world, it has not been immune to the loss of jobs, particularly in manufacturing, to lower-wage countries. A high level of employment is key to maintaining the welfare state and, by extension, the values of equality such a state upholds. The debate over employment has revealed that there is no one silver bullet for keeping jobs in Finland. Possibly effective partial solutions include a continued investment in education and research, a reform of tax policies, raising retirement ages, and moving younger people more quickly from school to work.

Globalization challenges notions of national identity. Since the nineteenth century, Finnish national identity has been based on the existence of a separate, if not independent, Finnish state. Globalization weakens the state's power over its borders and citizens, creating what the literary scholar Andrew Nestingen calls "inscrutable intrusions." The new threats to a society are external and strange, rather than internal and familiar. Finns have experienced these types of intrusions not only in daily life, but also in one of their favorite summertime activities—reading detective stories. Until the 1990s, the criminals in Finnish detective stories came out of the cracks from within society—

people whom the state, or more exactly, the welfare state, failed. Since then, the criminals increasingly have come out of a context created by globalization. Among the most popular detective novels in recent years is the Maria Kallio series by Leena Lehtolainen. In the installment published in 2005, the police-woman Maria Kallio faces collusion between a Russian-led prostitution ring in Helsinki and its clientele of influential Finnish men who seek to anchor Finland more firmly with the West. Even in an age of globalization, Finland is still a borderland between East and West.[16]

Globalization will contribute to the upward trend in immigration. Even though tolerance of immigrants has increased in recent years, xenophobia is still widespread. In a poll published by the Finnish Business Forum (EVA) in 2004, almost one-third of Finns believed that "the growing immigration of foreigners will result in a disadvantageous racial mixing and a weakening of [Finnish] national strength."[17] In facing the growth in immigration, Finland's people can draw on their long history of assimilating foreigners. As a borderland between East and West, outsiders have been coming to Finland since prehistoric times. Immigrant groups, whether the prehistoric Battle-Axe people or nineteenth-century Russian merchants, have enriched Finland and assimilated into the dominant culture. Finland is so homogenous because it has been able to assimilate diverse immigrant populations. There is no reason to doubt that, if offered the opportunity, Finland's new immigrants will become new Finns.

A FUTURE PRIVILEGE?

In spite of recent and future challenges, according to a 2004 survey more than 70 percent of Finns believed that it was a privilege to be a Finn. Considering Finland's level of prosperity, cultural achievements, and social peace, it is hard to argue against the majority opinion. The transformation of a borderland between East and West into a place of privilege has required hard work, realism, flexibility, and a bit of good fortune. Finns will need to possess these qualities in order to remain privileged in the future.[18]

NOTES

1. Viisi hallitusta on luotsannut Suomen EU-politiikka," *Helsingin sanomat*, 26 May 2005.

2. Heikki Arola, "Tutkijoiden mielestä EU-jäsenyys on ollut suomalaisille halpaa," *Helsingin sanomat*, 21 April 2005; "Finland mest gymnat av EU," *Hufvudstadsbladet*, 18 February 2005; Jukka Perttu and Merja Ojansuu, "Euroopan Unioni sai tavarat kulkemaan aiempaa vapaammin rajojen yli," *Helsingin*

sanomat, 9 January 2005; Minna Pölkki, "EU mullisti maatalouden," *Helsingin sanomat,* 2 January 2005.

3. "Valtioneuvoston turvallisuus- ja puolustuspoliittinen selonteko 24.9.2004," web site of Finland's Cabinet, http://www.valtioneuvosto.fi/vn/liston/base.lsp?r = 88857&k = fi&old = 40738 (accessed 10 February 2006).

4. *Statistical Yearbook for Finland 2005* (Helsinki: Statistics Finland, 2005), 253.

5. Tapio Bergholm, "A Short History of SAK," http://www.sak.fi/englanti/whatissak.shtml/02?10048 (accessed 15 January 2006); Katja Forssén, *Children, Families and the Welfare State: Studies on the Outcomes of the Finnish Family* (Helsinki: Stakes, 1998); Jason Lavery, "Finland at Eighty: A More Confident and Open Nation," *Scandinavian Review* 85, no. 2 (1997): 13–19; Matti Heikkilä and Hannu Uusitalo, "Jälkikirjoitus: Yhteenvetoa ja tulkintoja," in *Leikkausten hinta,* ed. Matti Heikkilä and Hannu Uusitalo (Helsinki: Stakes, 1997), 214–219; "Suomen köyhyysraja EU-keskiarvoa korkeampi," *Helsingin sanomat,* 30 November 2002; Pentti Virrankoski, *Suomen historia,* vol. 2 (Helsinki: Suomalaisen Kirjallisuuden Seura, 2001), 992–993.

6. Martti Häikiö, *Nokia OYJ:n historia,* vol. 2 (Heksinki: Edita 2001), 85–100; vol. 3 (Helsinki: Edita, 2001), 14–18, 116–117, 193; Antti Kasvio, "Tietoyhteiskunta—Edesmennyt idea?" in *Virtuaalihalleja ja hyvinvointia: Suomalaisen tietoyhteiskunnan kehitys ja haasteet,* ed. Antti Kasvio et al., Sitran raportteja 50 (Helsinki: Edita, 2005), 9–28; Hannu Salmi, "Tietoyhteiskunta ja talouskriisi: Informaatioteknkologinen näkökulma 1990-luvun lamaan," in *Lamakirja näkökulmia 1990-luvun talouskiriisiin ja sen historiallisiin konteksteihin,* ed. Helena Blomberg, Matti Hannikainen, and Pauli Kettunen (Turku: Kirja Aurora 2002), 321–340; Hannu Sokala, *Maailma taskussa: Kuinka matkapuhelimella tienattiin ja tuhottiin miljardeja* (Helsinki: Tammi, 2002), 10–17; Dan Steinbock, *Finland's Wireless Valley: From Industrial Policies Toward Cluster Strategies,* Publications of the Ministry of Transport and Communications no. 36 (Helsinki, 2000), 39–45; World Economic Forum's Information Technology Report 2002–03, http://www.weforum.org/pdf/Global_Competitiveness_Reports/Reports/GITR_2002_2003/Contents.pdf (accessed 10 February 2006).

7. Jason Lavery, "Finland at the Polls: A New President, a New Presidency," *Scandinavian Review* 87, no. 3 (2000): 4–9.

8. The Constitution of Finland, web site of Finnish Ministry of Justice, http://www.om.fi/74.htm (accessed 6 January 2006); Ilkka Saraviitta, *Valtiosääntöoikeuden perusteet* (Helsinki: Lakimiesliiton kustannus, 2001), 5; Virrankoski, *Suomen historia,* vol. 2, 974–975.

9. Minna Järvinen, *Hyvä yhteiskunta kaikenikäisille: Valtioneuvoston tulevaisuusselonteko väestöpolitiikasta ja ikärakenteen muutokseen varautumisesta* (Helsinki: Valtioneuvosto, 2005); Hannele Tulonen, "Lapsiperheiden määrä pudonnut vuoden 1950 tasolle," *Helsingin sanomat,* 20 January 2004; Tapio Wallenius, *Tuomitut vähenemään? Suomalaiset ja lisääntymisen vaikea taito,* (Helsinki: Elinkeinoelämän Valtuuskunta, 2003).

10. "Itä-Suomi venäläistyy hitaasti mutta varmasti," *Helsingin sanomat,* 7 March 2005; "Ulkomaalaistaustaiset keskittyvät edelleen Itä- ja Koillis-Helsinkiin; *Helsingin sanomat,* 12 April 2005; Riikka Venäläinen, "Maahan-

muuttajien osuus väestönkasvusta yli 40 prosenttia," *Helsingin sanomat*, 12 April 2005.

11. Lehtola, "Kaukaa olla seitsentähden," in *Suomen kulttuurihistoria*, vol. 4, ed. Laura Kolbe et al. (Helsinki: Tammi, 2004), 354.

12. "Lapseton avopari yhä yleisempi," *Helsingin sanomat*, 20 January 2004; "Syrjintäkielto 1995," *Helsingin sanomat*, 28 November 2004, "Yli puolet esikoisista syntyy avioliiton lkopuolella," *Helsingin sanomat*, 8 July 2003.

13. Kimmo Kääriäinen, Maarit Hytönen, Kati Niemelä, Kari Salonen, *Kirkko muutosten keskella: Suomen evankelis-luterilainen kirkko vuosina 2000–2003* (Tampere: Kirkon tutkimuskeskus, 2003), 26–28; Jussi Rytkönen, "Nuoret—kirkon ja ay-liikkeen viimeinen taisto?" *Kotimaa*, 18 November 2005; *Statistical Yearbook for Finland 2005*, 72.

14. Paula Tiihonen, "Good Governance and Corruption in Finland," in *The History of Corruption in Central Government*, ed. Seppo Tiihonen (Amsterdam: IOS Press, 2003), 99–118; Transparency International's Corruption Perceptions Index 2004, http://www.transparency.org/policy_and_research/surveys_indices/cpi/2004 (accessed 10 February 2006); Riitta Vainio, "Julkinen hallinto ja palvelut Suomessa mailman kärkitasoa," *Helsingin sanomat*, 14 May 2005.

15. Juha Siltala, "Idealismi ja realismi globalisaation aikakaudella," *Historiallinen Aikakauskirja* 103, no. 2 (2005): 129–134.

16. Andrew Nestingen "The Novel, the Police, and the Welfare State," paper read at the annual conference of the Society for the Advancement of Scandinavian Study, Redondo Beach, CA, April, 2004.

17. Kai Torvi and Pentti Kiljunen, *Onnellisuuden vaikea yhtälö: EVA:n kansallinen arvo- ja asennetutkimus 2005* (Helsinki: Elinkeinoelämän Valtuuskunta, 2005), 45.

18. Torvi and Kiljunen, *Onnellisuuden vaikea yhtälö*, 68.

Notable People in the History of Finland

The following entries do not represent an index of all persons mentioned in this book. The people cited here largely are drawn from a national opinion poll conducted in 2004 by the Finnish Broadcasting Company (YLE) concerning the 100 greatest Finns. Additional short biographies of notable Finns are available on the Finnish Foreign Ministry's Virtual Finland web site, http://virtual.finland.fi/, as well as the web site of the National Biography of Finland, http://www.kansallisbiografia.fi/english.html.

Aalto, Alvar (1898–1976). One of the world's leading functionalist architects. He first established his international reputation by designing the Finnish pavilions at the World's Fairs of 1937 and 1939. After World War II, Aalto drew plans for buildings all over the world, ranging from Finlandia Hall in Helsinki to the library of Mount Angel Abbey in the United States.

Agricola, Mikael (c. 1510–1557). Bishop, church reformer, and "Father of the Finnish language." Agricola championed the goal of sixteenth-century Protestant reformers to make the Word of God accessible in the language of the common people. Agricola published a spelling primer for the Finnish language in 1543. In the following year, he produced a prayer book in Finnish. In 1548, he published what is widely considered as the origin of Finnish as a written language—a translation of the New Testament in Finnish. Agricola's achievements helped him to win promotion in 1550 to the post of bishop of Turku, Finland's most prestigious religious office.

Ahtisaari, Martti (1937–). Diplomat and president. As a diplomat, Ahtisaari served his country as Finland's ambassador to Tanzania (1973–1977) and the Foreign Ministry's state secretary (1991–1994). In the 1980s, he served the United Nations as deputy secretary-general (1982–1983, 1987–1989). Ahtisaari served the UN in several capacities concerning the status of Namibia. In 1989–1990, he served as the UN's special representative in charge of guiding Namibian independence from South Africa. In 1994, running as the Social Democratic Party's candidate, he was elected president of the republic. During his presidency, Ahtisaari led Finland into the European Union and worked to end the conflict in the former Yugoslavia. Since leaving office in 2000, Ahtisaari's Crisis Management Initiative has worked to end conflicts such as the war in the Indonesian province of Aceh. For his work, Ahtisaari has been nominated for the Nobel Peace Prize several times.

Canth, Minna (1844–1897). Finland's first renowned Finnish-language female author. A writer of short stories, novellas and plays, Canth focused on the sufferings of ordinary people. She was a leader in turning Finland's literature away from national idealism toward realism and social criticism.

Chydenius, Anders (1729–1803). Enlightenment thinker and clergyman. His book, *The National Gain* (1765), argues for full economic freedom for all individuals. Chydenius's advocacy of free trade preceded Adam Smith's by more than a decade. In addition to advocating economic freedom, Chydenius was a noted proponent of freedom of the press.

Donner, Jörn (1933–). Author, moviemaker, public intellectual, and politician. Donner's vast literary works range from journalistic reports to novels. As a moviemaker, Donner made movies in both Sweden and Finland. In 1983, he won an Oscar for producing Ingmar Bergman's *Fanny and Alexander*. In politics, Donner served as a member of Parliament 1987–1995 and member of the European Parliament 1996–1999. In 1995–1996, he served as Finland's consul-general in Los Angeles, CA.

Engel, Carl Ludvig (1778–1840). The architect of Helsinki. Russian officials deputed Engel to design the central buildings of Helsinki, Finland's capital as of 1812. Engel's most significant achievement was Senate Square and the buildings that surrounded it: the Palace of the Council of State, formerly known as the Senate Building, (main wing completed in 1822), Helsinki's Lutheran Cathedral (completed in 1852), and the main building of Helsinki University (completed in 1832).

Gallen-Kallela, Akseli (1865–1931). Finland's most famous painter. Like many artists of his time, Gallen-Kallela lived in and painted both the world of agrarian Finland and urban Europe. In the course of his studies in Paris in the 1880s, Gallen-Kallela decided to break with realism and dedicate himself to portraying *The Kalevala*, Finland's national epic poem. Finland's National Gallery, the Ateneum, holds most of Gallen-Kallela's *Kalevala* paintings.

Halonen, Tarja (1943–). Finland's first female president. Before her election to the presidency in 2000, Halonen served as a member of Parliament, minister of justice, and foreign minister. As president, Halonen has focused on the challenges of globalization and economic disparities between rich and poor nations.

Jakobson, Max (1923–). Journalist, diplomat, and historian. During the 1940s and 1950s, Jakobson first became known to Finns as a newspaper correspondent based in London. Entering the foreign service in the 1950s, Jakobson rose to become Finland's ambassador to the United Nations 1965–1972. In 1971, he was a finalist for the position of U.N. secretary-general, a position won by Austria's Kurt Waldheim. Jakobson then served as Finland's ambassador to Sweden 1972–1974. He then helped found the Finnish Business and Policy Forum (EVA), an influential research and lobbying organization. A prolific author, his best-known work is *The Diplomacy of the Winter War.*

Jansson, Tove (1914–2001). Author and painter. Jansson is most famous for her Moomin series of children's books. During the 1990s, the Moomin book characters were commercialized in the form of toys, clothing, and even a Moomin park in the town of Naantali.

Juslenius, Daniel (1676–1752). Clergyman and scholar. Founder of the Fennophilia movement that sought to raise awareness and appreciation of Finland's cultural uniqueness. Using folklore as his source, Juslenius wrote fanciful histories that described Finland as having a highly developed ancient culture of its own that was destroyed with the arrival of the Swedes. Juslenius's work helped propel a search for that great prehistoric Finnish civilization that would last into the twenty-first century.

Kaurismäki, Aki (1957–). Finland's leading moviemaker. During the 1980s and 1990s, Kaurismäki developed a cult following outside of Finland for movies such as *Leningrad Cowboys Go America* (1989) and *La Vie de Bohème* (1992). In 2002, a film that he directed, *A Man Without a Past* (2002), won the Grand Prix du Jury at the Cannes Film Festival. Most of Kaurismäki's films focus on the underclasses and marginal groups of Finnish society.

Kekkonen, Urho (1900–1986). Finland's longest-serving president (1956–1981). During his term as head of state, Kekkonen continued the policy of his predecessor, J. K. Paasikivi, of building close ties with the Soviet Union. His ability to play the so-called Moscow card was a major factor behind his longevity in office. Believing that Finland's place in the Cold War divide allowed the country to make a special contribution to world peace, he initiated an effort that culminated in the Congress on Security and Cooperation in Europe in 1975. The Helsinki Accords that came from this meeting aided the causes of peace and human rights long after the end of the Cold War. In domestic affairs, Kekkonen focused on economic growth as well as on greater consensus among political parties and interest groups.

Kivi, Aleksis (1834–1872). The father of modern Finnish-language literature. In 1860, Kivi won a competition sponsored by the Finnish Literature Society for his first play, *Kullervo*, inspired by the tragic figure of *The Kalevala* of the same name. Over the course of a decade, Kivi produced several other plays and poetry. His crowning achievement was his novel, *The Seven Brothers*, published in 1870, the first Finnish-language novel.

Lalli (?–c. 1160). Peasant and rebel. According to legend, around the year 1156 Lalli killed Bishop Henry of Uppsala, who was working to establish the Catholic Church in Finland. Contrary to popular understanding, Lalli was not a pagan but, most likely, a Christian. He seemingly acted out of anger about new church taxes. Lalli has been understood in popular memory as a symbol of Finnish national self-determination. Bishop Henry later was made Finland's patron saint.

Leino, Eino (1878–1926). Author. Leino is recognized as the most versatile writer in Finnish, writing in almost every genre from poetry to literary criticism. He also translated many classics of foreign literature into Finnish.

Leskinen, Juhani "Juice" (1950–). Singer and writer. Leskinen is recognized as the father of Finnish rock music. His songs examine the Finnish condition.

Linna, Väinö (1920–1992). Author. Linna is widely regarded as the most influential author of post–World War II Finland. His novel about Finnish soldiers during the Continuation War (1941–1944), *The Unknown Soldier* (1954), has been through more than 40 printings and has twice been made into a motion picture. His other famous work, the trilogy *Here Under the Northern Star* (1959–1962), chronicles in epic sweep the transformation of a Finnish village between the 1880s and 1940s.

Lönnrot, Elias (1802–1884). A central figure in the growth of Finnish-language literature in the nineteenth century. While working a physician in the northeastern city of Kajaani, Lönnrot crossed Finland's eastern border to collect poems from the Finnish-speaking people of Russian Karelia. In 1835, Lönnrot published his collected poems as *The Kalevala*, an epic poem. A second, more extensive edition, was published in 1849. Lönnrot compiled this epic poem, with its heroic characters, as a work of literature. The widespread celebration of this work stemmed from the belief that *The Kalevala* was a work of history—a chronicle of Finland's lost past. *The Kalevala* sparked an interest in finding the country's roots from the east. Lönnrot also published the first Finnish-Swedish Dictionary (1866–1880) as well as books containing medical and practical advice.

Mannerheim, Carl Gustav Emil (1867–1951). Widely regarded as the greatest single figure of Finland's twentieth century. As a young man, Mannerheim left Finland to join the Imperial Russian army. Rising to the rank of lieutenant general, he was relieved of his duties by the Russian provisional government in September 1917. In January, 1918, he was given command of the Finnish Government's troops, which he led during the Civil War of 1918. In December 1918, he was made acting head of state until July, 1919. In 1920, he founded the Mannerheim League for Child Welfare. In the following year, he became chair of the Finnish Red Cross, a position he would hold until 1951. In 1931, Mannerheim returned to affairs of state by becoming chair of the National Defense Council. In 1933, he was promoted to the rank of marshal. During the years of World War II, he was commander in chief of Finland's armed forces. Parliament by emergency law elected him president in August, 1944. He resigned the presidency in March, 1946, and spent most of his remaining years in Switzerland.

Nurmi, Paavo (1897–1973). Long-distance runner. Nurmi, the "Flying Finn," won nine gold medals in three Olympiads (1920, 1924, 1928), tying him with three others for the most Olympic gold medals won. Only five other athletes have surpassed his total of twelve medals. His Olympic career was cut short before the 1932 games over charges of professionalism.

Ollila, Jorma (1950–). Chair and CEO of Nokia. Educated at the London School of Economics, Ollila joined Nokia in 1985. In 1990, he became head of its mobile phone division. He led Nokia's transformation from a national industrial conglomerate to a world leader in wireless communication.

Paasikivi, J. K. (Juho Kusti) (1870–1956). Political leader. A member of the Government that led Finland to independence in 1917, Paasikivi served as prime minister during May–November, 1918. Returning to politics in 1934, Paasikivi was elected chair of the conservative National Coalition Party. During his chairmanship, he ended the party's flirtation with authoritarianism. He then represented Finland as its ambassador to Stockholm 1936–1939. In the fall of 1939, Paasikivi led Finland's negotiations with the Soviet Union. During the Winter War, he served as minister without portfolio. After the war, he served as Finland's ambassador to the Soviet Union until the outbreak of the Continuation War in June 1941. In November 1944, he became prime minister. In March 1946, Parliament made him president by emergency law. As postwar prime minister and president, Paasikivi based his foreign policy on the acceptance of Soviet defensive interests in respect to Finland.

Porthan, Henrik Gabriel (1739–1804). Scholar and advocate of Finnish language and culture. Porthan believed that the people of Finland, regardless of language, shared a common country and a common past.

Ratia, Armi (1913–1979). Founder of the Marimekko company in the 1950s. By the 1960s, the company had established itself as a brand name internationally. Its horizontal- and vertical-striped shirts are Marimekko's best-known products.

Runeberg, Johan Ludvig (1804–1877). Finland's national poet. Runeberg's poetry painted the landscape of agrarian Finland. His collection of poems, *The Tales of Ensign Stål* (1848), is an account of the war of 1808–1809. The first of these poems, "Our Land," provided the lyrics for Finland's national anthem of the same name. He wrote his poems in Swedish and is recognized as one of (if not the) greatest poets to write in Swedish. Runeberg's contribution to the national cause lay in giving Finland's people a sense of uniqueness.

Ruotsalainen, Paavo (1777–1852). A leader of the religious revival movements of the early nineteenth century. An uneducated peasant, Ruotsalainen attracted a substantial following through his sermons. Persecuted by civil and religious authorities, Ruotsalainen was recognized decades after his death as not only having made a contribution to religious reform, but also to the creation of Finnish nationhood and civil society.

Schjerfbeck, Helene (1862–1946). Finland's most famous female painter. She lived most of her life as recluse, battling a variety of illnesses. Her best-known painting, *Toipilas* (*A Recovering Girl*) (1888), reflects the mysteriousness and challenges of Schjerfbeck's life. There is general consensus that, with some exceptions, Schjerbeck's paintings defy easy placement into any genre.

Sibelius, Jean (1865–1957). Finland's best-known composer. His music embodies a mixture of Finnish national and wider European influences. His first significant composition, the symphony *Kullervo* (1892), is recognized as the beginning of Finnish classical music. By 1924, he composed seven more symphonies.

Sillanpää, F. E. (Frans Eemil) (1888–1964). Author and Nobel laureate. Sillanpää's works depict the realities of agrarian Finland. In the fall of 1939, as Finland was threatened with attack from the Soviet Union, Sillanpää was awarded the Nobel Prize for literature.

Snellman, J. V. (Johan Vilhelm) (1806–1881). The most influential figure of Finland's nineteenth century. Snellman's Finnish-language nationalist ideology consisted of three basic elements. First, Finnish, not Swedish, was the true language of the nation. Second, the Finnish nation could survive only through an improvement of Finnish-language education. Third, the survival of the Finnish nation depended upon loyalty to the Russian emperor. Snellman pursued his agenda as a student, journalist, and professor. In 1863, Snellman's work influenced Emperor Alexander II to promulgate the Language Rescript in 1863. This decree placed the Finnish language on a path to becoming co-official with Swedish. His influence with the emperor was similarly significant in the creation of Finland's own currency, the mark, in 1860.

Sprengtporten, Göran Magnus (1740–1819). Aristocrat and military officer. In the late 1770s and early 1780s, Sprengtporten developed plans for an independent Finland with close ties to Russia. He believed that cutting Finland's ties with Sweden would ensure peace for Finland. Spengtporten entered Russian service in 1786, where he shared his plans with the Russian court. A lone wolf in the eighteenth century, Sprengtporten's plans and influence at the Russian court would make him a key person when Russia annexed Finland in the early eighteenth century.

Ståhlberg, K. J. (Kaarlo Juho) (1865–1952). Jurist and president. The chief author of independent Finland's first constitution in 1919, Ståhlberg was elected Finland's first president in the same year. He refused to serve a second term in 1925 in the hope that a change of power would advance Finland's new republican institutions.

Svinhufvud, Pehr Evind (1861–1944). Political leader. He established himself as a public figure through his leadership of the constitutionalist movement against Russian attempts to weaken Finland's autonomy before independence. In 1907, he became the first speaker of Finland's new single-chamber Parliament. In November 1917, Svinhufvud became head of the Government that would lead Finland to independence in December 1917. After the civil war in May 1918, Svinhufvud was made temporary head of state until December 1918. In 1930, he became prime minister. In the next year, he won the presidency as a candidate of the conservative National Coalition Party. A defender of law and order during his entire public career, Svinhufvud used his authority to peacefully disrupt the radical Right-wing Mäntsälä rebellion in 1932. He lost the presidency in his reelection bid in 1937.

Talvela, Martti (1935–1989). Opera singer. Talvela is regarded as the greatest bass of his generation. During the 1960s, he quickly rose into the elite of opera singers. His large six-foot, seven-inch frame made him an imposing figure on the stage. During most of the 1970s, he led the Savonlinna Opera Festival as its artistic director, making the festival a significant event in the world of opera. At the time of his death in 1989, he was leading the Finnish National Opera in a process of renewal.

Tanner, Väinö (1881–1966). Political leader and leader of Finland's cooperative movement. Tanner served as director of the Elanto cooperative from

1915 to 1946, during which time Elanto became one of Finland's largest businesses and one of the world's largest cooperatives. As a politician, he served as a member of Parliament intermittently 1907–1962. He served as prime minister in 1926 and in various ministerial posts 1937–1944. Recognized as the leading figure of the Social Democratic Party in the period between the world wars, Tanner formally served as party chair 1919–1926. After World War II, Tanner, along with seven other wartime leaders, was sentenced in 1946 to 5½ years in prison for war crimes. He was released from prison in 1948 and served again as Social Democratic Party leader during 1957–1963.

Topelius, Zachris (Sakari) (1818–1898). Writer, journalist, historian. Writing in Swedish, Topelius, like J. L. Runeberg, helped create a Finnish nationalism based on the country's history, natural environment, and culture rather than language. As a professor of history at Helsinki University from 1854 to 1878, he had a major impact on Finns' understanding of their history well into the twentieth century.

Valkeapää, Nils-Aslak (1943–2001). Writer, visual artist, and musician. Born in Enontekiö in Finnish Lapland, Valkeapää is the most influential Sámi cultural figure of modern times. Valkeapää's literary work has been translated into Finnish, Swedish, and Norwegian.

Virén, Lasse (1949–). Long-distance runner. Virén won both the 10,0000-meter and 5,000-meter runs in the Munich Olympics of 1972. He won the former event and broke the world record despite falling down during the race. His gold medals were the first won by a Finnish runner since 1936. Virén defended his Olympic titles at the Montreal games in 1976.

Virtanen, A. I. (Artturi Ilmari) (1895–1973). Biochemist and Nobel laureate. In the 1920s, Virtanen made an important contribution to food science by increasing the shelf life of butter through raising the pH level from 6.0 to 6.5. Virtanen's research then focused on the preservation of fodder for livestock, dairy cows in particular. His method improved the storage of green fodder (important during long winters) by adding diluted hydrochloric or sulfuric acid to newly stored grain. For the creation of this new AIV-fodder, Virtanen was awarded the Nobel Prize in chemistry in 1945.

Waltari, Mika (1908–1979). Author. Waltari's body of work encompasses virtually the entire range of literary genres, from detective stories to poetry. His short stories take place in urban, cosmopolitan settings. His historical novels embrace times and civilizations far away from twentieth-century Finland. Of these, the best-known is *The Egyptian* (1945).

Wirkkala, Tapio (1915–1985). A pioneer in Finnish applied art and industrial design. His work contributed to the reputation of Finnish design after

World War II. He is best-known as a designer of glassware for the Iitala glass works. His most ubiquitous creation is the bottle for Finlandia vodka.

Wright, Georg Henrik von (1916–2003). Finland's most internationally renowned philosopher. He served as a professor at both Cambridge University and Cornell University, as well as serving in various academic positions in Finland. He achieved fame through his research on logic, philosophy of science, and action theory. After his retirement from academia in the late 1970s, he became more noted for his work in cultural criticism and environmental advocacy.

Ylppö, Arvo (1887–1992). Professor of pediatric medicine. As a result of his scholarship and public advocacy for preventive prenatal and newborn care, Finland's infant mortality rate went from one of Europe's highest to one of the world's lowest. The centerpiece of Ylppö's program of preventive care was the creation of a network of maternity clinics.

Selected Bibliographical Essay

The body of publications in English and other major languages on Finland's history suffers from two major weaknesses. First, much of the scholarship is dated. Recent advances in interpretation and knowledge have only sporadically been published in English. Second, there is simply no detailed foreign-language scholarship for many important questions, such as the settlement of Finland and Finland's experience inside of the Swedish realm. In these cases, one must glean what one can from one of the general overview and specialized surveys listed below.

General Overviews

Eino Jutikkala and Kauko Pirinen, *A History of Finland* (Porvoo: WSOY, 1998) is the most comprehensive of the more recent general overviews. Originally written in the 1960s, it since has been updated regularly. A thinner, essay-style overview of Finland's past is Matti Klinge, *A Brief History of Finland*, 3rd ed. (Helsinki: Otava, 2000). Max Engman and David Kirby, eds., *Finland: People, Nation, State* (London: Hurst, 1989) is a collection of essays that, as a whole, makes a comprehensive overview. Seppo Zetterberg's *Finland Since 1917* (Helsinki: Otava, 1991) presents a short and meaty survey from independence until the end of the Cold War. Martti Häikiö, *A Brief History of Modern Finland* (Helsinki: Lahti Research and Training Centre, 1992) concentrates solely on the post-World War II era. D. G. Kirby's *Finland in the Twentieth Century* (London: Hurst, 1979) still offers interesting insights. One must keep in mind, though, that his treatment of the twentieth century ends in 1979.

Specialized Surveys

In addition to these general overviews, several works survey Finland's past with a narrower thematic focus. A thorough survey of Finland's modern political development is Osmo Jussila, Seppo Hentilä, and Jukka Nevakivi, *From Grand Duchy to Modern State: A Political History of Finland Since 1809.* (Carbondale, IL: Southern Illinois University Press, 2000). For economic history, turn to Riitta Hjerppe, *The Finnish Economy 1860–1985: Growth and Structural Change* (Helsinki: Valtion painatuskeskus, 1989). H. M. Tillotson, *Finland in Peace and War* (Norwich, UK: Michael Russell, 1996) gives a military history of independent Finland. Major turning points in women's history are covered in Merja Manninen and Päivi Setälä, eds., *The Lady with the Bow: The Story of Finnish Women* (Helsinki: Otava, 1990). For those interested in art and architecture, there is J. M. Richards, *800 Years of Finnish Architecture* (London: David & Charles, 1978) and Markku Valkonen, *Finnish Art over the Centuries* (Helsinki: Otava, 1999). Finland's literary past is surveyed in Kai Laitinen, *The Literature of Finland—An Outline* (Helsinki: Otava, 1994). The same topic is covered in even greater detail by George C. Schoolfield, ed., *A History of Finland's Literature* (Lincoln, NE: University of Nebraska Press, 1998). The history of law in Finland is addressed in a series of essays edited by Jaakko Uotila, *The Finnish Legal System* (Helsinki: Finnish Lawyers Publishing Company, 1985). A concise overview of the history of Finland's Sámi minority is provided by Veli-Pekka Lehtola, *The Sámi People: Traditions in Transition* (Inari: Kustannus-Puntsi, 2002). Finland's Swedish-speaking minority is surveyed in Kenneth D. McRae, *Conflict and Compromise in Multilingual Societies: Finland* (Waterloo, Canada: Wilfrid Laurier University Press, 1997). The history of science in is covered by Päiviö Tommila and Aura Korppi-Tommola, eds., *Research in Finland: A History* (Helsinki: Helsinki University Press, 2006).

Reference Works

Olli Alho, *Finland—A Cultural Encyclopedia* (Helsinki: Suomen Historiallinen Seura, 1997) is a useful reference work for those interested in culture. The book *100 Faces from Finland: A Biographical Kaleidoscope,* ed. Ulpu Marjomaa (Helsinki: Finnish Literature Society, 2000) has concise biographies of Finns from many historical periods. This work is a part of a larger national biography project whose web site http://www.kansallisbiografia.fi/english.html has additional biographies. George Maude's *Historical Dictionary of Finland* (Lanham, MD: Scarecrow Press, 1995) is a rich source of terms, people, and developments.

Finland before 1809

The dearth of English-language publications is most visible with respect to Finland's history before 1809. *The Cambridge History of Scandinavia,* vol. 1 (Cambridge, UK: Cambridge University Press, 2003) includes Finland in its comprehensive survey of prehistoric and medieval Scandinavia until the year 1520. Two specialized works on prehistoric Finland offer insights to a general audience as well: Mika Lavento, *Textile Ceramics in Finland the on the Karelian Isthmus: Nine Variations and a Fugue on a Theme of C. F. Meinander*, Suomen muinaisyhdistyksen aikakauskirja, vol. 109 (Vammala: Vammalan kirjapaino, 2001), as well as Hannu Takala, *The Ristola Site in Lahti and the Earliest Postglacial Settlement of South Finland* (Jyväskylä: Gummerus, 2004). The prehistoric settlement of Finland is also touched on in Thomas A. Dubois, *Nordic Religions in the Viking Age* (Philadelphia: University of Pennsylvania Press: 1999). This book also explores the ancient religions of Scandinavia as well as the spread of Christianity into the region. With respect to the Middle Ages, Finland is treated in a broader Scandinavian framework in Peter and Birgit Sawyer, *Medieval Scandinavia: From Conversion to Reformation circa 800–1500* (Minneapolis: University of Minnesota Press, 1993).

With respect to the early modern period, Finland is studied in a larger Baltic context in D. G. Kirby, *Northern Europe in the Early Modern Period: The Baltic World, 1492–1772* (London: Longman, 1990). Kirby continues his research to more recent times in *The Baltic World 1772–1993: Europe's Northern Periphery in an Age of Change* (London: Longman, 1995). The Lutheran Reformation is outlined in articles by E. I. Kouri, "The Early Reformation in Sweden and Finland," and Ingrid Montgomery, "The Institutionalisation of Lutheranism in Sweden and Finland," in Ole Peter Grell, ed., *The Scandinavian Reformation* (Cambridge, UK: Cambridge University Press, 1995). H. A. Barton investigates Finland's growing separateness and ultimate separation from Sweden in his masterful work *Scandinavia in the Revolutionary Era 1760–1815* (Minneapolis: University of Minnesota Press, 1986).

The Period of Autonomy: 1809–1917

For an explanation of Finland's political development during this period, consult Jussila et al., *From Grand Duchy to Modern State*. Keijo Korhonen investigates Finland from the Russian perspective in *Autonomous Finland in the Political Thought of Nineteenth Century Russia* (Turku: Turku University Publications, 1967). Juhani Paasivirta places Finland in the larger context of European interstate relations in *Finland and Europe 1815–1914: International Crises in the Period of Autonomy 1808–1914* (London: Hurst, 1981). An excellent book on the growth of nationalism is William A. Wilson's *Folklore and Nationalism in Modern Finland* (Bloomington, IN: Indiana University Press, 1976). An outstanding book on the development of Helsinki as Finland's capital is George C. Schoolfield, *Helsinki of the Czars* (Columbia, SC: Camden House, 1996). Tuomo Polvinen examines the conflict between Finland and Russia during the Bobrikov era in *Imperial Borderland* (Durham, NC: Duke University Press, 1996). The background of this conflict is drawn by Robert Schweitzer, *The Rise and Fall of the Russo-Finnish Consensus: The History of the "Second" Committee on Finnish Affairs in St. Petersburg (1857–1891)* (Helsinki: Edita, 1996).

Finland between the World Wars: 1917–1939

The best account of Finland's road to independence and civil war in any language is Anthony F. Upton, *The Finnish Revolution 1917–1918* (Minneapolis:

University of Minnesota Press, 1980). Risto Alapuro's work *The State and Revolution in Finland* (Berkeley, CA: University of California Press, 1988) studies the Civil War of 1918 from the broader historical perspective of Finland's experience as part of the Russian empire. Interwar Finland's foreign relations are examined in Juhani Paasivirta, *Finland and Europe: The Early Years of Independence 1917–1939* (Helsinki: Suomen Historiallinen Seura, 1988). James Barros, The *Aland Islands Question: Its Settlement by the League of Nations* (New Haven, CT: Yale University Press, 1968) covers the conflict over the archipelago between Finland and Sweden. The most comprehensive account of the conflict between Finnish and Swedish speakers is Pekka-Kalevi Hämäläinen, *In Time of Storm: Revolution, Civil War and the Ethnolinguistic Issue in Finland* (Albany, NY: University of New York Press, 1978). The radical Right-wing movements are covered in Marvin Rintala, *Three Generations: The Extreme Right in Finnish Politics* (Bloomington, IN: University of Indiana Publications, Russia and Eastern Europe Series 22, 1962). Rintala summarized his findings in an article in Hans Rogger and Eugen Weber, eds., *The European Right* (Berkeley, CA: University of California Press, 1965). A more recent study is Lauri Karvonen, *From White to Blue-and-Black: Finnish Fascism in the Inter-War Era* (Helsinki: Societas Scientiarum Fennica, 1988). The development of the welfare state in Finland and Scandinavia from the 1930s to present is chronicled in Eric S. Einhorn and John Logue, *Modern Welfare States: Scandinavian Politics and Policy in the Global Age,* 2nd ed. (Westport, CT: Praeger, 2003).

Finland at War: 1939–1945

The war years offer interested readers the largest body of literature in English on Finland's history. A solid survey of the entire period is Olli Vehviläinen, *Finland in the Second World War: Between Germany and Russia* (Hampshire, UK: Palgrave, 2002). The best work on the Winter War is Max Jakobson, *The Diplomacy of the Winter War* (Cambridge, MA: Harvard University Press, 1961). This was the first scholarly account of the Winter War, and a work that has withstood the test of time. In 1984, this book was republished under the title *Finland Survived* (Helsinki: Otava, 1984). A concise and thoughtful account of the Winter War is Anthony Upton's *Finland 1939–1940* (London: Davis-Poynter, 1974). Several military histories have been published in English. Two of the better ones are Allen Chew, *The White Death: The Epic of the Soviet Finnish Winter War* (East Lansing, MI: Michigan State University Press, 1971) and William R. Trotter, *A Frozen Hell: The Russo-Finnish Winter War of 1939–1940* (Chapel Hill, NC: Algonquin Books, 2000). A military history focusing on the Soviet war effort is Carl Van Dyke, *The Soviet Invasion of Finland 1939–1940* (London: F. Cass, 1997). The Allies' ill-fated attempt to intervene in the Winter War is illuminated by Jukka Nevakivi, *The Appeal That Was Never Made: The Allies, Scandinavia, and the Finnish Winter War 1939–1940* (Montreal: McGill-Queens University Press, 1973).

Historians have debated for decades whether Finland, after suing for peace with the USSR in 1940, could have avoided involvement in the German invasion of Russia in 1941. This debate was started by the American historian

Charles Lundin in 1957 with his book *Finland in the Second World War* (Bloomington, IN: Indiana University Press, 1957). In this book, Lundin questions the need of Finland to enter the war. This position was upheld by Anthony Upton in *Finland in Crisis 1940–1941* (London: Faber and Faber, 1964). The opposing position, that Finland could not have avoided war in 1941, has never been fully articulated in English. Finland's Petsamo nickel mines, a major factor in drawing Finland into the growing German–Soviet antagonism, is covered in Hans-Peter Krosby, *Finland, Germany, and the Soviet Union: The Petsamo Dispute* (Madison, WI: University of Wisconsin Press, 1968). Chris Mann, *Hitler's Arctic War: The German Campaigns in Norway, Finland and the USSR* (Surrey, UK: Allan, 2002) places Finland in the larger German invasion of the USSR Hannu Rautkallio's *Finland and the Holocaust* (New York: Holocaust Library, 1987) reveals the courage of Finland's political leadership in its refusal to ship Finnish Jews to Nazi concentration camps. Wartime relations with the United States are examined in R. Michael Berry, *American Foreign Policy and the Finnish Exception: Ideological Preferences and Wartime Realities* (Helsinki: Suomen Historiallinen Seura, 1987).

The central figure of Finland's war years, Marshal Mannerheim, has been the subject of two biographies. Stig Jägerskiöld's *Mannerheim: Marshal of Finland* (London: Hurst, 1986) is a condensed version of a work that first appeared as a multivolume biography in Swedish. J.E.O. Screen has produced a two-volume biography. The first volume, *Mannerheim: The Years of Preparation* (London: Hurst, 1970), chronicles the marshal's career before Finland's independence. The second volume, *Mannerheim: The Finnish Years* (London: Hurst, 2000) examines Mannerheim in the politics of independent Finland.

Finland Since World War II

Finland's new place in Europe after World War II is studied in Tuomo Polvinen's thorough work *Between East and West: Finland in International Politics 1944–1947* (Porvoo: WSOY, 1986). Defense policy during the Cold War is covered by Risto E. J. Penttilä, *Finland's Search for Security through Defence, 1944–89* (London: Macmillan, 1991). The research on Finnish–Soviet relations during the Cold War is very dated and filled with the political agendas of the time. Still-useful works from this time are Roy Allison, *Finland's Relations with the Soviet Union 1944–1984* (London: Macmillan, 1985), George Maude, *The Finnish Dilemma* (London: Oxford, 1976), and Max Jakobson, *Finnish Neutrality: A Study of Finnish Foreign Policy since the Second World War* (New York: Praeger, 1969).

Finland's place in Europe after the Cold War has been mapped out by Max Jakobson in *Finland in the New Europe* (Westport, CT: Praeger, 1998). The development of Finland into an information society has been analyzed by Manuel Castell and Pekka Himanen, *The Information Society and the Welfare State: The Finnish Model* (Oxford: Oxford University Press, 2002). A broader examination of Finland's current institutions is Pertti Pesonen and Olavi Riihinen, *Dynamic Finland: The Political System and the Welfare State* (Helsinki: Finnish Literature Society, 2002). Pesonen has also published a current survey of

Finland's political system in *Politics in Finland* (New York: McGraw-Hill, 1998). For a short but detailed treatment of the welfare state, see Pauli Kettunen, "The Nordic Welfare State in Finland," *Scandinavian Journal of History* 26, no. 3 (2001): 225–247.

Online Sources

Finland's public and private institutions furnish a wealth of English-language information online. The most comprehensive source is the Foreign Ministry's Virtual Finland web site at http://www.virtual.finland.fi. This site has a wealth of links to other online sources.

Index

About the Author

JASON LAVERY is Associate Professor of History at Oklahoma State University.